Poetry and Violence

Music in American Life

o o o

FOLKLORE AND SOCIETY

Series Editors
Roger Abrahams
Bruce Jackson
Marta Weigle

Lists of books in both series
appear at the back of the book.

Poetry and violence

The Ballad Tradition of Mexico's
Costa Chica

John H. McDowell

University of Illinois Press

Urbana and Chicago

Publication of this work was supported by grants from the L. J. and
Mary C. Skaggs Folklore Fund and from Indiana University's Vice
President for Academic Affairs and Bloomington Chancellor, the
Dean of Faculties, and the College of Arts and Sciences.

The photographs reproduced in this book were taken by and used
with the permission of Patricia A. Glushko.

Library of Congress Cataloging-in-Publication Data
McDowell, John Holmes, 1946–
Poetry and violence: The ballad tradition of Mexico's Costa Chica /
John H. McDowell.
p. cm. — (Music in American life) (Folklore and society)
Includes bibliographical references and index.
ISBN 0-252-02588-1 (alk. paper)
1. Corridos—Mexico—Guerrero (State)—History and criticism.
2. Violence in literature. 3. Politics and literature—Mexico—Guerrero
(State). I. Title. II. Series. III. Series: Folklore and society.
PQ7291.G84M3   2000
861.'04409355—dc21   99-051010

C   5   4   3   2   1

And if, as I believe, violence remains (almost) ineradicable, its
analysis and the most refined, ingenious account of its condi-
tions will be the least violent gestures, perhaps even nonviolent.
—Jacques Derrida

It is not enough to examine the anatomy of language, for
language is innocent and does not speak. It is in discourse, the
spoken word, the use of language, that the dialectic of violence
and meaning is born. Only in discourse will violence confront
meaning.
—Paul Ricoeur

Dime como mueres y te diré quien eres.
[Tell me how you die, and I'll tell you who you are.]
—Mexican proverb

Contents

Acknowledgments

I have been fortunate in the many helping hands and minds that have contributed so much to my efforts to understand the ballads of Mexico's southern Pacific coast. I place at the head of this list two gentlemen whom I consider my mentors. Américo Paredes, now deceased, spurred my interest in the traditional poetry of the Americas, then pointed me in the direction of Guerrero as a likely site for study of the living ballad, and remained a source of inspiration and knowledge throughout the many years of this quest. Miguel Arizmendi Dorantes, composer, musician, television producer, folklorist of his beloved natal state, has always received me warmly in Acapulco and has found many ways to facilitate my research. I like to think that the good spirit of these men pervades the pages of this book.

There are four extended families in Guerrero that have virtually adopted me and my research as their own, and I wish to express my gratitude for their assistance as well as my thanks for the pleasure of their company: Francisco Arroyo and members of his family in Chilpancingo; Miguel, Lucio, Benito, Isidro, Raul, and Carlos Arizmendi and members of their families in Acapulco and Ejido Nuevo; Juvencio, Moisés, and Meche Vargas and members of their families in Acapulco and Ometepec; and José and Victoriano Texta Torres and members of their family in Tecpan de Galeana on the Costa Grande. Three women among these families were particularly gracious in their hospitality: Noy, Miguel Arizmendi's deceased wife; Meche, daughter of Juvencio Vargas;

and Emperatriz, widow of Moisés Vargas. Finding myself in the company of such fine folks, I never felt alone or abandoned during my travels in the south of Mexico.

I thank in particular all the poets, composers, and musicians who have shared with me their passion for Mexico's local and regional music. Though I cannot possibly name all of them here, I would cite in particular Lucio Arizmendi, Miguel Arizmendi, Onofre Contreras, Alvaro Guillén Bracamontes (El Cobarde), Juvencio Vargas, Moisés Vargas, Enrique Mares, Tomás Navarrete, and Francisco Arroyo. In the different localities my research has caused me to visit, I have landed with generous people who immediately appreciated and supported what I was doing. In addition to those already mentioned, I cite here Hector Jesús Hernandez and Martín Díaz in Chilpancingo; Artemio Aguirre, Rafael Mesa, and Benito Hernández in Acapulco; Austreberto Gallardo and Raul Mayo in Cruz Grande; Juvenal Arrellanes in Cuajinicuilapa; and Joel Valverde and Baltazar Velasco in Pinotepa Nacional, Oaxaca. I think of these individuals as my trusted guides, and I thank them for helping me find my way into the rich musical scene on the Costa Chica.

I have benefited from the comments, suggestions, and assistance of numerous friends, colleagues, and students, and I thank, in this regard, Richard Bauman, Henry Glassie, Merle Simmons, Robert Dover, Carlos Fernández, Laura Lewis, Greg Urban, Peter Guardino, Catherine Héau, Gilberto Giménez, María Herrera-Sobek, Leonice Santamaría, Guillermo Hernández, Gustavo Ponce, Raymond Hall, Vania Castro, Juan Dies, Angela Martin, Heather Shirey, Luis Dávila, Olivia Cadaval, and many others who have shared classes, seminars, and conferences with me over the years. Naturally, the analysis and discussion presented in these pages are of my own invention, and these colleagues are absolved from any flaws that might be detected in this book.

I thank Judith McCulloh and Margo Chaney at the University of Illinois Press for their encouragement and help.

Financial support at different stages has come from the John Simon Guggenheim Foundation, the National Endowment for the Humanities, and from internal sources at the University of Texas and Indiana University. I thank Ken Gros Louis and Moya Andrews at Indiana University for their instrumental role in obtaining this funding.

I have saved until last the largest debt I must acknowledge, and that is to my wife, Patricia Glushko. She accompanied me to the Costa Chica in 1989, 1990, and 1996, when she took charge of the visual documentation through still photography and videocamera work. She has assisted in every phase of the project, talking through ideas with me, reading drafts as the manuscript progressed, readying for publication the photographs included in this book. Never was a man gifted with a better life-partner, and I thank her for all she has done to enable this project to flourish. She and our son, Michael, have been the best of sports as I have worked through my obsession with the corridos and corrido communities of Mexico's Costa Chica.

Poetry and violence

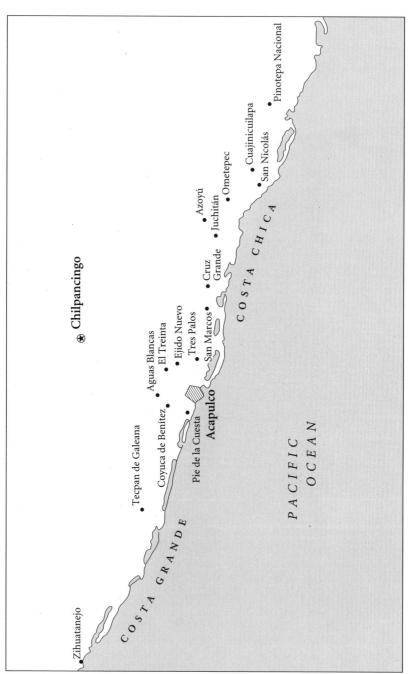

Map 1. The Costa Chica.

Miguel Arizmendi and his wife, Noy, Ejido Nuevo, 1989

Los Hermanos Vargas, Moisés (*left*) and Juvencio, Ometepec, 1989

Introduction

Señores, no hay que confiar
entre compadres y armas,
todo el que cargue su cuestión
que no se ande por la rama,
así mueren bonitos hombres
aunque sean de grande fama.

[Gentlemen, do not have faith
when *compadres* and weapons mix;
whoever carries a grudge
should not go out on a limb;
beautiful men die this way,
even if they are widely famous.]

Beautiful men die this way. This line holds the essential paradox of Costa Chica balladry, which at once adores the hero and warns of his imminent demise. Protagonists in this narrative song tradition are beautiful in their dedication to action, but they are not fated to live very long in this world. Juvencio Vargas, a prodigious source of regional corridos, recited with pride the stanza enclosing this line from an earlier, fading version of the well-known ballad "Simón Blanco." In the process of turning the longer original into a commodity, commercial performers have trimmed away this stanza along with others containing local detail. But connoisseurs of the tradition, like Vargas, keep alive the advice of the corrido poet, not to be casually set aside. The poet, and all singers who intone his words, stands back from the fray to philosophize for one moment. His reflections lead him to praise the beauty of defiance even as he spells out a recipe for disaster—blend together *compadres* and guns and carry a grudge to its logical conclusion. In one and the same breath, the poet and his legion of interpreters celebrate and constrain the violence motivating the song, for "Simón Blanco" is a tale of *compadre* murder, of killing where there should have been respect. This stanza, and more particularly this line of poetry, are emblematic of the thesis I will develop in the ensuing pages.

This is a book about violence and human responses to violence. It is stocked with songs about shootings, massacres, revenge killings, and the like. The reader will find it jolting at times, and cumulatively perhaps numbing, to be assaulted with these tales of mayhem and murder. My goal in writing this book is to add depth, texture, and nuance to the discussion of violence and poetic responses to it and, ultimately, to discourage facile conclusions regarding these matters. Coming to grips with violence and poetry on Mexico's Costa Chica involves a delicate balancing act. Violence has been a serious problem throughout Mexico's history, but the same can be said of the United States and most other nations. The Costa Chica is a scene of regrettable violence, but this state of affairs is closer to typical than unique in modern Mexico. The ballads composed and sung on the Costa Chica do contribute to the perpetuation of violence in this zone, but at the same time they strive mightily to contain the impulse to violence and heal the social rift in the aftermath of violent acts. We must fully appreciate the disjunctive effects of violence, its isolating and alienating character, while at the same time recognizing the ameliorative influence of ballad-making in these conflictive settings. Without denying the gravity of our subject matter, we will find that a story originating in the shedding of blood can lead, paradoxically, to a deeper appreciation of human resilience and resourcefulness.

My interest in the corrido was sparked by the power of its heroic narrative. As a student of poetry and music, I was intrigued by an expressive form of great artistic force that seemed so deeply embedded in the lives of ordinary people. Many a folklorist has made this leap from cloistered art to everyday art, so I am in excellent company here. I learned from my mentor, Américo Paredes, about corridos as a popular response to the currents of modern Mexican history, their role as a local and regional chronicle of the Mexican Revolution, and of the conflict between Mexicans and Americans on the Texas-Mexico border. When I came across a thriving ballad tradition on Mexico's Costa Chica, I was simultaneously hooked and baffled. The beauty and weight of these songs was palpable, but what were these people singing about? Who were their heroes?

I found that not all corridos are concerned with violence. There are joyful corridos singing the virtues of a hometown, the beauty of its women, its role in regional history. First-person laments tell of drinkers and prisoners who have squandered their chances in life. In Mexico, virtually any song telling a story can be labeled a corrido. But it was the *corrido trágico* (the tragic corrido), the *corrido de valentías* (the corrido of bold actions) and *de bravíos* (of outlaw deeds) that animated my hosts and friends on the Costa Chica and that ultimately became the focus of my curiosity. Prominent in a musical repertoire that includes the lively *chilena* and several romantic forms, the tragic corrido with its stories of mortal encounter strikes seemingly at the core of the coastal ethos. I turned to the tragic corrido because the musicians and audiences on the Costa Chica manifestly afforded this form their highest reverence. But it is important to recognize that these same communities revel in a delicate poetry singing the beauty of women and flowers and distilling in wise couplets the pleasures of life.

The Costa Chica, a littoral zone where the Sierra Madre del Sur approach and sometimes touch the Pacific Ocean, stretches east and south from Acapulco along the Guerrero coast and into the neighboring state of Oaxaca. Over the last one hundred years it has been one of those world settings where poetry and violence have been intimately entwined. This region offers a ready-made laboratory to investigate the effect that poetry about violence has had on the practice of violence and, conversely, that violence has had on the making and performing of narrative poetry. Here we can test the notion that such poetry celebrates, and thereby encourages, even incites, the practice of violence. We can search out alternative possibilities, that this poetry might to some degree contain the drift toward violence and that it might in some cases serve as a balm after the flaring of violent events. On Mexico's Costa Chica we are not confined to speculation on these matters, but can sample attitudes and habits of people directly involved in a living ballad tradition.

We will be entering a primarily masculine world, suggested by the corrido's root metaphor comparing the man of action to a fine fighting cock. Most composers and performers of corridos on the Costa Chica are male, and the main audience for corrido performances is male as well. The relative scarcity of female agents in the pages of this book is an artifact of this preference in the tradition itself. But women are hardly absent from the world of the corrido, and what is more, it can be argued that corrido poetry imposes an essentially feminine perspective on the manly world of heroic action. C. Colin Smith (1964:38) observes of Spanish heroic verse that "the masculine world and the bloodthirstiness of the epic correspond to the rough solidity of Norman architecture, whereas in the ballads we move into the gentler, more feminine and more delicate atmosphere of 15th century Gothic." We will encounter compelling evidence for a "gentler" and a "more delicate" dimension to corrido poetry on Mexico's Costa Chica as well, whether or not we choose to label these qualities "feminine."

In the cities, towns, and villages of the Costa Chica, women are active as performers of corridos, though rarely as corrido poets. Yet we know that women do compose corridos. A striking instance is Graciela Olmos, author of the well-known song "El Siete Leguas," a haunting inquiry into the mind of Pancho Villa, and several other corridos. Graciela Olmos was a remarkable soul, a companion of Villa and other generals during the Mexican Revolution. I have recorded several female performers of corridos, and one of them, the spunky Mercedes (Meche) Vargas, daughter of Juvencio Vargas from Ometepec, is featured in these pages. Meche is a talented singer of corridos and both scribe and singing partner to her father, a leading corrido authority and performer along the coast. She is a close observer of the regional corrido, and I have recourse to her thinking as I develop my ideas concerning the living ballad in the second chapter.

Women protagonists are ubiquitous in corrido narratives, often in the roles identified by María Herrera-Sobek (1990), and their appearances in these stories are frequently pivotal to the development of the plot. Most often it is a woman who warns the hero to avoid a specific setting, though the logic of the corrido requires him to disregard this advice and perish there. In these futile calls for circumspection, and in their realistic assessment of danger, women protagonists anticipate what I refer to as the regulatory function, the attempt to contain the spread of violence. Freed from the ethos of the macho code, women are the characters in corrido plots most likely to voice the wisdom of restraint as violence beckons.

Ethnic labels are as problematic on the Costa Chica as elsewhere. At play are slippages between the apparent meaning of the labels and the populations they denote as well as many nuances in local usage and discrepancies between local and external perspectives. It is easy enough to identify the three main ethnic strands in the region, though even here labeling proves to be deceptive. The "whites," *los blancos,* are in fact primarily *mestizos,* that is, a mixture of European and indigenous Mexican. The indigenous people, referred to as *los indios,* are of course not "Indian" at all but descendants of Mexico's original human populations. The black population, *los negros,* is not "black" or "African" but rather a mixed-race group with African, indigenous, and European antecedents.

The Costa Chica is distinctive in Mexico as a site of historical African influence, a circumstance that initially led outsiders to disdain its people but recently has stimulated interest among those in thrall to the romance of Africa in the New World. In *pueblos negros,* the towns and villages with the greatest evidence of black African ancestry, people prefer the label *moreno,* which translates as "dark-skinned," implying a mixture of black and indigenous Mexican ancestry. But the term *negro* is employed for the most dark-skinned individuals, regardless of ancestry, and in a range of other circumstances, for instance in jokes and insults (Lewis 2000). The terms *afromexicano, afromestizo,* and *afromixteco* have been introduced by outsiders to capture the salient detail of a biological mix that includes African ancestry, but these terms have little currency among the people they are meant to designate. Laura Lewis, whose research has taken her to San Nicolás, a village near Cuajinicuilapa on Guerrero's coast, reports that most of her friends and neighbors there are wary of the "Afro-" prefix, viewing it as a mechanism that perpetuates their erasure from the Mexican nation (n.d.).

This fluidity in ethnic terminology creates difficult choices for those who write about the coast. In this study, I employ the term *afromestizo* when I am referring to the *costeños,* the people of the coast, as a general category. But when referring to individuals within afromestizo communities, I use labels they prefer for themselves, in particular *moreno,* which stresses the mixing of African and indigenous Mexican ancestry, and, by implication, in Lewis's thesis, their participation in the popular vision of Mexico, customarily viewed as a nation forged from the conjunction of Native Americans and Europeans (see Vasconcelos 1958). This vision ignores the important contributions of Africans, and people descended from Africans, to the emergence of modern Mexico.

Unfortunately, when people do take note of the black presence in Mexico, they tend to draw upon racist and essentialist modes of thought, further obscuring the actual role of black contributions to the history and culture of the nation. One instance of this strikes close to our topic, a cluster of ideas I refer to as "the Africa thesis," linking alleged traits of Mexico's afromestizos to their African origins. On the Costa Chica, and in scholarly commentaries about the Costa Chica, this thesis makes several stipulations about blacks in Mexico, including prominently that they are more violent than other Mexicans and that this alleged propensity toward violence is rooted in their biology or history. While I hesitate to lend this thesis any credibility, I do think it needs to be addressed as a widespread expression of popular (and academic) belief.

Some readers may be surprised to find in these pages the term *Native Americans* used to refer to Mexico's first or indigenous peoples. I have opted to import this U.S. usage, preferring its ambiguities to those of alternative labels such as *indigenous peoples* or *American Indians.* In any case, it is time that we treat North America (and, indeed, the Americas) as a continuous world region, and standardizing our terminology (when possible) is surely a step in the right direction.

The pages of this book are saturated with texts brought back from the field, and they contain many citations from scholars writing in Spanish. Let me explain briefly the tactics I have employed in handling these materials. In the case of corrido poetry and interview excerpts, I offer the Spanish text as well as my translations, so readers familiar with Spanish can enjoy the flavor of the language and judge for themselves the virtues of the translations. Citations from the scholarly literature in Spanish, which abound in this book, appear only in my English translations; readers will have to place their trust in me as a reliable interpreter. In translating corrido texts, I seek to relay the meaning and verbal bulk of each line, in terms of syllables and stresses, rather than to produce English-language poetry of comparable worth. These translations attend closely to semantic detail in the original whenever possible, but stray from it on occasion in the interests of fashioning a viable English-language text. For English versions of interview excerpts, I try to convey meaning efficiently and to capture the social register of the original speech. The corrido texts and interview excerpts included here are rendered from field recordings and are ultimately dependent on acuity of ear for their value. I have strived to produce reliable transcriptions of these source materials, but cannot rule out the possibility of error in regard to the most recalcitrant passages.

This study of ballads on Mexico's Costa Chica offers a perspective, from one finite angle of vision, on issues and forces that have shaped modern Mexico. It is my hope that this dissection of a poetry absorbed with violence will illustrate how social conventions and shared attitudes influence the making and remaking of traditional song. These artistic productions incorporate but transcend the aesthetic, grounding aesthetic experience in the realities of social, political, and economic conditions. Elucidating the workings of a ballad tradition as seen from the vantage point of those who live within it, we see why people caught in violent settings might turn to narrative song as a resource and a refuge. The afromestizos on Mexico's Pacific coast nurture a living, heroic balladry, and I believe that our examination of its celebratory, regulatory, and healing dimensions has something of importance to tell us about these communities, about poetry, about violence, and about the course of Mexican history.

The analysis works outward from field data gathered over a quarter of a century on the Costa Chica to develop a framework for thinking about the relationship of poetry to violence. The first four chapters sketch the scene, the next three deliver the argument, and the concluding chapter opens the possibility of further applications. In chapter 1 I address the experience of violence from three angles of vision, that of perpetrator, victim, and witness, and depict verbal narrative as an instinctive response to violent events. In chapter 2 I draw a portrait of the living ballad, a song form pervading the life of the community. In chapter 3 I trace an outline of the Costa Chica ballad community, and in chapter 4 I examine the Africa thesis linking violence to African origins of the population. In chapters 5, 6, and 7 I take up in turn the celebratory, regulatory, and therapeutic theses, three models of poetry's connection to violent action. In chapter 8 I review the ballad process in light of Victor Turner's notion of social drama and apply my core ideas to the narcocorrido, gangsta rap, and school violence affecting communities in the United States.

In tribute to the many fine Costa Chica musicians who delighted my ear and captured my mind with their corrido performances, and as a treat and resource to you, gentle reader, we include a sampling of this balladry in an accompanying CD with the corrido texts, transcribed and translated, in the "Note on the Recording." My only regret is that I could not include a song from each and every one of the deserving artists I recorded over the years.

As we prepare to take up matters fraught with anxiety, I ask readers to treat this work as a gesture of peace, an attempt to stifle rather than fan the flames of violence. Like the corrido poet, I wish to offend none, nor do I wish my words to kindle or rekindle the resentments that lead to violent deeds. Corrido poets often initiate their songs with a plea, "Señores perdonarán," (Gentlemen, forgive me) and sometimes add for good measure, "no se vayan a enojar" (do not become angry). And I will take another phrase from their bag of tricks, "dispénsenme lo mal trovado," which translates here as "forgive me for any poor wording."

Violence and its Verbal Icons

Rage and the violence that sometimes—not always—goes with
it belong to the "natural" human emotions, and to cure man of
them would mean nothing less than to dehumanize or emascu-
late him.
—Hannah Arendt, *On Violence*

At first blush, poetry and violence seem unlikely companions. Violence beck-
ons to chaos, poetry to order; violence is wildly disintegrative, poetry, deeply
integrative. Violence enters our consciousness to sever all comfortable associ-
ations. Poetry, in contrast, delivers high doses of acoustic and grammatical
patterning and an overarching sense of wholeness. In spite of these fundamen-
tal differences, poetry (as we well know) is deeply intertwined with violence
in the oral traditions and literatures of the world's peoples. Narrative poetry
and song, building blocks of the world's most inspired literary expression, take
violent encounters as their preferred subject matter. The object of this study
is to assess the logic underlying the association between poetry and violence
in the ballad tradition of modern Mexico known as the corrido and, indeed,
in one particular manifestation of this tradition among afromestizos on the
Costa Chica in the states of Guerrero and Oaxaca.

We will explore three approaches to the intimacy of poetry and violence.
One of these posits an inflammatory spiral, wherein poetic expressions kin-
dle violent actions that in turn provide the grist for further poetic expressions.
In this paradigm, the poet's rhetoric inspires members of the community to
follow the example of the heroes. The argument goes like this: if the heroes
celebrated in the poetry find their place in the world through the exercise of
violent means, then those hearing the song are encouraged to do likewise. This
view further holds that poetry helps sustain an ideological climate conducive
to the employment of violent means. The most elegant statement of this po-

sition comes from Gonzalo Aguirre Beltrán, the distinguished Mexican social anthropologist. In a major ethnographic work, Aguirre Beltrán (1958) offers a vivid portrait of an isolated vernacular culture, the agriculturalists and pastoralists of the town of Cuajinicuilapa on the Costa Chica in the state of Guerrero. This region evinces a social structure partly determined by ancestry among a population with African, Native American, and European roots. In Cuajinicuilapa a small cohort of *blancos,* whom he labels *Euro-mestizos,* occupy positions of economic and political power. Surrounding the town are the *bajos* (lowlands), supporting settlements of *blanquitos,* a transitional group with some black African heritage, and *negros* or *morenos,* people with evident black African features. These labels are all native to the region, and they reflect a recognized social hierarchy there.

Aguirre Beltrán gives the local corridos a special prominence in his description of Cuajinicuilapa and its environs; for him they capture the essence of these communities, especially with respect to *la negrada.* Most of these corridos center around episodes of violence initiated by *las brosas* (gangs of armed men recruited from the outlying settlements), depicted by Aguirre Beltrán (1958:129) as "la arma ejecutiva de la negrada" (the executive arm of the black population), addressing through armed struggle the much-neglected needs of the afromestizo population. These *brosas* cultivate what Aguirre Beltrán refers to as "*un* ethos *agresivo*" (an aggressive ethos), which has served, in his estimation, to protect the region from outside incursion since its early days in the Spanish colony as a haven for escaped slaves.

In a key passage, Aguirre Beltrán (130) poses the essence of what I will refer to as the *celebratory* thesis, arguing for a link between the corrido and the activities of the armed gangs: "Between them [the gangs], the whites and the authorities there exists a fight unto death that has caused and continues to cause blood to flow in torrents. The regional corrido and the community itself, nevertheless, exalts them and their members. Aggressive and violent, they treat them as the ideal of the macho, as the prototype of the personality desired by the culture." In Aguirre Beltrán's account, the corrido plays a decisive role in shaping an "aggressive and violent" personality in the young men, thereby contributing to the cycle of violence. By celebrating the deeds of the corrido protagonists, he argues, the poets place the stamp of community approval on this pattern of behavior.

A second approach envisions a more contemplative role for poetry associated with violence. The poet, after all, lifts the violent episode from its actual setting and reframes it as a coherent narrative, a process that offers ample opportunity to assign credit and blame, to assess causes and consequences, and to sift meaning in a larger moral consciousness. In this vision, poetry about violence is more meditation than celebration. This position is advanced by Michael Meeker with regard to Bedouin legends (what he calls "ceremonial narrative") and poetry cultivated during the early decades of the twentieth century. These pastoralists were organized loosely into clans and bands, and warfare between shifting alliances was rampant. Meeker (1979:27) tells us that Bedouin society exhibited an emphasis on "personal deeds and words" in this context of violent exchanges. He finds a striving for something beyond the mere depiction of violence in the legendary material (98): "Inspired by the threat of political anarchy, the ceremonial narrator was preoccupied with a wish for a moral authority." Meeker (154) views the poetry as an attempt to exercise some form of control in the vortex of an unpredictable environment: "Men discover the possibility of a purely formal response to the pressure of a popular interest in aggressive resources. . . . As they work with such a formal expression, men feel they gain a certain power over their life situation, even though they accomplish nothing concrete."

In this analysis, the oral literary forms of the Bedouins provided a counterpoint to violence as a way of life. Nominally celebrating the deeds of the heroes, this oral tradition can be seen to advocate certain restraints on the uninhibited release of violence. As Meeker notes, impulsive violence begets drastic results in these expressions, and the wisdom of "men of peace" sometimes prevails over the inclination toward the use of aggressive resources. The poetry evinces a quest for a voice of moral authority and an assumption that God ultimately measures the deeds of men: "There is a final suggestion that a divine authority, which lies behind the sure design of human experience, is a support for all good men of firm intention" (162).

This point of view receives expression in the work the of the Mexican folklorist Miguel Angel Gutiérrez Avila. In reviewing the work of his mentor, Aguirre Beltrán, Gutiérrez Avila (1988:15) argues for a regulatory function for the Costa Chica corrido: "The corrido makes no apology for violence; by undressing it, it prohibits it when it is harmful, but it justifies it when it is considered useful. In this sense it performs the indispensable and major function of ideological *regulator* of violence. The corrido poet fully takes on the role of social critic." Drawing on the language of Gutiérrez Avila, I refer to this argument as the *regulatory* thesis, whose essence is the activation of a moral consciousness in transporting violent deeds into the confines of narrative poetry. The violence becomes comprehensible in reference to an encompassing moral universe.

I will present a third line of analysis that views the poetry as a form of individual and collective therapy in the aftermath of a violent scene. This thesis notes the disruptive impact of violent action and sees the need for mending through poetic remedies. Poetry dealing with violence normally evinces a strongly commemorative bent, adapting and modifying the experience of violent action to conform to models and archetypes widely accepted, even cherished, by members of the community. For all its commitment to factuality, the corrido has tolerance for equivocation in the cause of promoting the integrity of the community. As a commemorative discourse, it tends to absorb factional differences into a broadly acceptable surmise, playing down inconvenient details and playing up details consonant with a collective vision. I refer to this line of reasoning as the *therapeutic* thesis.

All three theses can be diagnosed in the living ballad tradition on Mexico's Costa Chica, and each offers insights into ballad production and consumption. There is ample evidence that young men in the ballad communities emulate heroic behavior as presented in the songs and that some of them engage in risky activity in hopes of achieving post-mortem fame in a popular corrido. "Chicharrón"[1] exhibits the relevant mindset:

Decía Pedro el Chicharrón:	[Pedro el Chicharrón said:
"De este mundo me despido,	"I take my leave of this world;
lo que les encargo muchachos	what I ask of you boys
que me troven un corrido,	is that you write me a corrido,
pa' que quede de recuerdo	so it can be a reminder
a toditos mis amigos."	for every one of my friends."]

At the same time, it is not difficult to trace in the lyrics of the ballads—in the way corrido poets handle violent episodes and comment on them—an urge to reflect on the legitimate and illegitimate uses of violence, to assess the consequences of violent actions, and to assign a broader meaning to violent episodes that have disturbed the social equilibrium. The deployment of narrative poetry as part of a healing process is less evident on the surface of the ballads, but it comes into view when one inspects the dynamics of ballad composition, performance, and reception. The commemorative impulse of poetry associated with violence offers ample scope for adjusting historical fact to fit paradigms of collective identity. The healing function is evident in the way composers address the feelings of both sides in a factional rift, in the way performers select ballads appropriate to a particular social gathering, and in the fervent identification of audiences with the heroes of their districts.

Experiencing Violence

In the reams of pages written on violence, only an occasional scholar examines closely the actual experience of violence as lived by those who are caught in its grasp (Arendt 1970; Gilligan 1996). To appreciate the interplay of poetry and violence, we must fashion an experiential framework, that is to say, an account rooted in perceptions and emotions of those who experience violence. Violent encounters can be thought of as communicative acts taking place within finite scenes or tableaus and feature two primary roles, that of perpetrator and victim, and one secondary (and optional) role, that of witness. I offer this construction as a finding device rather than as an all-encompassing model, as a means to isolate key elements touching on poetry's handling of violence. In this take, the *perpetrator* plans and initiates the action and in the early phases, at least, controls the sequence of events. The *victim* plays (unwillingly, in most cases) a counterpart to the perpetrator, receiving, deflecting, or absorbing the perpetrator's incursions. The *witness* can be found at varying distances from the epicenter of action, ranging from an eyewitness present at the scene to those who "witness" the action vicariously—through family members' accounts, news stories, oral histories. Preeminent among the corps of witnesses are the makers, performers, and audiences of corridos.

The role of the perpetrator is cloaked in ambiguity and ambivalence. Those who plan and initiate violence may be seen as freedom fighters or rebels without a cause, as heroes or villains, as noble warriors or common criminals, depending on the perceiver's angle of vision. But many—perhaps most—perpetrators see themselves as crusaders for justice, even as they initiate actions that are normally condemned in society. Often enough perpetrators view themselves as victims, and the violence they plan and execute as the means for correcting a painful imbalance. Perpetrators of violence are often motivated by the conviction that the world is unbalanced, that a score remains to be settled, and only through the exercise of violent means can this disparity be resolved. James Gilligan (1996) found that violent criminals viewed themselves as just avengers in a world that had badly mistreated them. He portrays them as dead souls or the living dead, caught in an untenable existence and hardened by indignities they have suffered, souls who seek redemption or at least a modicum of self-respect through physical aggression. Gilligan (1996:12; italics omitted), drawing on the lessons of classical tragedy, proposes that "the attempt to achieve and maintain justice, or to undo or prevent injustice, is the one and only universal cause of violence."

These observations transfer rather well into the world of Costa Chica corridos. Some corridos do chronicle despicable deeds beyond the reach of any moral framework, but for the most part, violence is presented as a calculated response to wrongs heaped upon perpetrators by a corrupt government or by a vicious rival. Wicked men and women in the world of the corrido initiate violence for personal gain or for mere caprice, but the hero typically acts to avenge the death of a close relative, friend, or ally. The archetype is the man who seeks revenge for the death of his brother. The corridos encourage a positive response to such actions, which are characterized as bold, decisive, justified, and even necessary. In many a Costa Chica corrido, the hero is a wronged man bent on exacting revenge for mistreatment he or his family has received at the hands of enemies. These heroes resort to violence in the absence of conventional systems of justice. It is widely accepted in Mexico that the public authorities are incapable of dealing with criminal activity; indeed, they are thought to be largely responsible for much of it. On the Costa Chica, this lack of confidence in legal agents and institutions, coupled with the prevalence of revenge killing, makes citizens reluctant to step forward and cooperate with the authorities. Without the prospect of swift and secure punishment for violent crimes, people feel obliged to seek direct personal solutions. The celebratory mood of the corrido derives largely from a recognition of the courage and decision of the avenging hero. "Son hombres muy decididos" (They are very determined men), "hombres de resolución" (men of firm resolve), as the corridos have it.

Commentaries surrounding corridos provide additional evidence supporting this profile of the perpetrator of violence. Alejandro Gómez Maganda (1960), in his memoir of coming of age in Acapulco, offers a vivid portrait of the all-pervading uneasiness within a family during the interim between the moment of loss when a relative has been killed and the moment of revenge. In this portrait, the matron of the extended family gives voice to the impossibility of the situation, and the only release from these flames of purgatory is revenge. Interestingly, James Greenberg (1989), in his study of sectarian violence among the Chatino people residing in the mountains above the Costa Chica, also notes the central role of women in fanning the fires of local rivalry. But it would be unfair to cast the blame upon the women, for entire networks of people, held together by kinship or alliance, experience a deadening of the spirit and an almost sacred obligation to settle the score in the wake of aggression. In these scenarios, the perpetrator of violence is celebrated as a righteous hero settling a skewed account through acts of personal bravery.

How different is the experience of the victim when violence seems to strike out of the blue. Violent events create their own schemes of time and space, and they rearrange the familiar landscape of the imagination. Violence is disruptive, antithetical to our efforts to sustain an orderly existence. Victims may never fully comprehend what has hit them, or perhaps they gain a glimmer of comprehension as the action unfolds. If they are fortunate, they will have an opportunity to respond to the aggression, a prerequisite for heroic status. But it is likely they will never be the same as before. These anarchic dimensions of violence, experienced with intensity by its victims and vicariously by witnesses, call for redress through various mechanisms, including revenge on the perpetrators, their kin, and their allies. When legal remedies are lacking, one violent act tends to beget another unless a range of inhibitory reflexes can stem the tide. Among the customary responses are verbalizations in all forms, from the wounded cry of surprise to well-crafted narrative renderings.

Perhaps each of us is a witness to violence; as persons with at least some direct experience of violence, we possess a rubric for interpreting the numerous accounts of violence that come to our attention. For most people, violence is most often experienced vicariously: we hear practically every day about violent confrontations. To say that we experience this violence vicariously means that we are capable of drawing on our own experience to project ourselves into the stories we are told. Violence is such a primordial experience that we cannot help but inhabit the accounts we hear of violent actions, especially when they are contrived to engage our attention and affect our emotions. Violence is inherently dramatic, and tales of violence feed on this natural drama to engage the imaginations of those who hear them.

Violence is a communicative exchange between two parties, sometimes unilateral, sometimes mutual, in which destruction of property and the infliction of physical harm (sometimes unto death) is the essential mode of signification. Like conversation, violent actions possess a systematic reciprocity, a parry and thrust binding aggressor and victim in an intimate grasp of mutual regard. This kernal communicative event is embedded within an immediate and ambient context. The immediate context is defined by a set of central factors: the lapse of time, the chronology of action, the physical setting, the people on hand, and the people's relationship to one another. The ambient context reaches out more broadly to encompass the sources of hostility that have conditioned the possibility of violence. Cleavages in social enclaves mark individuals as potential adversaries, and the weight of accumulated frustrations inclines certain individuals toward violence.

A violent act presupposes either madness or an aggrieved sense of separation. Yet violent action necessarily binds people experiencing this sense of separation into a momentary intimacy, as partners—willing or otherwise—in a joint, sustained nexus of behavior. Violent behavior, like joking behavior as analyzed by Mary Douglas (1968), establishes a common frame of interaction while pointing to perceptions of structural discontinuities in society. Aggressors typically seize upon difference between themselves and their victims, though an outside observer may detect far more in the way of commonalities. In other instances, the points of social demarcation between aggressors and victims are crystal clear, and the aggressor's sense of difference mirrors society's own. The violent action either creates or reinforces a perception of social division, and where none was evident before the event, a widening rift may appear in its wake.

Violence brings about acute suffering to those who are its victims, to their next-of-kin, and in attenuated form to those who vicariously experience it. It exposes a flaw in the social contract, proposes the impossibility of harmonious coexistence. In this sense, violence challenges the assumption that people can work together toward common goals—indeed, that society can prosper. It threatens not only the abstract vision of human cooperation but also the very personal and immediate hopes for a peaceful and rewarding life. Ultimately, violence experienced vicariously reaches out to rattle our sense of security and stability in life. Herein lies perhaps the strongest goad to the invention of narratives that will heal the open wounds lingering in the aftermath of violent deeds.

Some violent scenarios display a mutuality of attitude and action in perpetrator and victim. Both parties to the violence have entered knowingly and freely into the exchange. This state of affairs obtains in the many descriptions of shootouts between rivals in Costa Chica corridos. Consider the case depicted in "La Carta Blanca."[2] The hero has been drinking in a cantina named for a Mexican beer. The local police officer arrives and asks him to surrender his weapon. The hero responds by alerting his companions to take cover: "'Muchachos, no se hagan bola / yo me he de matar con Adolfo / ya se nos llegó la hora'" ("Boys, don't crowd around; / I am going to die with Adolfo; / now our time has come"). He then turns to his adversary and addresses these words to him:

"La tuya es cuarenta y cinco   ["Yours is a forty-five,
la mía escuadra veintidós,   mine is a squad twenty-two;
te vas a matar conmigo   you are going to die with me—
encomienda tu alma a Dios,   commend your soul to God;
dejaremos en el mundo   we will leave in the world
una historia de los dos."   a history of us two."]

The two men face off, draw their guns, and fire. Each is aware of what is happening and each chooses to pursue the confrontation to its conclusion. The corrido poet tells us that although they had been friends, they became adversaries that day. Held together in the vice-grip of mortal combat, the two protagonists find themselves on opposite sides of a line dividing citizens from authority. We do not know what other factors may have played a role in the perception of social distance, but in many corridos men from rival gangs or factions oppose one another. Sometimes the quarrelers are close friends or *compadres* divided by the haze of inebriation.

Other scenarios are less symmetrical. In these settings we must distinguish between perpetrators and victims, but the roles may not be clear. The perpetrator has a plan and thus at least some foresight concerning the sequence of events. The victim is caught in the perpetrator's scheme of action. "Los Torres"[3] describes the classic asymmetry of an ambush. Two men have a disagreement and one of them, with assistance from his brothers, arranges an ambush for the other man and his brothers. They lure the father of their enemy to a funeral, knowing the sons will follow to assure his safety. The corrido poet summarizes the result:

> Todo fue así en un momento   [Everything happened in an instant—
> los Torres sin saber nada,   the Torreses didn't see it coming;
> cayeron al mismo tiempo   they fell at the same time,
> vilmente en una emboscada.   wickedly, in an ambush.]

The perpetrator, as author of a plan, holds the initiative, makes choices, and controls the first flow of events. Naturally, even the best laid plans may go astray, and a perpetrator may quickly lose tactical advantage and must respond to the actions of a quick-thinking adversary. Such is the fate of the protagonist in "Gomecindo Pastrana,"[4] who sets out with a companion to eliminate Aquilino for a remuneration of ten thousand pesos. Aquilino is vulnerable as he drinks in a cantina but his assailants mistakenly shoot the wrong man. The tactical advantage shifts to Aquilino, and Gomecindo is reduced to begging for his own life: "'Ya no me tires, Aquilino / yo soy tu primo hermanito'" ("Don't shoot me anymore, Aquilino— / I am your own first cousin").

Costa Chica corridos record many reversals along these lines, a warning to those who might think that initiating violence guarantees success. These ballads make clear that the roles of perpetrator and victim can shift very quickly in the fury of violent action, and the perpetrator may forfeit an initial tactical advantage. Indeed, in "Los Torres," the father watches his three sons fall to the ground but he extracts a measure of revenge by killing two of the attackers.

But in many cases the aggressor does succeed with impunity, leaving the hapless victim with no recourse other than a defiant oath like this one from "Lalo Reyes":[5]

"Hombres viles y cobardes	["Cowardly and vile men,
¿por qué en las piedras se esconden?	why do you hide in the rocks?
Sálganse a campo razo	Come out into open country—
que así se mueren los hombres."	that's how real men die."]

For participants and witnesses, the violence has created a hiatus between what was happening before it took place and what has happened since. There are three relevant experiential frames: the world as it was before, the violent scene itself, and the world as it is in the aftermath of the violence. A corrido poet captures the dissociation between the first two frames in "Los Dos Comandantes": "que lejos estaban Ramiro y Marciano / de lo que les esperaba" (how far removed were Ramiro and Marciano / from what awaited them).[6] In one corrido after another the poet retraces this journey from a prior state of innocence through the cataclysm of violence to a radically different world, a state of experience, at the other side of the sequence. The shock of the victim, even of the perpetrator converted to victim, and the pleasure of the perpetrator are central nodes in the corrido's thematic development. Corrido narratives are anchored in our awareness of violence as an essential—perhaps the quintessential—human experience and in our shared ability, or shall we say compulsion, to inhabit reports of violent episodes that come to our attention.

Verbal Responses to Violence

The dramatic realignment in experience occasioned by violent actions naturally activates a process of mental adjustment. Those who have directly experienced violence are perhaps most in need of this reprocessing, but others are similarly affected as the impact of the violent action radiates outward from its epicenter. Immediate kin, close friends, and bystanders may experience the dislocation with an intensity equal to that of the actual victim, who is sometimes protected by trauma-derived shock. Indeed, even those who hear of a calamity befalling an unknown victim are prone to an intense vicarious experience, especially if there are grounds, such as shared social characteristics, for identifying with the victim. The rift caused by a violent act may trigger a general convulsion as immediate victims, their associates, and a larger public engage in a process of reconstitution aimed at establishing a postviolence equilibrium. This process may be channeled away from further violence through the operation of several devices, including efforts at mediation, the resistance afforded by cross-cutting loyalties, and the production and performance of narratives emphasizing the common ground.

Verbal instruments are critical in this process of reconstitution. We can begin with the instinctual cry or shriek at the sudden realization that violence has crashed in upon the normal routine. Perhaps all subsequent verbalizations can be interpreted as glosses of this immediate response. Initial responses may be vocalizations—screams—rather than verbalizations with semantic content. The importance of verbal instruments in response to violence appears to derive from a couple of elements. For one thing, verbalization helps people crystallize a fluid mental process into a more stable, and hence finished, product. An emergent line of thought can be snared and conserved in a verbal object. It can, in a sense, be rescued from the stream of consciousness and fixed into a representation with some degree of permanence. Verbalization can also activate a social arena in which the search for a new equilibrium can be shared and provisional versions can be tested and revised in a collaborative process. The most common verbal instrument involved in this reprocessing is narrative, a verbal icon that images the event through description of its action sequences and, in some cases, through replaying parts of the original verbal and gestural segments.

Firsthand narratives are produced as part of an effort to reconstruct systematically what actually happened. Often it is necessary to collate as many of these as possible to arrive at a plausible account of the event. Frequently narratives from those involved in the action fail to cohere or may even contradict one another, creating in some instances an indeterminacy in the precise sequence of action and reaction in the violent encounter. Fresh narrative culled soon after the event from participants or witnesses may contain accidental or deliberate inaccuracies, and these can sometimes be difficult to identify. It is the mission of forensic and legal professionals to sort through this body of evidence to flush out a convincing overview—a master narrative—of the event. The closing arguments of lawyers in a criminal prosecution are normally competing master narratives weaving together the body of fresh, firsthand narrative into an account that will be bought by the jury. But this type of spade work is carried out to some degree by those who are affected even remotely or indirectly by a violent deed, as people seek to ground their vicarious experience of the event in a plausible interpretation. On the coast of Guerrero, among those sifting through the firsthand narratives, and seeking out even second- or thirdhand accounts to supplement these, are relatives of people killed or wounded in violent encounters and the makers of corridos;

the former are deciding what course of action to follow in response to the violent event, whereas the latter are searching out the facts upon which to base their poetic expressions.

As the aftermath extends beyond the immediate postviolence phase, fresh narrative gives way to more considered narrative. Narrative accounts that initially flowed in response to the excitement and shock of dislocation now begin to acquire the trappings of a meditated response. In the earlier phase, the highest priority might have been a coherent rendering of a narrative sequence, replete with as many details as can be mustered from memory of the event. Were there two people or three who came to the door? Did one of them wear a hat? Did they knock before speaking or speak before knocking? Who spoke first, and what did he say? Fresh narratives are often absorbed in this level of recounting, leaving relatively little scope for the development of interpretive frameworks. Seasoned narrative has the luxury of consulting the body of fresh narrative as a foundation for a different kind of narrative product that selects among the available facts to construct an account informed by a theory.

Like the master narrative of the prosecuting or defending attorney, the seasoned narrative might locate evidence within an overarching thesis, but unlike litigators, those who fashion seasoned narratives are not primarily concerned with proving innocence or guilt. Instead, they seek to design narrative objects that respond to communal and aesthetic concerns. The communal issue enters the picture when narratives about violence are put forward as collective representations, that is, as representations that project, explore, and fortify the common basis of affiliation within a society. The aesthetic concern is to create a narrative that captivates its audience by virtue of enticing formal structures and arresting formulations of themes. These concerns take seasoned narratives in the direction of commemoration, a mode of signification characterized by its stylized discourse and by removal to a heightened plane of understanding (McDowell 1992).

Seasoned narratives occur in several varieties. Those who initially tell fresh narratives about a violent event may later perform seasoned narratives about the same event. During a process of maturation, these stories become more cohesive as narrative objects, with more touches of dramatic intensity. Eventually, such tales may lose their connection to the source event and become emblematic of a particular value or emotion, or they may wander away from specificity and acquire the exemplary character of legend. Other makers of stories, working within familiar expressive genres, create contemplative art objects for community perusal, along the lines of the Costa Chica corridos.

The societies of the world offer a multitude of poetic treatments of violent episodes. The movement from informative utterance style, marked by what Dwight Bolinger (cited in Ladd 1980:219) refers to as "constant and subtle ups and downs of pitch," to commemorative utterance style, with its leveling of pitch, can be characterized as a process of formalization in the material substance of the channel of communication. Commemorative speech is endowed with regularized prosodies through the introduction of rhythmic effects such as rhyme and isochronic stress. An autonomous aesthetic system is given leave to organize the production of speech into parallel and periodic structures. At the same time, the plane of reference is now curtailed, revolving around the set of symbols and archetypical narrative elements that resonate most deeply for members of the community. Such measured and allusive speech acquires remarkable levels of efficacy, beyond that associated with discourse in the informative mode. We may speak of *speech narcosis* when poetic discourse attains the capacity to alter the mood of its recipients as it works upon their central nervous systems, and under the influence of its sonorous medium, listeners receive and elevate the encoded messages.

Corridos as Artistic Objects

The Costa Chica corrido, a regional variant of a ballad tradition of great depth and extension, is dedicated to the problem of human violence. Its roots lie in the Spanish *romancero,* the ballad tradition that flourished in Renaissance Spain and came across the Atlantic to take on a new life in the American colonies. The Spanish romance was a balladry of such importance in expansionist Iberia that it was carried by soldiers, explorers, traders, and settlers to every corner of the empire. The dean of Spanish ballad scholars, Ramón Menéndez Pidal (1939:16), addresses the importance of the *romancero* among Spaniards who first came to the Americas: "Surely in the memory of every captain, of every soldier, of every merchant, went along something of the extremely popular Spanish *romancero,* that would often spring up as a reminder of childhood to sweeten the sentiment of loneliness for the home country, to lessen the boredom of those endless trips or the fear of the adventures awaiting them in the unknown world they set foot on."

Old romances are known from the southern tip of South America to the highlands of New Mexico, persisting as reminders of the Iberian past. In its poetic forms and narrative subjects the Mexican corrido is essentially true to its roots. The term *corrido* is probably a shortening of the term *romance corrido,* meaning a through-sung ballad, as attested in Spanish usage during the sixteenth century (Simmons 1957:8). Corridos are found, as a minor song tradition, in several parts of Latin America, but it is only in Mexico that these roots from the colonial period have produced a progeny of comparable magnitude (Paredes 1963; Simmons 1963). The indigenous cultures of Mexico, with their emphasis on recording history through narrative poetry and painted books, must have added something to the mix, though the corrido has evolved primarily as a mestizo cultural form, one associated with the rise of a national consciousness especially during the early decades of the twentieth century and in the context of border conflicts with Mexico's northern neighbor. Catalina Héau de Giménez (1998) identifies the popular Spanish broadside ballad, infiltrating Mexico in the years after independence, as the immediate precursor to the Mexican corrido, especially the octosyllabic ballad of the north. Still, the roots of both Spanish broadside ballad and Mexican corrido lie in the vast heritage of Iberian narrative poetry originating in the medieval epics and culminating in the *romancero*.

The afromestizos of the Costa Chica have nurtured one of Mexico's most significant regional corrido traditions. Like the *ranchera* corrido of the northern frontier, the Costa Chica corrido is an enduring tradition that has continuously produced ballads from at least the early decades of the twentieth century to the present. Just as the resurgence of the corrido in late-nineteenth-century Mexico is shrouded in mystery, we cannot say for certain when the making and singing of corridos gained popular acceptance on the Costa Chica. One tantalizing stanza is preserved from a Costa Chica corrido about a land dispute, brought to a head in 1891, between two afromestizo communities (Salazar Adame 1987:56):

Juchitán y Huehuetán   [Juchitán and Huehuetán
andan peleando terrenos,   are fighting over land;
Juchitán dice ganamos   Juchitán says we beat you;
Huehuetán dice veremos.   Huehuetán says we shall see.]

The first mention of corridos in writings about the Costa Chica, according to Gabriel Moedano (1988), is this problematic statement by Carlos Basauri (1943:15), who visited the area in the 1930s: "They sing *sones* and corridos with the accompaniment of the *jarana;* these corridos were brought to those regions by the mestizos, and the *negros* entone them deforming both the melodies and the words." It is fitting that this first mention drips with scorn for the afromestizo, for this posture is characteristic of a deep-seated racial and cultural prejudice in the Mexican literature on the Costa Chica. What he calls the "deformation" of word and tune is most likely the adaptation of the genre to the local speech dialect and musical idiom. As for the source of the material, it may be as Basauri says or it may be that Costa Chica residents came into contact with corridos elsewhere and brought them back to their native land. Was it the *zapatistas* swarming the area during the revolution who implanted the ballad as an expressive form? Or was it Costa Chica muleteers or laborers making the trek between the coast and Tixtla or Puebla who returned home with corridos on their lips? For that matter, we cannot rule out the possibility that musicians from the coast were themselves active in the rebirth of balladry that swept through Mexico in the 1920s.

This formative period in the rise of the corrido in Guerrero is necessarily a matter of speculation, but we have firm and extensive information beginning in the late 1940s when Gonzalo Aguirre Beltrán conducted field research in Cuajinicuilapa and its environs. Aguirre Beltrán, aware of the bias toward *lo índio* in Mexican ethnology, took advantage of the available airplane service to the area and spent several weeks in 1948 and 1949, in and around Cuajinicuilapa, documenting the culture of the afromestizos. Aguirre Beltrán (1958:14) writes of a two-week period in February 1949: "We especially dedicated our efforts to collecting folkloric material, managing to record more than sixty regional and local *sones* and corridos." Apparently some forty of these songs are corridos, including many early versions of ballads still circulating on the Costa Chica.

Following in the footsteps of Aguirre Beltrán, a number of field researchers have documented the Costa Chica ballad tradition since then. The North American ethnomusicologist Thomas Stanford (or one of his assistants) traveled through the area twice, in the 1950s and again in the 1960s, and found a flourishing ballad tradition in the towns and villages of the Costa Chica. In 1972, I visited Cruz Grande, Ometepec, and Pinotepa Nacional, recording an ample body of regional corridos. More recently, the Mexican folklorists Gabriel Moedano (1988) and Miguel Angel Gutiérrez Avila (1988) have affirmed the persistence of a living balladry in these regions. In the course of trips to the Costa Chica in 1989, 1990, and 1996 I have found that the corrido continues to occupy a position of prominence in the area.

In the towns, villages, and hamlets along the Pacific coast and inland toward the foothills of the Sierra, the afromestizo population of the Costa Chica cultivates a corpus of balladry focused primarily on local events featuring mortal conflict. Crucial to this enterprise are the corrido makers, the *compositores* or *trovadores*, as they are locally known, who have the skill to fashion the lines and stanzas of the poetry and set their verbal creations to music. Each locality has at least one person gifted in this craft, and community members turn to these artists for corridos as reminders of family members and friends fallen in action. Often a father or brother of someone killed in a violent episode approaches the ballad maker to request a corrido. In several cases, a man who senses his end is near arranges in advance for a corrido upon his demise. Not all corridos are solicited; in some cases, ballad makers are inspired by the weight of events to create a new corrido.

Performers of corridos, *trovadores* and *juglares,* are of course vital to the perpetuation of the tradition. The primary medium for disseminating corridos on the Costa Chica is live performance, and perhaps the majority of men, as well as a significant minority of women, are competent singers of corridos. It comes as a surprise to find this flair for artistic performance in an assembly of rough-hewn farmers and fishers. Beyond this common level of interest and competence, each extended family, and each barrio, has at least one group of musicians especially noted for performing corridos and other local and regional music. These ensembles are professional in that they are available for hire at social gatherings such as weddings, *santos* (birthday celebrations), and fairs. Few of these musicians earn their living at making music, however, but rather play at public events to supplement their primary income, typically from farming, fishing, or petty commerce.

The third component in the Costa Chica ballad ecology is the audience. Afromestizo communities have a strong following for corridos. Men and women request them from singers and respond fervently to performances. During the course of a performance, audience members contribute a variety of *gritos* (shouted comments and vocalizations), most of them expressing pride in local identity. At such moments it seems as if the corridos encapsulate the afromestizo experience, as if they stand for the most valued achievements of the community. It is easy to see how Aguirre Beltrán found in the corrido a key to the afromestizo personality. Composers, performers, and audiences are bound together in the cultivation of these songs telling the stories of violent episodes affecting local communities.

Just what kind of an object is this artistic response to violence? The corrido is a song form consisting of anywhere from a handful to a score or more stanzas. Each stanza contains four, six, or eight lines of poetry sung to a corresponding musical phrase. The lines are most often octosyllabic, though a regional variant known as the *bola suriana,* with various mixings of eight- and twelve-syllable lines, is quite popular (Serrano Martínez 1989). Syllables will be elided or sustained to match the pattern of stress present in the musical phrase, creating the effect of an isochronic poetic line with three strong beats in the case of eight-syllable verse and four for its twelve-syllable counterpart. Rhyme or assonance occurs at the end of each even-numbered line within the stanza and is not held constant from one stanza to the next. Composers seem to work with two-line units, often making use of formulaic bits and phrases in arranging these basic building blocks. The stanza, typically, evolves as a stacking of two or three of these two-line components (McDowell 1972).

Performances begin with an instrumental statement of the complete melody, and musicians are likely to insert complete or partial restatements between stanzas. Corrido performances normally end with the singing of the final verse of the poetry; there is no instrumental coda. The minimal performance unit is a singer with a guitar, and ensembles of all sorts can be found performing corridos in the different regions of Mexico. On the Costa Chica I have heard corridos performed with ensembles containing guitars of various sizes, violins, a harp, an accordion, a synthesizer, even a brass band. Corridos can be performed with one voice though there is a preference for two- or three-part harmony. The preferred voice quality, on the Costa Chica at least, is strong and forceful rather than sonorous.

Corridos are fairly simple musical constructions. The melodies trace a harmonic journey to the dominant and back again to the tonic, with a detour to the subdominant in some of them. One distinctive feature of Costa Chica corridos is that they are often in minor keys; approximately half of the corridos performed among afromestizos are. Elsewhere in Mexico, corridos are performed exclusively in major keys. Meters may be in three or four, and cut time and 6/8 meter are not unusual. New corrido texts usually are given their own musical setting, by probing new options in one of several families of corrido melodies.

Corridos exhibit a fairly standard thematic progression. They normally open with a greeting or announcement in which the singer directly addresses the audience. In this opening gambit, the singer seeks a performer's immunity, for the topics of the songs are often inflammatory. From this beginning, the corrido poet typically sets the scene by supplying facts, such as the time and place of the encounter and the identities of the principal antagonists. Many corrido narratives mirror the sequencing of violent scenes by describing first the initial situation, then the violent exchange, and at last the resulting situation. The narrative body of the corrido is most often punctuated with lines and stanzas of reported speech, and it is these segments that arouse the most passion among audiences. The corrido often finishes with a *despedida* (leave-taking), wherein the singer (or in some cases, the protagonist of the song) says farewell to the audience.[7]

Corrido narratives are almost always in third-person discourse, apart from the first- and second-person pronouns in segments of reported speech. The

Corrido with brass band accompaniment sung by El Trovador de la Sierra, Savanillas, 1989

tone of the narrative is serious and objective to a degree, though there are ample opportunities to insert editorial commentary. Such commentary can present a decidedly partisan view, emphasizing loyalty to one faction or another or striking a political stance. But it is more likely to adduce a common wisdom that all parties can subscribe to, such as the notion that *aguardiente* (alcohol) and guns do not mix or that agents of the government cannot be trusted.

Violence and the Literary Impulse

What is it about violence that awakes the literary impulse, the tendency to distill experience into artistic verbal objects? Does it possess inherent drama that transfers readily into poetic narrative? According to Roland Barthes (1977:160), "violence always organizes itself into a *scene*"; it is "the most transitive of behavior . . . also the most theatrical." Violent encounters are finite communicative sequences, occurring in scenes that preserve the classical unities of time and space. To this extent, they seem to be ready-made for reconstitution as verbal narrative. Artistic representations of violence can take their cues from the boundaries and sequences of the experiential substrate itself. Américo Paredes (1958) notes that corrido narratives typically move through a sequence of finite scenes or tableaus as they tell their tales. Dramatic intensity derives in large measure from the high stakes of violent encounters, their potential to transform a prior situation into a radically different resulting situation. Human emotions reach cathartic levels in the embrace of such high-profile effects.

The quest for vengeance, a central theme in many narratives of violence, offers insights into these issues. Around half the corridos on the Costa Chica are about successful or failed attempts to avenge previous wrongs. People in this region are highly sensitive to the demands of honor and to the agony of shame. The heroic mentality operative in these communities stresses the importance of maintaining one's dignity. Demeaning behavior toward oneself or one's family creates a tension that can be resolved only through violent retaliation. The code of *machismo* can define something as slight as sustained eye contact as a cause for violent response. Other provocations include verbal insults, the carrying-off of a female relative in the traditional practice of bride capture, and the murder of a close relative, friend, or associate. Any homicide can easily expand into a feud, with two extended families permanently on the prowl for the enemy. These situations of blood revenge (Boehm 1984; Greenberg 1989) sometimes feature preemptive strikes, can involve major shootouts with many resulting deaths, and may persist over generations.

The typical corrido focuses on an aggrieved individual or group seeking revenge for a fallen relative. In "Pedro Torres,"[8] two sons of a woman who was brutally raped and murdered by an influential man wait for an opportunity to avenge their mother's death. The boys were youngsters when the crime occurred; now they are grown and have become soldiers in the Mexican army. One day their mother's killer stops in a car at a checkpoint along a highway. The two young men step out from behind the barrier and shoot him. Corrido poets make use of a proverb in assessing such events: "Lo que se debe se paga" (What is owed must be paid). More generally, people speak of those who have killed as "owing" (from the verb *deber*) with the sense that at any moment they may be called to account for past deeds through the mechanism of blood revenge.

What is it about vengeance that lends itself to treatment in verbal art productions? John Kerrigan (1996:vii) argues that "its impulse towards structure, its ethical ambiguity and emotional turbulence have helped authors, acting companies, and (in a broader sense) entire cultures produce major works of art." As Kerrigan notes, several aspects of revenge are conducive to dramatic handling: the high level of emotional intensity, a symmetry through which the victim (or associates) become the aggressors, the moral ambiguity of violence that proceeds from admirable causes, such as self-respect and loyalty to kith and kin. The web of intrigue spun as people seek revenge possesses elements of structure and affect that play very well in artistic representations.

Costa Chica corrido poets show a special interest in the words, or alleged words, of people locked in mortal combat. Indeed, the coverage granted to the speech of the heroes equals or exceeds the coverage given to their actions. The corrido in its tragic mode may attend to violent scenes, but the focus is generally on alleged thoughts, sentiments, and especially speech of story protagonists. This is not to say that descriptions of stabbings, shootings, beatings, and the like are absent from corrido poetry. But reading through a group of these ballads one is struck by the prominence of reported speech. This proclivity of corrido poets to repeat the sayings of the heroes is a generic trait in need of explanation. On inspection, this trait strikes at the heart of what we might call the "literary" mission of the genre, its essential take on the violence it versifies.

Corrido heroes and villains are men and women of words as much as of deeds. In episodes of reported speech corrido poets indulge their muse, producing colorful and often metaphorical expressions that draw on the popular vernacular. If the experience of violence can be organized into three stages— a prior moment, the violent moment, and its aftermath—corrido poets find each one appropriate for the delivery of reported speech. In the moments prior to violent action, heroes can be heard discussing their plans, as in this sequence from "Apolonio"[9] in which Fabián is requesting assistance from Apolonio to go after an enemy:

Y entonces dice Apolonio:
"'Ora sí, me voy a rajar,
porque estoy escaso de parque
no te puedo acompañar."

[And then Apolonio says:
"This time I'll have to back down;
because I am low on ammo,
I cannot come along with you."

Entonces dice Fabián:
"Me engañas con la verdad,
si le escribo a mi patrón
dos cajas me va a mandar."

Then Fabián tells him:
"You're playing tricks with me;
if I write to my boss
he will send to me two cartons."

Entonces dice Apolonio:
"'Ora sí, no veo la hora,
con mi escopeta del doce
la que le nombro La Tora."

Then Apolonio says:
"Now I can hardly wait—
with my twelve-gauge shotgun,
the one I call La Tora."]

As the violence draws near, heroes will reveal to their companions doubts about the outcome or they will exhort them to stand bravely in the action. When the rival parties come into sight of one another, heroes are likely to speak of their unflinching loyalty to their friends and family, to boast of their prowess and courage, and to assign specific targets to their cohorts. Consider this exchange from "Nicho Esteban"[10] between two heroes as they contemplate the rival gang from a medium distance:

Allí le dijo Preciliano:
"Dime quíen es tu contrario,
para írmele de frente
pa' ver si puedo matarlo."

[There Preciliano told him:
"Tell me which one is your rival,
so I can go confront him
to see if I can kill him."

Ahí le contesta Juvencio:
"Si usted se haya suficiente,
el de trajesito azul
es el que viene de frente."

There Juvencio responded:
"If you think that you can do it—
the one wearing a blue outfit,
he's the one riding in front."]

Here action is contemplated in a dialogue between two companions, one of them displaying courage and dedication to his friend by insisting on attacking his arch enemy.

Often enough, before the engagement with lethal weapons begins, there is a verbal engagement with barbed comments, taunts, and boasts tossed across the divide separating the contraries. At the decisive moment in corrido narratives, when a death is imminent, corrido poets once again report the words of the heroes. The aggressor may declare to the victim his fate, as in this segment from "Juan Colón":[11]

Onésimo contestó:	[Onésimo responded:
"Colón, como te parezca."	"Colón, just as you wish."
Colón que da media vuelta	Colón turns half-way around,
ya mero se hizo a la izquierda:	just then he moved to his left:
"Ya te moristes, Colón	"Now you are dead, Colón,
con uno de punta negra."	with a black-pointed bullet."]

The victorious hero may announce the cause of his action at this critical moment, as in "Antonio Veles":[12]

Manuelo Peláez gritaba	[Manuel Peláez shouted
al público y todo al grito:	to all present and fully shouted:
"Tú me tenías que pagar	"You were going to pay me
la muerte de mi hermanito."	for the death of my little brother."
Y metió otros dos balazos	And he sunk in two more bullets
con una cuarenta y cinco.	with a forty-five pistol.]

The falling hero is also allotted a turn at speech in many Costa Chica corridos. Often he will mock his adversaries and belittle the significance of the death they have arranged for him, as in "Villarreal":[13]

Fue cayendo poco a poco	[He was falling little by little
con el sombrero en la cara,	with his hat in his face;
dice: "Está bueno, muchachos"	he says, "That's just fine boys,"
y soltó una carcajada.	and let out a big laugh.]

Not infrequently, the dying hero warns his adversaries of a loyal companion who will avenge his death, as in "El Culebro":[14]

Al consentir los balazos	[On feeling the bullets land
él les habló fuertemente:	he spoke to them in strong words:
"Ya se hartaron al Culebro	"Now you have finished Culebro;
'ora se sienten valientes,	now you think that you are bold,
pero allí dejo un buen caudillo	but I leave there a fine leader,
que es el Juvencio Clemente."	who is Juvencio Clemente."]

Sometimes the fallen hero is given ample scope to indulge his final fancies, as in "Chicharrón," in which the hero addresses his girlfriend with these admonitions:

Su compadre cayó adentro	[His *compadre* fell inside,
y Pedro al pie de una palma,	and Pedro at the foot of a palm,
le gritaba a su querida:	he shouted to his girlfriend:
"Te quedas, negra del alma,	"You'll stay behind, darling girl,
vas a abrazar a otros hombres	you will embrace other men—
que no sabes ni como hablan."	you don't even know their voices."
Decía Pedro el Chicharrón	Pedro the Chicharrón spoke
cuando estaba agonizando:	when in the throes of death:
"Arrímate, Crescenciana	"Come closer, Crescenciana,
que ya me estoy acabando,	as I will soon be done;
te quiero morder el brazo	I want to bite your arm,
pa' que te andes acordando."	so you will remember me."]

The aftermath of violent actions also lends itself to reported speech. In another ballad called "Chicharrón"[15] the corrido poet even has a corpse do the talking:

Dijo Candelario Río:	[Candelario Río said:
"La culpa la tengo yo,	"I am the one to blame;
en este velorio mío	in this wake of mine,
el diablo aquí se esmeró."	the devil cleaned up here."]

Victors in mortal encounters can be heard bragging as they head off to celebrate their good fortune, and through reported speech many corridos offer a portrait of the dealings required to smooth over problems created by violence, as in "Juan Colón":

Amaba fue 'onde Demetrio	[Amaba went to Demetrio's
a que le dieran consejo:	so that they might advise him;
"Le voy a decir la verdad	"I will tell you the truth:
yo no me puedo rajar,	I cannot back down now;
Onésimo mató a Juan	Onésimo has killed Juan—
'ora ¿cómo le haremos?"	now what are we going to do?"
Demetrio le contestó:	Demetrio answered him:
"Váyanse al monte del potrero,	"You all go to the meadow on the hill,
mientras que voy a Acapulco	while I go to Acapulco
y doy una declaración,	and make a declaration;
yo me meto Enrique al centro	I'll get Enrique to go downtown;
con Cárdenas lo arreglo."	I'll arrange things with Cárdenas."]

Here the conspirators are pictured making use of political contacts to mini-mize the fallout from the killing of Juan Colón.

These are just a few examples. Costa Chica corridos are so infused with sim-ilar episodes that one could say the stories are told through vignettes of he-roes in conversation with one another. What is going on here? Are the *costeños* actually this loquacious? Do people engaged in mortal struggle have the pres-ence of mind to so neatly articulate their predicaments as events are unfold-ing? Or are corrido poets making use of a literary conceit by endowing their subjects with poignant speeches? And if this is the case, what does this tell us about poetry centered on violence?

We certainly cannot rule out the possibility that some speech episodes in Costa Chica corridos are faithful renderings—after all, corrido poets make strenuous efforts to ascertain the facts of the events they narrate. But it seems unlikely that every instance of reported speech can be traced to an actual ex-change of language. Some portion of them, like the speaking corpse mentioned above, is certainly the invention of corrido poets. It appears that composers of corridos are conceptualizing their narratives as sequences of finite social scenes conducive to the exchange of words. They are capitalizing on the in-herent dramatic potential of violent encounters and expanding this potential by working within a theatrical matrix placing a small group of key persons in close proximity with one another.

In this light, we can characterize corrido poetry as a measured response to violence, one that imposes order on the flux of events by creating narratives moving from one dramatic exchange of words to another. The blood and gore of slaughter are of little interest to these poets, who are drawn instead to the archetypes of speech under duress: the bold and defiant words of the heroes, the conniving words of the villains, the demurring words of the cowards. Heroic archetypes are transcended in moments of self-doubt as heroes voice their fears and concerns. The centrality of speech episodes in this balladry indicates a poetry drawn not to violence but to the play of human emotion in the grip of violent situations. Poets seize on and augment the dramatic possi-bilities of violent encounters by fashioning a narrative discourse featuring chains of reported speeches. This technique enables them to move their audi-ences by presenting compact vignettes deeply revealing of human character.

The corrido's artistic intentions are made evident in the central role allot-ted to reported speech in the narratives. Corrido poets organize and drama-tize their stories by channeling the daunting multiplicity of actual events into sleek narratives driven by periodic episodes of reported speech. This technique tends to idealize the action by assimilating it to a paradigm that emphasizes the display of emotion and character in the face of life-threatening situations. Violence, which tends to occur in scenes, is molded in this poetry into a theatrical framework featuring face-to-face verbal exchanges. If the graphic details of aggressive deeds are slighted in this program, corrido poetry can claim for itself a higher truth, as a window into the human soul.

Notes

1. "Chicharrón" tells of a hero who is betrayed by the government and by a *compadre* as he is drying his ammunition in the sun. *Chicharrón* refers to a fried pork rind and is often used as a nickname for people with pockmarked faces. This version came from Juvencio Vargas and Meche Vargas in their home in Acapulco on February 4, 1989. A variant of this text is reproduced in Gutiérrez Avila (1988:54–55) from a performance in San Nicolás, Guerrero.

2. "La Carta Blanca" is a traditional ballad from the coast. I have two versions from Cruz Grande, Guerrero, separated in time by twenty-seven years.

3. "Los Torres" was composed by Lucio Arizmendi (originally from Ejido Nuevo but living in Acapulco) at the request of Elpidio Torres, the father of the three brothers slain in an ambush.

4. "Gomecindo Pastrana" is a corrido of the coast, centered around San Nicolás. José Albines sang this version at the home of Juvencio Vargas in Acapulco in February 1989.

5. "Lalo Reyes" is a well-known corrido of the coast, of some antiquity, about a killing by ambush. Juvencio Vargas and his daughter, Meche, sang this version at their home in Acapulco in February 1989. Another corrido about the same protagonist appears in Gutiérrez Avila (1988:59–60).

6. "Los Dos Comandantes" was composed by Onofre Contreras about a 1985 shootout in Acapulco between representatives of two police agencies. Tomás Navarrete sang it in Acapulco in February 1996.

7. Américo Paredes, in conversations and in correspondence with me, insisted that a *despedida* is "a complete and irrevocable farewell" rather than a temporary leavetaking.

8. "Pedro Torres" is a corrido of the coast about the death of a prominent underworld figure from Maguey. This version was sung by Juan Saguilán and Teódulo García Pastrana in Cuajinicuilapa in May 1996.

9. "Apolonio" is a corrido of the coast telling of a failed assassination attempt and revealing the dangers of *compromisos* (commitments). I have recorded Juvencio Vargas singing it on several occasions. A shorter version of this corrido appears in a chapbook made from the third encounter of corridistas of the Costa Chica, which took place in Copala in 1992.

10. "Nicho Esteban" tells of the demise of one of the coast's most brutal killers. The

name of this protagonist, and corridos about him, are somewhat variable in Costa Chica tradition, which includes the variants "Leonicio Esteves" and "Nicho Esteves." I have an excellent version of "Nicho Esteban" from Juvencio Vargas and from his nephew Isaac in Ometepec. I also recorded it from two blind marketplace singers, Juan Savaleta and José Figueroa, in Ometepec.

11. "Juan Colón" tells of the death of a police agent who chooses to celebrate in the wrong barrio. This version is from the singing of Pablo and Laurencio Gallardo in Cruz Grande in August 1972. A variant of this text appears in Salvador Memije Alarcón (1992:17), who calls it "one of the most pleasing to the people of Guerrero."

12. "Antonio Veles" is a classic tale of rival *brosas* on the Costa Chica. This version was sung by Audón Ramón Juárez at the Gallardo home in Cruz Grande, Guerrero, on August 11, 1972.

13. "Villarreal" tells of two rival factions on the Costa Grande. Victoriano Texta Abarca and his father, José Texta Torres, performed it in Tecpan de Galeana in July 1972.

14. "El Culebro" tells of the death of Cirilo Hernández, known as "the Snake," one of the legendary heroes of the Costa Chica. I have versions of it from singers in Cruz Grande, Ometepec, and Acapulco.

15. This ballad called "Chicharrón" is about vengeance extracted at a funeral on the coast. This version was sung by Pablo and Laurencio Gallardo at the home of the Gallardo family in Cruz Grande, Guerrero, on August 5, 1972.

2 The Living Ballad

A throng of people without skill to read or write . . . gathered in
festal mood, and by loud song, perfect rhythm, and energetic
dance, expressing their feelings over an event of quite local ori-
gin, present appeal, and common interest.
—Francis Gummere, *The Popular Ballad*

Imagine this scene: we are in the main room of an adobe-walled house with
ceramic tile roofing, an earthen floor; with the demise of a scorching afternoon,
people have started assembling at this home, arriving on foot along the mud-
cracked paths cut by gullies connecting these houses. The town is Cruz Grande,
the month is August. There will be an evening of music and song.

Some men are arriving in pairs, bringing with them a guitar; a few just
wander in on their own to the salutations of those present. The woman of the
house is stirring about in the adjacent kitchen; she calls out a word of greet-
ing from time to time. Her husband enters and greets each person heartily,
makes each of us welcome in his house. In spite of these formalities, or per-
haps because of them, and certainly in part due to my presence—an outsider,
a gringo—there is a stiffness to the moment. I send out for a bottle of tequila
and shots are passed around the room. The stiffness eases, guitars are tuned,
and music is in the offing.

Most of these men are related to one another, as brothers, cousins, and in
the close kinship bond known in Mexico as *primo hermano* (first cousins whose
mothers are sisters). The four brothers—Modesto, Angel, Honorio, and Roge-
lio—are first cousins to Austreberto, the man of the house and, incidentally,
the *presidente municipal* (mayor) of Cruz Grande. Another pair of brothers,
Pablo and Laurencio, are cousins to these cousins, a degree of kinship further
removed. Policarpo Piza is a friend and neighbor to this gathering of the Gal-

lardo clan. Some wives have accompanied their husbands, and children of various ages move in and out freely among the group.

There are no opening ceremonies. Instead, after a period of readying the instruments, the first chords are struck and the chatter comes to a halt. Pablo Gallardo is singing a corrido about his cousin, Gonzalo Gallardo, next-of-kin to several of those present in Austreberto's house that evening. The guitar strokes are clean and direct in a triple meter, with a formulaic arpeggio inserted between stanzas and developed into an instrumental break after every third or fourth stanza. The voice of Pablo Gallardo, forceful, at moments even shrill, rises into the tenor range as he sings the opening stanza:

Voy a cantar un corrido	[I will sing a corrido
de un caso que sucedió,	about a case that happened
a los muchachos del cerro	to the boys of the highlands;
Chico Bernal les cayó,	Chico Bernal fell upon them—
ahora ¿qué vamos a hacer	now what can we do
si así lo dispusó Dios?	if God willed it like this?]

At the close of this stanza, as the guitars carry the song forward toward the next stanza, one of the men in the audience calls out loudly, in timing and tone consonant with the singing: "¡Así es Guerrero!" (That's how it is in Guerrero!). Another man chimes in: "¡Así es la costa, puro gallo!" (That's how it is on the coast, nothing but fighting cocks!). With those words resonating in the air, the singer launches into the second stanza:

Chico Bernal les cayó	[Chico Bernal fell upon them
con todita su gallada,	with all of his gang;
de valiente se llevaron	boldly they carried off
a ese mentado Gonzalo,	that famous Gonzalo
porque querían emparejar	because they wanted to get even
la muerte de Tadeo Gallardo.	for the death of Tadeo Gallardo.]

The audience is absorbed now in the performance; the men sit with their eyes mostly directed toward the ground, concentrating on the story; women are standing at the edges, surveying the scene. Only the children seem indifferent to the song in progress as they continue to circulate according to the logic of their play.

The singer and the two guitarists move through successive stanzas without faltering. The song comes into its pivotal section:

Ahí dijo Diego Bernal:
"Nito de mi corazón,
tú te llevas la guitarra
y yo me llevo el acordión,
y Palemón esta hamaca
envuelta en un pabellón."

[There spoke Diego Bernal:
"My dearest Nito,
you carry the guitar
and I'll carry the accordion,
and Palemón this hammock
wrapped up in a fine cloth."

Ese Palemón Felipe
hombre de valor sobrado:
"Párense, guapos cabrones
¿por qué están tan afanados?"
Les gritaba Palemón:
"Ahí les va tercio pesado."

That Palemón Felipe,
a man of surpassing valor:
"Hold it, my fine bastards—
why are you in such a hurry?"
Palemón shouted to them:
"Here comes the real heavy."]

We understand at this moment that the calculations of the raiding party have gone awry. The dramatic reversal of expectations here, from anticipation of a fiesta in celebration of a victory to an encounter with a deadly adversary, signals our arrival at the "emotional core" of this ballad (Coffin 1957), its most powerful and memorable narrative sequence. The power of these stanzas is further enhanced by the use of metaphor (*tercio pesado* literally means "the heavy load") and vulgarity (*cabrones*) in the reported speech. The audience responds with shouted interjections at the close of this segment in the song. Perhaps the most telling of them—"¡Así es la casa!" (That's how this house is!)—underscores the connection between the protagonists of the song and the people performing the song and witnessing its performance.

The corrido comes to a close with a variation on the conventional formula:

Ya me voy a despedir
por no seguirlo más largo,
aquí termina el corrido
del cerro y de los Gallardos,
aquí termina el corrido
del cerro y de los Gallardos.

[Now I will bid you farewell
so as not to carry it further;
here the corrido ends
of the highlands and the Gallardos;
here the corrido ends
of the highlands and the Gallardos.]

In winding up the final stanza, the singer slows the pace and the guitarists stroke a few closing chords. The performance ends with cheers and parting volleys from the audience: "¡Viva la costa!" "¡Viva Cruz Grande!" (Hurrah for the coast! Hurrah for Cruz Grande!). As the gathering breaks into dispersed conversations, the bottle of tequila is passed around once again and the men—plus a few of the women—serve themselves another shot.

The evening continues in this vein, moving through a series of songs as one singer after another offers a sampling of his repertoire, with voice and guitar accompaniment provided by various members in the gathering. After a while the turn at singing comes to rest with Pablo and Laurencio Gallardo, brothers who combine their voices with uncanny precision. The bottle of tequila is finished but there is no need of more fuel: the singing has already acquired its own momentum and nothing will stop it until well into the night when the hostess lets us know the hour is getting late. Toward the end of the evening Pablo and Laurencio sing an extended version of "Juan Colón," 156 lines of poetry in 26 stanzas, a singing that lasts almost one-half hour. The pattern of audience involvement remains constant, as ballads are sung about heroes known to the group personally or through local tradition. The occasional *chilena,* a lively dance rhythm cultivated in this region, offers a sprightly interlude, and boleros such as "Los Dos Perdimos," from the popular repertoire of recorded trios, keep alive the ever-present theme of tragic love. Among the mix that evening were one crafty and one impassioned love song in a rhythm the singers call the *colombiana* with its stutter-step beat. As most of the guests are leaving, I start out the door to fetch a blanket from my car, for I have been invited to sleep in a hammock. But my hostess dissuades me from leaving the house as the night is uncertain and all about are men carrying guns.

The living ballad is a curious notion for those who come to ballads through the study of literature, through participation in the folksong movement, or as consumers of commercial music. In these venues the ballad stands as a finished, fixed, and distanced object. It is easy to admire the evocative lyrics and the haunting melody of "Mary Hamilton" or "The Unquiet Grave" and to discover in these fossilized songs an early manifestation of Britain's poetic muse. In the United States, we are aware of ballad traditions that flourished once among miners, loggers, and cowboys, among union activists, in African-American communities along the lower Mississippi River, and in Scots-Irish communities of the upland South. But our experience of the ballad tends to be removed from our primary sense of who we are and of the kind of world we inhabit. To most of us, the ballad is a curiosity, a narrative song retrieved from another people, another time, another place. In this scheme of things, ballads are cherished for their ability to transfer human emotion and experience across the chasms that separate historical periods and distinct ethnicities.

The *living ballad,* as I intend the term, is another matter altogether. It is the ballad in its source community, typically a community that embraces a visionary heroic worldview. In this setting, the ballad is not a distanced object but rather an intimate one; it is neither finished nor fixed but always evolving, adapting to the needs and desires of those who cultivate and value it. The living ballad emerges from the shared life of the community and connects with the mental world and social practice of its members. It engages the aspirations, beliefs, and values of its adherents to a point where familiarity with the repertoire actually shapes people's expectations, their plans of action, and their responses to events. The ballad world and the world outside the ballad are merged.

My cue for isolating the living ballad comes from an insight by Américo Paredes. In an exchange with Merle Simmons, my friend and colleague at Indiana University, on the question of the ancestry of Mexico's corridos, Paredes (1963:231) draws a distinction between "traditional ballads" and "a ballad tradition." The former are "survivals of a moribund tradition," whereas a ballad tradition consists of "a crystallization of those survivals at one particular time and place into a whole ballad corpus, which by its very weight impresses itself on the consciousness of the people." Paredes and Simmons engage in debate on this theme: did the corrido spring into the world as a full-blown novelty in the latter part of the nineteenth century when it is first documented or had it existed sporadically in Mexico and elsewhere as a continuation of a wide-ranging Hispanic narrative song tradition? Simmons (1963) brings forward evidence of corrido-like fragments dating as far back as the early eighteenth century and from several sites, including Argentina, Colombia, Venezuela, and Cuba, arguing that the origin of the corrido must be treated in the context of this Spanish and Spanish-American tradition.

Paredes's response pivots on the definition of key terms. It is one thing, says he, to nuture a repertoire of historical ballads carried into the present as heirlooms from a distant past. It is something else to sustain a practice of creating and singing ballads in response to the events of the day. In the first instance, we have the maintenance of a store of traditional ballads, in the second, the cultivation of a living ballad tradition. This distinction is not a frivolous one, for it entails real differences with regard to how one hears and experiences the ballad. In a culture maintaining a corpus of traditional ballads, the experience is mediated through the passage of time, the succession of generations, the movement of peoples. Where the living ballad flourishes, the ballad is experienced as a vital component of the culture; it resonates with all other attributes of being and identity. It is the difference between knowing some verses from a classic such as "Tam Lin" and feeling the impact of a ballad commemorating the death of a friend, relative, or community figure. The living ballad addresses issues and events of direct personal relevance in the context of a whole corpus of balladry known to articulate the experience and values of the community.

The living ballad is an expressive artistic form that emerges from the conditions of ordinary life and reflects upon those conditions through the device of poetry set to music. The ballad is a rooted meditation on ordinary life. It is a familiar medium of communication that is constructed upon commonplace associations but that accomplishes a reframing of routine experience by introducing and pursuing an interpretive framework. The living ballad is not mysterious to those who know it. Such ballads are composed by individuals with a talent for verse and performed by individuals with a talent for singing and playing music. The composers and performers are known personalities in the community. People inhabiting ballad communities are acquainted with the ballad process—working from the dire events deemed worthy of commemorating to the unveiling of a newborn corrido. They know that young men strive to emulate (or avoid) the heroic models presented in the songs. They know that aggrieved or grieving individuals will seek out composers and commission from them a corrido to honor the memory of a fallen relative. They have seen how composers pass their songs on to performers and how one performer learns from another and then deviates according to his or her genius, all along the chain of dissemination. People in corrido communities are accustomed to the interplay between life and poetry. They find in the corridos, taken as a whole, the most revealing account of their own history.

Let us return momentarily to "Gonzalo Gallardo" as recreated and witnessed that evening in Cruz Grande, Guerrero. The narrative concerns a personage of note to those assembled, a senior male relative who attained a certain local status in life and in death. To an outsider like me the song is opaque at many points. Who is Chico Bernal? When we hear in a stanza near the end these words,

Ahí dijo Agustín Román:	[There spoke Agustín Román:
"'Ora sí que voy a ir,	"Now I'll surely leave;
a Cuatro Bancos no voy	I won't go to Cuatro Bancos
porque me puedo morir,	because I could die there;
esta burla me la pagan	they'll pay me for this trick,
los hijos de Chocotí."	the sons of Chocotí."]

it is clear enough that this is an embittered speech of renunciation, a vow for vengeance to follow, but who are the children of Chocotí? The outsider lacks the local knowledge assumed as a backdrop for the song narrative. With persistent questioning it is possible to discover that Cuatro Bancos is a settlement about halfway to the Pacific Ocean from the town of Cruz Grande and that the Chocotí are a clan residing in and around that settlement. It is not necessary to know these details to appreciate this corrido as a narrative of clan warfare. But two different modes of experience are implicated here: the local audience keys upon these references as emblems of a local identity; such details anchor and animate the narration, encouraging identification with the protagonists in the plot. The outsider passes over these details in securing a general impression of two groups in conflict with one another.

Conclusive and Permeable Texts

The discipline of folklore studies has drawn sustenance from a remarkable body of research exploring the history and literary qualities of the European ballad in all its regional manifestations (Entwistle 1939; Richmond 1989). Ballad scholarship has generated some powerful analytical tools, concepts such as "the emotional core" (Coffin 1957), "incremental repetition" and the "leaping and lingering" narrative technique (Gummere 1959), "communal recreation" (Barry 1933), and many others. But it is a curious fact of ballad scholarship that these significant insights have come about primarily through remote sensing, that is, in the absence of access to ballad communities and their living traditions. Ballad scholars have, for the most part, worked within the literary framework and treated ballads as literary expression. Some ballad scholars have discussed the social and cultural ambience of balladry (Buchan 1970; Renwick 1980; McCarthy 1990), but even this work has little to tell us about central features of ballad process, such as the motives for composing ballads, the occasions for singing them, and the response of audiences to performances of them.

Much of the earlier work on ballads is replete with hazy speculation regarding the operations of ballads and balladry in human sociability. Particularly troublesome is the matter of origins. Most ballad scholarship treats the ballad as a deviant form of literature without the linkage between authorial intent and consecrated text that has been generally assumed in literary studies. Ballads were seen to participate in a performative economy radically different from the conventional triad of author, book, and reader. In the prevailing account of nineteenth-century scholarship, ballads were seen as a poetry that invents itself either virtually independent of human volition or else through the device of a mythopoetic choral dance or throng. The assignment of balladry to the liminal period before the establishment of literacy or to pre- or quasi-literate incrustations in the modern setting occasions a dislocation of scholarly orientation, a loss of bearings, that has resulted in remarkable speculations on ballad origins.

Without documentation concerning the nature of oral poetry in its social and cultural contexts, literary scholars sought to exorcise their enchantment with the ballad through the creation of ingenious etiological myths. The assertions of George Lyman Kittredge, that giant among Shakespearean scholars, that "a ballad has no author," that "there are no comments or reflections by the narrator," leads to a remarkable denouement: "If it were possible to conceive a tale as *telling itself,* without the instrumentality of a conscious speaker, the ballad would be such a tale" (Sargent and Kittredge 1904:xi). One hears lurking behind these comments the mischievous formula attributed to the brothers Grimm, *das Volk dichtet,* the people as a whole composes poetry. Yet the denial of authorship is probably less bizarre than some attempts to imagine authorship, such as the once influential theories of Francis Barton Gummere, who concocted the "singing, dancing throng" as the imaginary source of ballad poetry.

It would be fair to say that ballad scholars have been seduced by the formal perfection of the ballad text to the extent that it became standard procedure to touch up any perceived imperfections to attain this ideal product. The perfect text is a *conclusive* text, that is, an end in itself, a final destination. Pursuing the conclusive text made it possible to chart the migration and evolution (often conceived as devolution) of songs, to speculate on the origins of poetry, and to analyze texts as complete verbal designs. But this approach divorces poetry from its makers. It severs the organic relationship between poetry and life, obscuring the social process that brings ballad texts into existence and sustains them in oral (and mixed oral-literary) tradition.

Immersion in a living ballad tradition teaches that the ballad text is permeable, an open artifact registering the impact of those who collaborate in its invention and reinvention through performance. Ballad texts, so cherished by generations of antiquarians and literary scholars, are the residue of a ballad ecology linking those who create and perform ballads to their audiences. My encounter with a living ballad tradition convinces me that ballads cannot be effectively treated as mere literary texts. In the following pages I develop an account of the ballad process that charts the positioning of composers, performers, and audiences with respect to the corridos and to the events they narrate. The general thrust of these considerations is to return this poetry to its makers, who are not after all invisible ciphers in a mechanical process, but instead vital agents in the creation and preservation of a poetry that tells their story as they would like it to be remembered.

The Ballad Process

The corrido is atmospheric in the state of Guerrero; it exerts a tremendous influence over patterns of thought and expression. Perhaps it possesses something of the weight attributed to the Spanish *romancero* during the Siglo de Oro, the famed Golden Age of Spanish arts and literature, when the themes and verses of balladry dominated the national consciousness. In Acapulco and down the Costa Chica, corridos are heard on the radio; they are played by local brass bands; they are performed in dimly lit cantinas; and they are composed and sung by popular artists in every barrio, pueblito, and rancho. This salience is most evident among the working class in cities and towns and among rural peasants, but the ballad presence is hardly confined to this element, as attested by the Arizmendi brothers—urbane professionals in fields such as teaching, libraries, and tourism. Those with roots in a town or village along the coast have a life-long acquaintance with the corrido tradition.

Perhaps even more significant than the active presence of the corrido in the daily lives and thinking of coastal people is its emblematic status as a symbol

Acapulco pays homage to the Arizmendi brothers, 1989

of local identity. Frequently after a performance of one of these songs of defiant heroism, one hears the exclamation, "¡Así es la costa!" (That's how it is on the coast!). Surely among the working classes, the heroic worldview of the ballads coincides with the idealized conception of the collective self. Exactly how far into the web of Costa Chica society this connection extends is uncertain. I suppose some individuals would very much like to be rid of the familiar stereotype link-ing the coastal population to violence. But to wander the popular neighbor-hoods of Acapulco or to visit any of the small towns along the Costa Chica or to drop in on the provincial cities of Ometepec or Pinotepa Nacional is to im-merse oneself in a world partly defined and totally perfused by the corrido.

Here the intersection of life and art is total. Corridos serve as a kind of blue-print for the honorable life; they hold up to ridicule the timid responses of the cowardly and exalt the bold deeds of the courageous. Corridos provide a char-ter by holding before the people a code of behavior. This vision of the honor-able life exists within an essentially tragic worldview, evident in the following very popular closing formula: "De estos hombres pocos nacen / y si nacen no se logran" (Few men like these are born / and if born, they don't last long). There is a single conceptual paradigm that perhaps most fully expresses this heroic worldview, *la pelea de gallos* (the cockfight). Corrido discourse can be highly metaphoric, especially in the bold and clever words spoken by the pro-tagonists, but this one extended metaphor—the valiant life as a stand-off be-tween two pugnacious fighting cocks—is so pervasive as to constitute a base or root metaphor for the entire tradition. The epithet "Es un gallo bien juga-do" (He is a proven fighting cock) is among the most common of corrido commonplaces. But the popular muse does not stop with such allusive refer-ences to the cockfight. A passing familiarity with the cockfight is essential in interpreting Costa Chica corridos, for the whole array of artifact and custom associated with this diversion can grace corrido plots.

Lucio Arizmendi, for example, refers to the *pelea de gallos* in "Juan Carmo-na."[1] After the death of the young protagonist, the father relays his son's ear-lier self-characterization:

Decía Carmona a su padre:	[Carmona said to his father:
"Si el destino no me falla,	"If fate doesn't let me down,
cuando busquen a este hombre	when they come looking for me
he de morir en la raya."	I will die standing my ground."]

Here "la raya" indicates the line drawn in the dust at the outset of a cockfight, marking the exact point where the two cocks will engage in battle. Carmona's words evoke this scenario and express his determination to stand fast at the line of battle just as the fighting cock does. The tradition frames this defiant attitude as exemplary.

I am suggesting a transference of values between the contrived realm of the cockfight and the realm of manly demeanor. There are ample ironies in this transference: roosters, who are taught to fight as human surrogates, are subsequently elevated as the epitome of human defiance. In turn, human conflict is readily portrayed through the extended metaphor of the cockfight. First roosters are humanized; then humans are equated with these elevated animals. This root metaphor and its transferences exist within a broader metaphorical rubric, that of the *macho,* the human male as an irrepressible natural force best exemplified in the cantankerous males of various species, especially the *toro* (bull), *borrego* (ram), and *gallo* (rooster).

It is clear that more than mere imagery is involved because the heroic figures commemorated in the ballads are often *galleros* (keepers of fighting cocks) and almost always avid participants in cockfight events. Many a corrido tells of ambushes at cockfights, where normally reclusive heroes have ventured forth to play their fighting cocks. The hero, known as *un gallo de traba* (a real fighting cock), is himself a connoisseur of the cockfight. It would be misleading to treat the *gallo* as merely a fortuitous metaphor, however, since awareness of the social context indicates a deeper relationship between poetry and life, one in which the heroes actually identify with the attitude and destiny of the animal they have elevated into a symbol. Véronique Flanet, the French anthropologist who visited the Costa Chica in the 1970s, noted the identity forged between *valiente* and *gallo* (1977:203): "The trainer becomes one with the cock; the game unto death of the cock allows him to live his own death, to play out his own death."

Corridos portray the ideal male role as one ultimately of defiance unto death. Like the fighting cock, the hero must stand his ground firmly to the bitter end, even if it costs him his life, in the corrido formula, *aunque me cueste la vida.* The ideal man in the world of Costa Chica corridos is also a man who can speak well, even artfully, a man sensitive to the pathos of poetry. There is a strong cultural emphasis on artful language on the Costa Chica, evident in the *versos* that are interspersed in conversation and song, the rousing *chilena* lyrics, ceremonial jests at weddings, and proverbial inscriptions placed on machete blades (Tibón 1961; Memije Alarcón 1995). Participation in the corrido tradition, as composers or singers, is so widespread on the Costa Chica as to provide further evidence for this claim of a collective appreciation of poetic speech. The complete man in these communities is a person who cultivates in public performance some variety of poetic speech, be it recited poetry or song. On the coast the production of live music often takes precedence over the replaying of recorded sound, and one is never far from the strumming of guitar strings, often enough as an accompaniment to the singing of corridos.

Scholarship normally treats ballads as literature, albeit deviant literature, marked by curious infelicities, repetitions, and lapses that can be attributed to an irregular mode of creation. Ballad scholars have poured over collections of ballad texts as their primary (sometimes exclusive) contact with these traditions. Exposure to the living ballad radically alters the picture; suddenly ambient factors leap into sight. It turns out, not surprisingly, that ballads are composed, performed, and savored by human beings who are connected in specific ways to the tradition, to the events narrated, and to the other persons active in the ballad process. The ballad text, like other documentary records of aural and verbal performances, is an artifact, a partial reconstruction of a complex web of human action and intent. It is this reliance on texts that has perpetrated the illusion of the disembodied ballad.

This is not to deny the importance of text, which remains a transportable and tangible relic of performance. In fact, acquaintance with a living ballad tradition inspires a new interest in the notion of "text," since members of the ballad community recognize an ideal form of each song, a "textualized" version that may or may not be captured in writing. The living ballad proposes a realignment of focus, locating "the text" as an indicator of social process culminating in the performance of corridos in public arenas. Ballad texts derive from narrative song events implicating at least three roles (which can on occasion collapse onto a single actor), those of composer, performer, and audience.

Composers of corridos are much revered on the Costa Chica. "Es un don de Dios" (It's a gift from God), one hears. My friend Juvenal Arellanes used a phrase for composers that is often lavished upon corrido heroes: "De esos hombres pocos nacen" (Few men like that are born), leaving off the clause that usually follows, "y el que nace no se logra" (and the one who is born doesn't last). The process of composition can be divided into primary and secondary components. Primary composers are those who invent a new song by harnessing new words to a familiar ballad tune or by forging a new association between verbal and musical resources. The limiting case is the composer who slightly modifies an existing ballad; here we border on secondary composition, wherein an existing ballad is only minimally altered, most often inadvertently in the act of performance. Albert Lord (1960) has alerted us that composition and performance can coincide in a single expressive moment, and this coincidence has a place in the ballad ecology as secondary composition (see McDowell 1972).

These observations lead us to the moment of performance, which always entails some nuances, however slight, of secondary composition. In the limiting case, the performers can so disfigure or reconfigure an existing song that the process closely resembles primary composition, the key difference being perhaps one of intent (the performers have not intended to create a new song). The corrido tradition provides recurrent instances of stanzas switched or stanzas dropped, of lines shuffled about or altered, of phrases provided with divergent grammar and diction. Often accidental features of the performance event force these departures from the prototype, as performers search for words that elude them or deliberately modify the song to please or to avoid angering someone present.

What is interesting, in the corrido of the Costa Chica at least, is that performers themselves acknowledge the sanctity of the prototype, however vaguely they apprehend it. The text is a valuable artifact in this ballad tradition, even though performances are almost never fashioned directly from printed scores. Juvencio Vargas, the best of the ballad singers in Guerrero, would say of other singers, "Ellos lo dañan" (They ruin it) or "Ellos lo cantan como es" (They sing it as it is). Many corrido singers keep written texts out of respect for the proper form of songs. Francisco Arroyo owns a cherished notebook in which his sons have gathered typed versions of his own and other ballads. Juvencio Vargas relies on the writing and reading skills of his daughter, Meche, who will recite the words of songs to refresh his memory. The Arizmendi brothers, especially composers Lucio and Miguel, commit the words of their own songs to paper as they create them. They even prepare illustrated photocopies of their songs for distribution within their circle of friends. But these occasional incursions of literacy into the tradition do not modify its essentially oral character.

Performers must likewise be grouped into primary and secondary categories. Every corrido performance elevates one or a few individuals to a position of accountability for the successful completion of the song. I have never witnessed a total breakdown in the system such that a performance in progress might grind to a halt, though I have witnessed a few shabby performances that did little justice to the song. The central figure is the main singer, who takes responsibility for carrying the narrative from its opening to its closing. This person may be flanked by subsidiary singers who provide harmonies and by musicians who provide a musical surround for the narrative. Secondary performers visibly cue on the main performer, and they are subject to his wrath if they overstep their supportive role. Likewise, I have seen musicians scolded for not providing instrumental breaks at the appropriate moments. There is plenty of intense ensemble work in these group performances, all keyed to the initiative afforded by the main performer.

At the boundary between the role of performer and audience member is

Miguel Arizmendi, a man of words, Acapulco, 1996

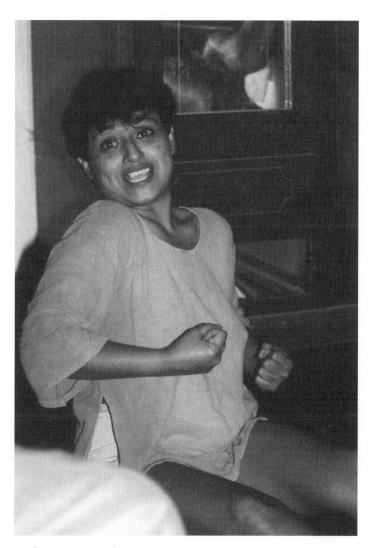

Meche Vargas, Acapulco, 1990

the space allotted for especially vocal members of the audience. Corrido performances are punctuated by audience vocalizations ranging from the proto-verbal to the fully verbal, and one of the shortcomings of the text as artifact is that it rarely comprehends this emotive counterpoint to the narrative discourse. In fact, an adequate account of corrido performance must necessarily include the commentaries and shouts interjected by members of the audience, for these are tailored to interact both musically and semantically with the song in progress. There is nothing random about the timing and the tapering of the *grito*, and the primary and secondary performers of corridos are themselves reassured and inspired by these gestures of solidarity on the part of audience members, who might be thought of as tertiary performers.

This structure of roles identifies the generic process in the making and presenting of corridos. We must now investigate the positioning of individuals who fill these roles. In the following anecdotes depicting corrido composition and performance lurks the essential character of the corrido as a permeable expressive form.

The Composer's Niche

We are concerned here with primary composition, with those who originate new ballads in this expanding narrative song tradition. I spoke with several composers of Costa Chica corridos: Lucio Arizmendi is an urban professional who works at the airport in Acapulco; El Cobarde is a barber in the provincial town of Ometepec; Moisés Vargas owned and managed El Rincón Bohemio (the Bohemian's Corner), a picturesque salon for food and drink in Ometepec; Onofre Contreras is a professional musician in Acapulco whose corridos have become popular on the coast. The common elements in each biography are a deep commitment to the corrido tradition forged over the course of the person's lifetime coupled with some degree of personal detachment from the immediate environment of the violent events. These composers seem to exist at some remove from the heroic world of corrido events. Typically, they live in a city and are approached for corridos by people from nearby towns or they live in towns and attract clients from the surrounding villages. Much as one might travel to a city or to a town for a service not readily available at home, people would journey to nearby commercial centers to locate composers when they found themselves in need of a corrido. El Cobarde, the barber, offers parallel services, providing villagers with haircuts and with corridos.

On the Costa Chica it would be impossible to find anybody unaware of the ballad tradition. In an environment pervaded by ballad consciousness, every individual is affected to some degree. The composers I interviewed had all come of age in the ballad community and had accepted the corrido as a principal means of poetic and musical expression. The musical environment of the Costa Chica includes dance forms like the *chilena*, many romantic and tropical forms (*huapangos, bambucos, valses peruanos*), and the narrative corrido, each of them contributing an essential flavor to the bohemian persona of the coast. Some composers of corridos were active as well in adjacent genres in the local repertoire; others restricted their compositional talents to the corrido, and specifically to the *corrido trágico*.

When I asked Meche Vargas how people came to write corridos, she stressed the experiential aspect: "Porque estas son cosas que la gente ha presenciado, lo ve y de allí les llega la idea, especialmente cuando la persona es respetado en el pueblo, les hacen su corrido para que quede en la mente, para recordar a una persona que fue importante para ellos, de allí nace el corrido" (Because these are things that people have witnessed, they see them and that's where they get the idea, especially when the person is well respected in the town, they make them a corrido that will stay in people's minds, to recall a person who was important to them, so that's how the corridos come about). Meche told me that certain individuals are recognized as specialists and that they work within a climate that favors their composition. She describes composing as managing poetic units such as lines and stanzas and fitting these to music. Much of the material for ballads found in her home town of Ometepec comes from the small settlements, often referred to as *bajos*, on the periphery of the more substantial towns. The events selected for treatment in the corridos are substantiated by independent evidence, as they lie within the experience of the community. Not just anybody is a likely target for a compositional effort; instead the composers tend to select the more notable personages of the town to leave behind a verbal memento of them.

The Costa Chica composers I spoke to confirmed these general principles. El Cobarde (the Coward) is well known as a musician and composer in Ometepec. He is a slim, handsome man with dark skin and mostly European facial features. This kindly gentleman embraces his nickname contentedly. As he explained to me, he comes from a family of *amigos*, the local term for the tough characters enshrined in the Costa Chica corridos, but he decided early on that he did not want to participate in that way of life: "Me dicen así porque no me quedé a pelear" (They call me that because I didn't stick around to fight). Something of his wry wit can be discerned from this public announcement scrawled on the walls of his shop:

Oyeme cliente mi amigo:	[Listen to me, client my friend:
no importa que no tengas estudio,	it doesn't matter if you don't have education,
no importa que no tengas riquesas,	it doesn't matter if you don't have wealth,
no importa que no tengas nada,	it doesn't matter if you don't have anything,
pero pórtate como los hombres,	but act like a man,
ten verguenza, y no me pida fiada la pelada.	have some pride, and don't ask for your haircut on credit.]

In the course of his workday he hears about notable events in and around town and quickly turns these accounts into corridos. He told me with some pride about one occasion when he began composing even as one of his clients described a recent shooting in his home town of Azoyú; within a few days he had the entire corrido done, complete with music.

El Cobarde is typical of Costa Chica composers in his placement within the ballad tradition. He assimilated the corrido outlook as a birthright, coming of age in the very matrix of the *brosas*. But he has established a slightly detached perspective on his place of origin, preferring a perch that affords him a safe reprise on the violence that continues to plague the communities along the coast. For several years El Cobarde taught music in the Acapulco schools, only returning later in life to his native region. It appears that these shapers of poetic narrative thrive in a niche that lies beyond active engagement in the corrido lifestyle, a position that gives them the liberty to adopt a reflective attitude toward the events they commemorate.

Nonetheless, El Cobarde and the others do write songs about people and happenings that have touched them personally if indirectly. El Cobarde prefaces a performance of his composition, "Abel Torres," with this comment: "ahora pues el corrido de un individuo que no fue matón; era profesor y fue mi compañero de escuela" (now the corrido of an individual who was not a killer; he was a teacher and my classmate in school). The thread of personal involvement, either with a person or with a place or with a community, runs through most of the accounts I have gathered about motives for composing a specific corrido. Another instance is provided by Enrique Mares, who composed a corrido about his uncle, Alejandrino Ambrosias, in response to a request from a companion:

Ese era mi tío, era mi tío y sabía tocar muy bien la guitarra. Se enamoró de una mujer de un rico y lo mandó matar pues. La mujer lo quiso a él, era pobre pero lo quiso. Entonces el rico lo mandó matar con pistoleros.

Pero estando en la guardia donde trabajo, yo estaba con el maestro de música, y empezamos a tocar la guitarra, pero entonces me dice: "¿Por qué no le haces un corrido?"

Le digo yo: "Pero yo no me acuerdo pues, yo era chamaco."

El otro dice: "Yo me acuerdo."

Otro compañero dice: "Andaba conmigo cuando lo mataron."

Entonces me empezaron a decir. El maestro de música dice: "Yo lo voy a co-ordinar."

Así hice ese corrido que oyó.

[He was my uncle. He was my uncle and he played the guitar very well. He fell in love with the woman of a rich man and so he arranged to have him killed. The woman loved him—he was poor but she loved him. Then the rich man had him killed by hired gunmen.

But one time we were at the police station where I work. I was with the music teacher, and we began to play the guitar, so then he says to me: "Why don't you write a corrido about him?"

I tell him: "But I don't remember, I was just a child."

He says: "I remember."

Another companion says: "He was with me when they killed him."

So they started telling me about it. The music teacher says: "I'm going to put it together for you."

That's how I made the corrido you just heard.]

Here we have an account of a joint compositional process—but not a singing, dancing throng—motivated through a complex network of associations linking the composer and the protagonist. The immediate motive is the kinship that ties the primary composer, Enrique Mares, to Alejandrino Ambrosias, his uncle. Beyond that is the common interest among the full team of composers in the theme of music-making as a life's commitment. The story concerns a man who in some sense gave his life in the service of the bohemian lifestyle. There is also a class consciousness that operates in this account: a rich man eliminated a poor man and a philistine arranged the death of a poet and musician. The basis for identification with the story protagonist begins with the kinship linkage but then moves outward into the arenas of shared lifestyles and ideologies. The process of consultation between composer and eyewitness, in this case expanded into a joint act of composition, is also a common thread in accounts of corrido origins.

As a composer Lucio Arizmendi has adapted the traditional ballad to a heightened poetic sensibility, yet he clearly works within the corrido tradition and his ballads are popular among all segments of the Guerrero population. Arizmendi was born and raised in the town of Ejido Nuevo, inland from the Pacific coast but still part of the Costa Chica region. The ballad tradition is active in this area, and Arizmendi remembers ballad heroes of Ejido Nuevo and nearby towns who were commemorated in songs he heard as a child. As a young man he started composing corridos, achieving his first major success with "Tiene Lumbre el Comal" (The Hearth Has Live Embers), a ballad about the capture of a rogue police patrol in Ejido Nuevo. Again, the basis for selecting this theme is its resonance in the life and mind of the composer, a native son and a staunch advocate of democracy for the state of Guerrero.

Arizmendi has modified the traditional corrido, formally by introducing

Lucio Arizmendi (*left*) with the author, Acapulco, 1989

poetic diction and idiosyncratic metaphor, topically by including overt statements of political orientation. One of his ballads opens with the strikingly original phrase "Señores, soy el corrido" (Gentlemen, I am the corrido), a personification of the genre itself as bearer of news. Lucio Arizmendi has also completed a corrido about Salvador Allende. It is clear that this composer has chosen not to reject but rather to adapt and expand the corrido tradition as he has matured as an artist. Throughout a process of artistic experimentation, he remains rooted in the corrido tradition that shaped his outlook and his musical strivings from youth.

When Arizmendi began to achieve some notice as a composer of corridos and other songs, he found that people would come to him with requests for songs on topics dear to their hearts. He comments regarding the origin of his composition "Los Torres":

Elpidio Torres es un personaje, un señor de Ejido, de los principales como le llaman de un pueblo. Tenía tres hijos, dos de ellos gemelos. A que uno de ellos, Catarino, que no era gemelo, tuvo problemas con unas gentes que viven cerca de Ejido Nuevo, en otro pueblecito que no tiene nombre, es una ranchería.

Aquellos señores mandaron a traer a Elpidio Torres sabiendo que sus hijos iban a ir en seguida a estar con él. Esa es la clásica emboscada, ¿no? Invitarle al padre, llegaron los hijos, y los mataron.

Pasaron unos días, eso fue el primero de diciembre. Después de dos meses, el señor Elpidio Torres era mi compadre, me contó la historia. El quiso que la tragedia de sus hijos se quedara en la mente del pueblo a través de un corrido.

Me contó toda la historia, cómo sucedió, cómo los mataron a ellos, tres hijos, los tres cayeron al mismo tiempo. Pues le prometí hacerles un corrido, se lo escribí y le canté, le gustó mucho y quedó.

[Elpidio Torres is a figure, a gentleman of Ejido, one of the pillars, as they call them, of the community. He had three sons, two of them twins. It happened that one of them, Catarino, the one who wasn't a twin, had some problems with some people who live near Ejido Nuevo, in another little town without a name—it is a small settlement.

Those gentlemen sent for Elpidio Torres knowing that his sons would come along right away to be with him. It's the classic ambush, right? Invite the father, the sons came along, and they killed them.

A few days went by, that was the first of December. After two months, Mr. Elpidio Torres was my *compadre*, he related the story to me. He wanted the tragedy of his sons to stay in the mind of the community by virtue of a corrido.

He told me the whole story, how it happened, how they killed them, three sons, all three fell at the same time. So I promised to write them a corrido. I wrote it and I sang it, he liked it very much, and it has remained in currency.]

The characteristic themes of the compositional process reappear in this account. Lucio Arizmendi is drawn to the story by his connection to the place where it happened and also by kinship—this time ritual kinship—to one of its principal figures. In this instance there is a catalyst, the *compadre* who requests a corrido about his slain sons. Note that Elpidio Torres is not just anybody around Ejido Nuevo—he is a pillar of the community. As in other cases, the person who witnessed the event relays his firsthand account to the composer-poet, who takes great interest in specific narrative detail. The aggrieved father recognizes the importance of commemoration through corrido; he wants the tragedy of his sons to stay in people's minds. The resulting composition was pleasing to the petitioner, but perhaps more importantly, it has earned its way into currency in the local ballad repertoire.

The connection between composer and story protagonist is not necessarily left in the background, as the case of "Los Torres" demonstrates. When Lucio Arizmendi or one of his brothers sings this ballad, he usually makes mention of his friendship with the Torres family at the outset of the performance. Moreover, acknowledgment of the relationship is built into the opening and closing stanzas of the ballad, the very segments that normally index the extranarrative circumstances of the occasion:

The opening:

Voy a cantar un corrido	[I will sing a corrido—
que me llena de dolor,	it fills me with sorrow;
yo de los cuatro fui amigo	I was a friend of these four,
amigo de corazón.	a friend from the heart.

The closing:

Ya me despido señores	Now gentlemen, I bid farewell;
ya desahogué mi dolor,	now I have relieved my sorrow;
para Carlos y los Torres	to Carlos and the Torres family
dedico yo esta canción.	I dedicate this song.]

These personal touches fly in the face of the standard wisdom concerning the ballad's impersonality. The innovative methods of Lucio Arizmendi are partly responsible for this departure from the conventional stance, but I think it important to note that the ballad's celebrated objective stance leaves room for personal affirmations.

Direct connections linking composer to ballad subject are common but not always present. Some personages along the coast are so widely known (and feared) that their demise is fair game for any aspiring corrido-maker. Moisés

Moisés Vargas (*right*) with his nephew, Isaac Vargas, Ometepec, 1989

Vargas, who died in 1995, was a genial, swarthy gentleman, highly regarded as a poet and composer. He begins his account of the composition of his corrido "La Mula Bronca" as follows: "Ese señor era muy famoso aquí en la región de la Costa Chica, y fue conocido en el puerto de Acapulco. Algunos funcionarios del gobierno, generales, coroneles, todo eso, le tenían mucho miedo, porque era un hombre peligroso" (This gentleman was very famous here in the region of the Costa Chica, and he was known in the port city of Acapulco. Some functionaries in the government—generals, colonels, and the like—feared him greatly because he was a dangerous man). La Mula Bronca (the Angry Mule), who fell into the hands of the government less than ten years ago, is a throwback to the outlaws of old. Having established the viability of this theme as a legitimate corrido topic, Vargas goes on to speak of his compositional technique:

> Y yo, sobre ese tema, quise componerle sus versos, más o menos cómo fuera la tragedia, el suceso, el caso, ¿verdad?
> Para escribir un corrido yo lo que hago es orientarme, cómo fue el suceso, cómo fueron los encuentros, cómo fueron los atracos, con quiénes personas

estaban, de dónde irían, de qué pueblo, cuáles eran sus hazañas, y yo empiezo a escribir, sacando la partitura, la forma en que se les haga todo, cuadrado, con metáfora, de música, todo.

[And I, on this theme, wanted to write him some verses, more or less about how the tragedy, the event, the case, took place, right?
In order to write a corrido what I do is get oriented—how the thing happened, what the encounters were like, which people was he with, where were they coming from, from which town, what were his deeds—and I begin to write it, arranging the stanzas, in the form that these things are done—well-shaped, with metaphor, set to music, everything.]

Once settled on a worthy ballad theme, Vargas is then anxious to "get oriented," that is, to secure a bundle of information on the particulars in the case. This commitment to history runs throughout these accounts, and it is safe to say that whatever the ultimate historical value of the corrido, the primary composer invests considerable energy in the attempt to obtain facts and to present the story accurately, at least in its essentials. Moisés Vargas, like other corrido makers, was highly conscious of the corrido as an artistic form with its own poetic and musical requirements. Composers use the term *cuadrado* (squared, well-formed), to refer to the finished product of their labors. The mention of *metáfora* (metaphor) is less customary and marks this maker of corridos as a man of more literary ambition than many of his peers.

Reverence for factual detail was expressed to me by another coastal composer, Onofre Contreras, a nervous, intense man in his midforties, dashing in his charro outfit inspired by the *norteño* style. Contreras emphasized the importance of obtaining accurate information "para no decir mentiras" (so as not to be telling lies). Working in Acapulco with stories from that city and from nearby towns, he consults newspaper accounts and tunes into discussions he hears around him, attempting to form a clear impression of the violent event that will be the centerpiece of his corrido. Assembling data from all these sources, he gradually comes to an understanding that he can work with in designing his corrido. He portrays this preparation stage as a process of closing in on the truth: "¿Cuál será la verdad? Me voy a inclinar por este lado, a veces no le yierro mucho, pero uno más o menos se está dando cuenta de, se está imaginando, esto vino así, esto fue así, pudo haber sido más fácil de esta manera que de esa, y este dato me quedo con él. Hay que chequear . . . y veo lo que más puede estar acercado a la realidad" (What could be the truth? I think I'll lean to this side. Sometimes I'm not far off, but one more or less figures it out. One is imagining, this came like this, this was like this, it would be more likely this way than that way, and I'll hang onto this detail. It's important to verify . . .

and I see what may be coming closest to the reality). Contreras told me that at times he tries to imagine himself in the middle of the action to sort out which elements in conflicting accounts have a greater likelihood of being true. "En el centro de un palenque, voy a cantar un corrido, pa' recordar un valiente caballero muy conocido, pero ya estoy imaginándome, por decirlo así, que yo estoy en el palenque, me estoy imaginando yo en el palenque" (In the middle of a thatched shelter, I am going to sing a corrido, to bring to mind a well-known bold gentleman, but I am already imagining myself, to say it this way, that I am under the shelter, I am imagining myself in that shelter).

For Onofre Contreras, the compositional process begins with the music. He makes every effort to create a melody that is sufficiently distinct to be accepted as original to him. From this starting point he devises poetic lines to match his melodic phrases and to tell the story as he has constructed it in his imagination. He will often insert a specific detail to ground his narrative in the appropriate environment; for example, he will mention that people are relaxing in the shade of a tree that is native to the region. He stresses that a corrido works "cuando tiene de imaginación" (when it shows the results of an active imagination).

Contreras, like other composers along the coast, writes corridos on request as well as on topics that have captured public interest. He mentioned *compadres,* fathers, brothers, and wives of fallen heroes as likely sources of personal requests for corridos. On occasion, the hero himself, knowing that he is in mortal danger, will approach the composer with a request like this one: "'Oyeme, yo quiero que me compongas un corrido; si puedes, componémelo antes de que me muera, y si no por lo menos házmelo aún cuando yo no pueda oirlo'" ("Listen, I want you to compose for me a corrido; if you can, compose it for me before I die, and if not, at least do it for me even when I can no longer hear it"). Contreras told me about a very rough character, a man named Félix Salas Zequeida, a known murderer, who always treated him "de maravilla" (marvelously well). "Tal que parece que sabía que yo le iba a componer su corrido" (It seems that he knew I was going to compose his corrido). In some cases, the composer is inspired to make a corrido for a friend: "Pues, digo, bueno, pa' que quede un recuerdo, porque de todas maneras, eso es lo único que va a quedar, yo voy a hacer un corrido, a mi camarada, mi cuate, a mi amigo, yo le voy a hacer un corrido" (So, I say, fine, so it stays as a reminder, because in any case, that is all that will remain. I am going to make a corrido, for my comrade, my pal, for my friend—I am going to make him a corrido).

The positioning of corrido makers that emerges from these individual cases is a mixture of detachment and involvement. Composers are involved by virtue of coming of age in the ballad community and by virtue of their interaction with those who solicit corridos for themselves or for their fallen relatives. At the same time, most of the composers I spoke with had removed themselves from the grasp of the ballad community, and they made little effort to affect the lifestyle of the heroes portrayed in their ballads. Composers are regarded with some reverence on the Costa Chica, as persons gifted with the ability to create moving tales of violent encounters set to sonorous corrido melodies. They are held accountable by their public, and, as we shall see, by the authorities, for the contents of their compositions. The composers I interviewed think of their talent as a *don,* a gift from God that they are obliged to develop for the good of their community.

Performers and the Bohemian Lifestyle

The term *bohemio* is a current one in the state of Guerrero, where a necessary attribute of the complete person, especially the complete man, is a devotion to poetic expression. The *bohemio* has an abiding love of poetry and song and periodically enters a kind of expressive warp given over to indulgence in the performance and appreciation of poetic language. *Bohemio* is also used to designate social events featuring performance of song and poetry in a casual gathering of friends. More than a few cantinas in Guerrero have names like the restaurant managed for many years in Ometepec by Moisés Vargas, El Rincón Bohemio. The bohemian lifestyle is typically ascribed to heroes in the corridos; the notion is that they live it up for a time until their inevitable destiny carries them away in their prime.

If the composer of corridos normally stands apart from the people and events celebrated in the ballads, corrido performers often occupy a less peripheral location. In fact, the best performers I witnessed along the Costa Chica aspired to the reputed lifestyle of the corrido hero. These singers and musicians devoted themselves to the bohemian night replete with music and song, and they often admired the tough characters commemorated in the ballads. Cultivating a competence in the balladry was a means of declaring one's affinity with the heroes and the heroic worldview featured in the songs.

In several corridos, the heroes are presented as participants in a bohemian lifestyle that includes love of song. One of the most famous of Costa Chica figures, Juan Colón, calls for guitars and music on his fatal visit to the barrio of Tres Palos. Another corrido protagonist, in "Claudio Bahena,"[2] cannot wait to get his hands on a guitar; when he does, he starts singing corridos. Interestingly, the man he is with, who intends to murder him, tries to harmonize but lacks the skill to do so. The Costa Chica is suffused with singers express-

Artemio Aguirre, a corrido singer, and friends at a *bohemio,* Acapulco, 1989

ing admiration for the heroes of their songs and heroes who share the sing-
ers' love of music. Dwight Reynolds (1995:79) notes in Egyptian epic perfor-
mances a "mirroring" between poets and heroes, involving a "complex nego-
tiation of relationships between the figures of poet, hero, and patron." A similar
pattern is manifested in the affinities linking corrido performers and heroes
on the Costa Chica.

Performing the Living Ballad

The efforts of composers and performers come to fruition in social gatherings
where corridos are sung. At the beginning of this chapter we glanced at one
of these sessions. There are many occasions for singing corridos on the Costa
Chica. Corridos are performed in public spaces such as marketplaces, canti-
nas, fairs, and cockfights. Américo Paredes (1976) pointed to a distinction on
the Texas-Mexico border between "lonesome" singing and singing at social
events. On the Costa Chica I heard very little about solitary singing. Instead,
as Gabriel Moedano (1988:124) indicates, there is a pivotal distinction between

singing at informal and formal gatherings. Informal occasions take place in private homes and outdoor shelters in the absence of a special motive for assembly and without the benefit of elaborate arrangements. The more formal end of the scale includes occasions such as *santos* (birthday celebrations), *bohemios* (evenings of poetry and song), baptisms, weddings, wakes, and *fandangos* (organized parties and dances).

As we have noted, the typical session alternates between corridos and other popular music forms. A series of corridos might be followed by an interlude featuring a string of *chilenas*. As happened at the gathering in Cruz Grande, the musicians may work in *colombianas* and *boleros* to further vary the musical idiom. In more casual settings, the turn at initiating and leading a song performance is likely to pass around from one qualified person to another, with musicians filling in as they deem appropriate. Formal occasions are more likely to feature set combos working through their musical repertoires. Both settings allow for requests from the audience for particular items, and in either casual or more formal settings audience members contribute actively to the performance with their shouts and whistles.

When a corrido is on the agenda, whether by audience request or initiative of the musicians, there is a probable sequence of events. The arrival of a particular corrido is announced by the strumming of its tonic chord or the picking out of its first melodic phrase. The singing may be preceded by a prologue, in which performers and audience members talk about the episode, its protagonists, and personal associations with the material. In the interlude before the singing begins, musicians often try to "coax" the corrido by rehearsing in muted tones its initial words and musical phrases.

The threshhold of the actual performance is clearly marked as the musicians turn to face the audience squarely, and the leader calls out something like "¡Sale!" (Here goes!) or "¡Vámonos!" (Let's go!). The corrido performance invariably begins with a rather deliberate guitar statement of the melody as musicians gradually orient themselves to the song in progress. If there are two singers, their vocal combination may be a bit halting in the first stanza, but as the singing moves through the early stanzas the ensemble finds a comfortable groove, the pace picks up, and the musicians coordinate their efforts seamlessly. The lead singer continues to exercise control over the performance, setting the pace by initiating each vocal line. Between each stanza the musicians insert adornments or partial statements of the melody, and after every third or fourth stanza the singing pauses to allow for an instrumental statement of the complete melody. Throughout the singing, audience members are free to toss in statements and shouts, timed and trimmed to complement the performance.

At the completion of the song, audience members signal their appreciation by applauding and by contributing additional shouts. An epilogue, a meditation on the persons and events presented in the corrido, often follows. This discussion may overlap with the beginning of a new cycle as another corrido is brought forward for performance.

At every juncture in this sequence, the living ballad opens to the experience of its audience. Prologues and epilogues stress personal connections to the persons and places featured in the songs. Juvencio Vargas, the most prolific of the ballad singers I have recorded on the coast, is a fount of information on the histories, nicknames, and other attributes of the heroes he sings about. He was once given a ride between towns by La Mula Bronca: "¿Qué tal que le hubieran caído sus enemigos?" (What if his enemies had fallen upon him then?). He knew Chante Luna's righthand man, known as El Patotas (the Bigfeet), having learned the butcher's trade from this ill-fated man. He identified Juvencio Moreno, one of the most famous of the Costa Chica *amigos,* as his *tocayo* (name-sharer), and supplied anecdotal information about him: he lives like a hermit in a house on a hill, and if you want some job done (such as the elimination of an enemy), just go to him and arrange it. Vargas laughingly described his *tocayo*'s deadly business in terms appropriate to an office, with secretaries, schedules, and deals struck over a handshake. Vargas packs the prologues and epilogues to his corridos with supplementary details manifesting a deep personal involvement in the local history underlying the ballads.

Personal involvement and identification in this ballad tradition sometimes lead singers and audience members to exchange knowing comments in the midst of ballad performances. As Ernesto Gallardo and Alejandro Mejía sing "Sidonio," Gallardo tosses out a series of comments to my friend Raul Mayo, a member of the audience directly related to the protagonist of the song. When one gang is portrayed as seeking revenge on another, Gallardo sends Mayo a sarcastic comment: "Estaba sencillo" (It was easy). Later, as one fighter is pictured as waiting in the bushes to fill his antagonist with lead, Gallardo says to Mayo: "Lo quería mucho" (He was really fond of him). In the epilogue to this performance, Mayo clarifies his connection to Sidonio, who was his father's *primo hermano* (first cousin), and provides additional details on the bitter feud between the two extended families implicated in song.

The living ballad, with its permeable text opening toward the experience of the community, is a platform upon which composers, performers, and audience members meet to celebrate and commemorate regional history. Composers, situated at some distance from the heroic lifestyle, are inspired by the familiar corpus of balladry to invent new songs to keep pace with the swirl of

The author with Raul Mayo (*right*), Cruz Grande, 1989

Ernesto Gallardo (*left*) and Alejandro Mejía, Cruz Grande, 1989

local events. Performers, more involved in the lives of the heroes, maintain a stock of ballads in their repertoires to satisfy the demands of their audiences. And audience members solicit corridos on musical occasions as embodiments of local pride and identity. At every stage of this ballad process, personal associations bind individuals to one another, to the tradition, and to the events narrated in the songs.

Notes

1. "Juan Carmona" was composed by Lucio Arizmendi at the request of the fallen hero's father.

2. "Claudio Bahena," a corrido of the Costa Grande, was performed in Acapulco in February 1996 by a trio, Los Dinámicos, consisting of the brothers Andrés and Rolando Cruz and their cousin Oscar Villasana.

3 The Ballad Community

Whenever a people in the course of its development reaches a
certain moral and intellectual stage, it will feel an impulse to
express itself . . . in . . . narrative verse. . . . The condition of a
society in which a truly national or popular poetry appears [is]
a condition in which the people are not divided by political
organization and book culture into markedly distinct classes,
in which consequently there is such community of ideas and
feelings that the whole people form an individual.
—Francis James Child, "1874 Essay from Johnson's Universal
Cyclopaedic and Atlas"

During a series of visits to the Costa Chica, I have witnessed hundreds of bal-
lad performances and overheard scores of conversations about regional cor-
ridos. More than elsewhere in Mexico, excepting the northern frontier with
its narcocorrido, ballads are on the public agenda on Guerrero's Costa Chica.
It is true that I was looking for ballads, but I readily found them in towns and
settlements in this region, in currency and in great numbers. Until I stumbled
upon the rich vein of local balladry in Cruz Grande in 1972, I was not certain
that the corrido was a living tradition, especially in light of the common wis-
dom that the ballad tradition in Mexico had fallen into a period of decadence
after 1930 (Mendoza 1954; Paredes 1963). Américo Paredes suggested that I trav-
el to Guerrero in search of a living balladry. On arriving in Chilpancingo, the
state capital, my initial efforts seemed to confirm the corrido's demise. Work-
ing with the affable Francisco Arroyo and his son, Paco, I gathered fine per-
formances of a largely residual corpus of ballads in the national repertoire,
songs like "Gabino Barrera," "Valentín Quintero," and "El Siete Leguas" that
over the years have lost their connection to specific locations. But there were
hints of a more situated ballad corpus, in songs done by the Arroyos such as
"Simón Blanco," "Chante Luna," and "El Ciruelo."

Francisco Arroyo, Chilpancingo, 1989

These enticing signs led me to the coastal region of the state, where (I was told) I would encounter real balladry as well as real danger. I landed first in Acapulco, the gateway to Guerrero's coasts, where I became acquainted with the splendid Arizmendi brothers, singers and composers whose repertoire includes a number of original and very polished corridos. A venture into the Costa Grande was rewarding, bringing me into contact with the Texta family in Tecpan de Galeana and their repertoire of regional corridos. These songs had a local connection but they seemed to belong to an earlier time. There was the flavor of the archaic in the ballads I heard on the Costa Grande. The people I spoke to had only limited associations with the songs, for the most part, and the local repertoire was not very extensive.

At last, as the summer of 1972 moved into its final weeks, I managed a visit to the Costa Chica. Navigating the coastal highway in my green VW Bug, I sustained (and survived) contacts with armed police and armed citizens and found the object of my quest, the living ballad. First at the home of Austreberto Gallardo, *presidente municipal* in Cruz Grande, later in the open market in Ometepec, I listened with reverence to the strains and stanzas of heroic songs closely tied to local community. Singers and audience members identified strongly and personally with the protagonists of these ballads, and though some of the songs were from earlier generations, many of them had been recently composed about current events. Unlike the sophisticated ballads of the Arizmendi brothers, these Costa Chica ballads had that aura of graceful impersonality that attaches to products of the oral tradition. I felt that I was in the presence of a legitimate heir to *El Cid* and the great Iberian *romancero,* persisting in this enclave as a living ballad tradition within a true ballad community.

José Texta Torres, Tecpan de Galeana, 1972

Subsequent visits to the Costa Chica, in 1989, 1990, and 1996, have only strengthened this impression. These visits brought me into contact with admirable poets and musicians from Ometepec: El Cobarde, Enrique Mares, and members of the Vargas family, especially the dean of Guerrero's corrido singers, Juvencio Vargas. In May 1996 I was fortunate to work with two pairs of musicians in Cuajinicuilapa, thanks to the assistance of my good friend Juvenal Arellanes. Representing the older generation and singing an earlier stratum of local balladry were Taurino Colón, a nephew of the famed Moisés Colón, and Agustín Mayo. Proof that the younger generation in Cuajinicuilapa is engaged in the ballad tradition is found in the excellent performances of Juan Saguilán Peña and Teódulo García Pastrana, whose repertoire deals with events and protagonists of the recent past.

These happy encounters have allowed me to amass a recorded archive of well over two hundred Costa Chica corrido performances as well as dozens of interviews and discussions with musicians and audience members regarding the contents of these songs. All these indicators—the ubiquity and quantity of corridos, the familiarity with plots and protagonists, the direct personal involve-

Taurino Colón (*left*) and Agustín Mayo, Cuajinicuilapa, 1996

Teódulo García Pastrana (*left*) and Juan Saguilán Peña, Cuajinicuilapa, 1996

ment in the tradition—point to the existence of a ballad community on the Costa Chica. But can we take seriously this notion of a "ballad community"? Scholars have used the term loosely to refer to human populations that generate living ballad traditions. Following this criterion, one can allocate the term to entire peoples and nations or to much smaller entities, such as regions within a country or a specific class within a larger social complex. Thus we might think of the Iberian Peninsula in the fifteenth and sixteenth centuries as a ballad community by virtue of the production and performance of *romances* in most Iberian regions, and by most Iberian social groupings, during that period. A comparable argument can be made for Mexico during the turmoil of the revolution, roughly from 1910 to 1930, though one would have to concede a much lesser degree of participation in the ballad culture on the part of Mexico's indigenous peoples. Américo Paredes (1958) characterizes the Texas-Mexico border region at the dawn of the twentieth century as a ballad community, pointing to the importance given in particular to ballads emerging from intercultural strife. He notes parallels between this border region and another one famous for its balladry, the lowland zone where England meets Scotland, where a living ballad tradition flourished well into the seventeenth century.

A scanning of William Entwistle's valuable survey of European balladry suggests many other candidates for inclusion on the list of ballad communities, and a vast body of ethnographic literature offers additional possibilities in and beyond Europe. In assessing the social history of the coast of Guerrero, specifically the Costa Chica, I will argue that it makes sense to speak of a ballad community, that is, a community to a considerable extent organized and conceived around the living ballad tradition cultivated in this region. It was not by chance that Aguirre Beltrán made use of stanzas from local corridos in framing each chapter of his ethnography of Cuajinicuilapa, a prominent town on the coast. The people of the Costa Chica have been making and singing corridos in earnest since the early decades of the twentieth century, and what is more, they have been inhabiting the plots of their ballads, using the examples in the corridos as touchstones for proper and improper behavior and advancing them as the authentic history of their communities. These people have formulated a sense of themselves as a distinct group in large measure through the agency of corridos, which summon regional heroes and describe rivalries and alliances linking the various settlements, villages, and towns into an imagined community.

Since any human group can be epitomized in any number of ways, it is necessary to be very clear about the attributes that lead to denomination as a ballad community. In the language I am developing here, I call the *ballad community* the natural habitat of the living ballad. What we observe in this stretch of Guerrero and in other comparable settings is a pervasive presence of ballads and a pervasive ballad mentality. As Paredes (1963:231) alerts us, a living ballad tradition acquires a "weight," a social force that "impresses itself on the consciousness of the people." In such moments, the ballad is in the air, on people's lips and minds. It serves as a point of reference for processing experience and as a resource for expressing deep-seated feelings and notions of personal and collective identity.

Let us try to isolate the main attributes of a ballad community. For one thing, the ballad tradition must be firmly rooted in the everyday consciousness of the community. It will not do to have a corpus of ballads known to several people but not generally available to members of the community. Nor will it do to have a handful of ballads that people can recall when they set themselves to remember the old days. To speak of a ballad community, the ballads must be lurking in people's minds at all times; there must be an obsession with them. On the Costa Chica people speak of "living" the ballads; they are routinely aware of them and tend to measure their experiences using the ballad narratives as a yardstick.

There must be a dynamic intersection between balladry and life. If the corpus of balladry is kept segmented into a special sphere, such as "literature" or "art," then the ballads are not connecting actively with people's real-life concerns. In a ballad community the words to the ballads are permeable, and corridos admit into their lines and stanzas the biographies of real people known personally or by word of mouth to participants in the tradition. It will not do to sing of kings and queens from the old country, of wars and heroes from another time and place. Ballads in a ballad community do not accrue from a mysterious process of cultural retention. Instead, they are produced through a social process witnessed by members of the community.

In addition, a taste for ballads in a ballad community is not restricted to a particular social segment. Instead, the ballads are known and appreciated all across the social spectrum. In Spain of the Golden Age, the *romance* was cultivated by rustic *juglares* as well as by the most distinguished literary artists; it was performed in the rural market and in the king's court. Naturally, the style would vary from one setting to another, but the essential form and content of the genre remained constant. Similarly, on the Guerrero coast today no social element is indifferent to the corrido; it is a viable genre for the "literary" art of the Arizmendi brothers as well as for blind singers of the village plazas. In a ballad community the ballads are ubiquitous, crossing the major social boundaries of generation, social class, gender, and ethnicity.

In the towns and villages of the Costa Chica, ballads are a primary vehicle for rendering the experience of the community. People find in their images and dialogues a mirror of their own circumstances. The ballad heroes talk the familiar lingo of the local vernacular. They stand up for values held dear by the community or are chastised for betraying these values. As in other ballad communities, in the Costa Chica ballads make a strong statement of local identity, typically in resistance to the encroachment of outside influences. The living ballad is not archaic or arcane. It is an accessible outlet for articulating widely shared convictions about human nature and the history of the community. Its power is evident in the passionate responses of audiences and in passionate affirmations of the truth value of corridos. On the coast of Guerrero, the corrido, not the newspaper, is portrayed as the conveyer of reliable information.

Two Coasts and a Port City

Guerrero is one of the most isolated, poorest, and least studied areas of Mexico, and the coastal region of the state manifests these same qualities in the extreme. Without a doubt, the Costa Chica is one of Mexico's forgotten regions. Even Acapulco was difficult to access by land until the completion of the Mexico City highway in the 1950s. The coastal highway linking Acapulco to towns and villages on the Costa Chica and eventually connecting them to Pinotepa Nacional and other coastal settlements in Oaxaca was not finished until the mid-1960s. Prior to that date, routes on the Costa Chica were limited to dirt tracks impassable during the rainy season. To this day many out-of-the-way settlements on the coast are inaccessible after the rains begin in June.

Although Acapulco received attention from the federal government, which began to develop it in the 1920s as a tourist destination, the remainder of the state was virtually abandoned from the days of the *porfiriato*, when the technocrats running the economy opted to send resources to less conflicted areas of the nation (Salazar Adame 1987:44). Through the early 1970s even Chilpancingo, the capital city, remained suspended in provincial isolation. According to Donald Hodges (1995:31), the support among the people of Guerrero for the armed rebels Genaro Vásquez and Lucio Cabañas, who took to the hills in the late 1960s, finally persuaded the federal government to invest in social programs in Guerrero. But Guerrero remains largely excluded from the flow of money that has removed the blight of dire poverty from many other sections of the country. It is still fertile soil for the mounting of armed rebellion against the central government.

The isolation of coastal Guerrero has deep roots. In the colonial period the Spanish and mestizo population thought the coast was largely uninhabitable, preferring the cooler forested areas in the mountains for their towns and cities (Gerhard 1993:40). Partly for this reason, the coastal area became a refuge for escaped slaves and a target of periodic pirate activity. The littoral, with its lagoons, lakes, and rivers intersecting the coastal plain, at places extending inland many kilometers but pinched to a narrow strip where the mountains come down to the edge of the sea, is mostly a hot, semi-arid zone, though areas of higher elevation may be forested and less inhospitable.

At the time of the Spanish conquest the Pacific coast was fairly heavily populated, in small-scale, localized native enclaves sometimes loosely organized into regional alliances but more often persisting as independent units. Three districts established by the Spanish authorities governed what is now the Guerrero coast: Acapulco, running from the top of the Sierra Madre down to the coast and centered on the bay of Acapulco; Zacatula, to the north and west along the coast and comprehending the area between the top of the Sierra Madre and the ocean (what is now the Costa Grande); and Igualapa, running inland to the foothills of the Sierra Madre del Sur and reaching to the ocean to the south and east of Acapulco (what is now the Costa Chica). The adjacent portion of the Costa Chica, in what is today the state of Oaxaca, corresponds to the colonial district that was known as Xicayán.

Although each of these zones displays some particular features, the entire region does harbor certain common elements. Indigenous settlement was fairly dense but compact, reflected in the numerous languages and dialects spoken in the area. Mexica, or Nahuatl, the language of the Aztec Empire, was present intermittently, indicating only a tenuous presence of highland power on the coast. The Costa Grande may have had a few Tarascan outposts, but for the most part its communities lay beyond the control of the Tarascans and the Triple Alliance of the central plateau. From Acapulco and southeast along the coast several independent and allied states held sway; Yopes or Tlapanecos and Amuzgos (speaking a Mixtecan language) controlled specific territories and sought freedom from the expanding influence of the Mixteca kingdom of Tutetepec and from the garrisons of Mexican forces. Typical of the region at the moment of the Spanish conquest was the indigenous province of Ayacastla, now the eastern portion of Guerrero's Costa Chica, which had rich ethnic and linguistic diversity. Its heart was the area around Ometepec and Igualapa, but its influence reached outward to the coastal zone that is today Cuajinicuilapa, San Nicolás, and Maldonado (de los Angeles Manzano 1991). Several languages were spoken in this province, including Tlapanec, Mexica, Amuzgo, and Ayacasteca, the language of the dominant group.

The Spanish first came to this area in the early 1520s. Rodrigo Alvarez Chico explored the coastline, arriving in Acapulco in the fall of 1521. A force led by Gonzalo de Sandoval conquered the Aztec tributary states in 1523, though the Yopes remained intransigent well into the 1540s. One of Cortes's main lieutenants, Pedro de Alvarado, led an expedition to the Costa Chica in 1522 and encountered little resistance until he came into areas controlled by the Yopes. Within a few years the entire coastal region had been assigned by Hernán Cortes as *encomiendas* (entitlements to an area and the Native Americans resident within it) to prominent *conquistadores* and other allies. These lands and their Indian populations were passed along within the families or were reassigned to other Spanish families well into the next century. The *encomenderos* were responsible for looking after the conversion of the Indians, but in return they were entitled to a tribute in kind and in labor from their Native American charges.

As elsewhere in North America, a series of epidemics decimated the indigenous population here. The policy of congregating the Native Americans into accessible settlements, pursued starting in the 1590s, further contributed to their decline, as did the often harsh conditions of labor exacted in the mines and on cacao and sugar plantations. Within one hundred years of Spanish penetration into these coastal areas, the native population had declined to well less than one-tenth of its initial numbers, many indigenous villages and settlements were permanently destroyed or depopulated, and the great majority of languages and dialects spoken had ceased to exist. Nonetheless, significant indigenous communities persisted on the Costa Grande at Tecpan, Coyuca, and Atoyac and on the Costa Chica at Ayutla, Ometepec, Jamiltepec, and a number of inland sites.

The Guerrero coast was only gradually transformed under the Spanish. Each administrative district acquired its *alcalde mayor* or *corrigedor* to manage the affairs of the crown, and Spanish settlements were founded as the century of the conquest progressed. Royal shipyards were built in Acapulco and where the Balsas River enters the Pacific Ocean, and parishes and churches were established in the more populated areas. A settlement was formed at Acapulco in 1550, and in 1573 the first galleon bringing goods from Asia arrived. The arrival of *nao de china,* as these ships were called, after their trans-Pacific voyages from Manila became an annual event of some magnitude, bringing merchants, muleteers, and others into town for trade and associated revelries. Fort San Diego in Acapulco became permanently garrisoned in 1617, but Acapulco was to remain a backwater for the next three centuries.

With the decline of the indigenous population, and with a growing need for labor in the fields, mines, and cattle ranches, by the 1550s the Spanish began importing African slaves, first from the Antilles and later primarily from the Cape Verde Islands and Guinea Coast (Aguirre Beltrán 1972). Before the end of the sixteenth century there were more Africans than Europeans in Mexico, and an additional 120,000 Africans were brought to Mexico in the seventeenth century (Whetten 1948:50). Africans came to work in the mines in the Sierra Madre and on sugar and cacao plantations. The Spanish brought black Africans to oversee Native American work crews and, as the cattle industry expanded in the region, to work as *vaqueros.* The *encomenderos* brought people of black African descent from Barbados and other Caribbean sites—and eventually directly from Africa—to supplement the diminishing Native American work force. The isolated littoral of the Costa Chica became a refuge for freed and escaped slaves, and to this day a population with pronounced black African features persists in settlements on Guerrero's and Oaxaca's Costa Chica.

The demographics of Guerrero's coast are marked by the dwindling indigenous population and the growing population of black Africans in the context of a rather small and constant European presence. In addition, in Guerrero as elsewhere in Mexico, *mestizaje* (race mixing) became the most significant factor in shaping the physical identity of the new generations. The colonial administrators made use of an elaborate code to classify the various mixtures of people, and rights and privileges attached to the different levels in the hierarchy. At the top were the *gachupines,* those actually born in Spain of Spanish parentage. The *criollos* were those born in Nueva España of *gachupín* parents. The other primary categories were people of mixed blood, Native Americans, and *negros* (those of black African origin). The category of mixed-bloods was calibrated into groups like these (Whetten 1948:52):

mestizo	one Spanish and one Indian parent
castizo	one Spanish and one mestizo parent
mulato	one Spanish and one African parent
morisco	one Spanish and one mulato parent
albino	one Spanish and one morisco parent
torna-atrás	one Spanish and one albino parent
lobo	one Indian and one torna-atrás parent
sambaigo	one Indian and one lobo parent
cambujo	one Indian and one sambaigo parent
albarazado	one mulato and one cambujo parent
baroino	one mulato and one albarazado parent
coyote	one mulato and one baroino parent
chamizo	one Indian and one coyote parent

This system indicates an obsession with *mestizaje* on the part of the Spanish authorities, but it also charts the many patterns of intermarriage prevalent among the people of Nueva España, nowhere more fully articulated than on the Pacific coast.

Cultural factors were important in determining racial categories even in the colonial period. Work by Raymond Hall (1999) with parish archives in the area around Tamiagua, Veracruz, shows that this system for classifying human beings underwent significant changes toward the end of the seventeenth century. Fewer racial labels were used in baptismal records, suggesting that families found ways to persuade the parish priests, who made these assignments, that they belonged closer to the "white" end of the continuum regardless of their physical appearance. But this slippage toward "white," we should note, only reinforced the racist pattern of thought underlying the entire scheme.

Documents indicate that toward the end of the colonial period a majority population of free mulattos lived at the port city of Acapulco and in Coyuca on the Costa Grande (Gerhard 1993:41). On the Costa Grande toward the close of the seventeenth century, there were relatively few Spanish families and somewhat more mestizos and mulattos (Gerhard 1993:396). On the Costa Chica, the

1791 census indicates 235 Spaniards, 594 mestizos, and 5,206 Negroes and mulattos (Gerhard 1993:151). The population formed on Guerrero's coasts through the conquest and the colony consisted of a numerically small but powerful group of Spaniards, a number of small, isolated Native American and black African communities, and a broad mixed-blood base with a strong admixture of black Africans. Perhaps most distinctive, and centered on the Costa Chica, was the emerging afromestizo population containing various combinations of Native American, African, and European people. The prevalent pattern in this region involved Africans having children with Native Americans and Africans having children with *mestizos* (Flanet 1977:146).

In view of the similar background of Guerrero's two coasts it is interesting to observe their contrasting roles in the struggle for Mexican independence. As Peter Guardino (1996:51) notes: "No group in Guerrero directed more hate at the European Spanish than the mulatto sharecroppers and Indian villages who grew cotton on the Costa Grande." When Father José María Morelos, a leader in the rebellion against Spanish authority in Mexico, entered the region, he immediately received the support of the Costa Grande population, with the exception of Acapulco's wealthy merchants. In stark contrast, the Costa Chica remained loyal to the royalist cause. Guardino (1996:53–54) characterizes the Costa Chica population at the time as "mulatto sharecroppers" who "lived dispersed along the banks of rivers used to irrigate their cotton crops" and expresses puzzlement at their political role in the independence period since "the Costa Chica was socially and economically similar to the Costa Grande." The answer apparently lies in the isolation and independence of the Costa Chica. Its dispersed population was less subject to tributes, taxes, exploitative loan policies, and other programs of the Spanish merchants and authorities. Moreover, with a history of fierce opposition to outside authority, Costa Chica settlements had maintained their own militias and nurtured a spirit of proud independence since the previous century. As a consequence, Spanish administrators sought accommodation and tempered the imposition of royal policies. The Costa Chica militias joined the royalist cause with enthusiasm.

Heroes and Rebels

The people of Guerrero are proud of the heroes they have lent in the epic of Mexican history: Cuauhtémoc, the last of the Aztec leaders, whom legend associates with the northern stretches of the state; Vicente Guerrero from Tixtla, scourge of the royalists; Hermenegildo Galeana from Tecpan on the Costa Grande, righthand man of José María Morelos, a leader in the independence movement; Ignacio Manuel Altamirano from Tixtla, man of letters and soldier during the French invasion; Juan Escudero from Acapulco, martyr to the cause of worker unionization in the early 1920s; Valente de la Cruz and Amadeo Vidales, agrarian leaders on the coast in the turbulent years after the Mexican Revolution; and Genaro Vásquez and Lucio Cabañas, leaders of guerrilla movements based in Guerrero during the late 1960s and early 1970s. These regional heroes are celebrated in Guerrero along with national heroes such as Francisco Madero, Emiliano Zapata, and Francisco Villa, in traditional corridos preserved from earlier decades as well as in newly composed tributes in corrido form. They constitute a pantheon of noble resistance to *mal gobierno* (mis-government), a theme running throughout the panorama of Mexican history and still current in troubled areas of the southern highlands and littoral. Differences in historical period and political context erode in the face of this all-encompassing theme, and contemporary figures entering into conflict with government forces are assimilated.

Vicente Guerrero is preeminent among these figures in the insurgency of the eighteenth century leading to Mexico's independence from Spain in 1821. A man of the people, of mixed-blood, he had been a muleteer plying the trails between the coast and the highlands. Rising early to the call for independence issued by Padre Morelos, Guerrero stayed in the battle after the death of Morelos and eventually helped promolgate the Plan de Iguala, which recognized the rights of all Mexicans, regardless of their position in the racial hierarchy, to participate in the Mexican nation. In league with Santa Anna, Guerrero became president of Mexico in 1829. A corrido by Miguel Arizmendi commemorates Vicente Guerrero as a *guerrillero,* the prototype of the rebel who rises up against tyranny, a theme with continuing resonance in contemporary Mexico. It is seldom noted that both Padre Morelos and Vicente Guerrero, heroes whose names were given to states in the new nation, were partly of black African ancestry.

The mulatto sharecroppers of Guerrero's coasts have provided fertile ground for political organizers advancing populist causes. There was already a strong workers' movement on the Costa Grande by the end of the nineteenth century, and the animosity between workers and the wealthy elite has stimulated a regional class war that shows few signs of abatement. The town of Aguas Blancas, adjacent to Coyuca de Benítez on the Costa Grande, is the setting of the latest round of violent confrontation. During the *porfiriato* Aguas Blancas was the home of a major development project, a large cotton mill known as El Ticui managed by the Spanish commercial houses in Acapulco, and the region experienced severe strains associated with worker exploitation and labor unrest. The Costa Grande became an important enclave of agrarian agitation in the early decades of the twentieth century and sustained the radical politics of Juan Escudero and the Vidales brothers. Aguas Blancas, and the region around it extending outward to encompass much of the Costa Grande, persists as one of the hotbeds of local activism in Mexico.

On June 28, 1996, a new guerrilla force went public, the Ejército Popular Revolucionario (EPR) or Popular Revolutionary Army. This armed group chose Aguas Blancas as the site to make its initial public appearance. Although government representatives immediately dismissed the group as "a gang of mere delinquents," within a few months the EPR had mounted a series of actions in several regions of Guerrero and Oaxaca, and the government had begun mobilizing a major military operation to seek out and destroy this new manifestation of armed resistance. The EPR was not the first guerrilla force to step forward in Guerrero. It follows in the footsteps of Genaro Vásquez, founder of the Asociación Cívica Nacional de la Revolución (National Civic Association of the Revolution), and Lucio Cabañas, leader of el Partido de los Pobres (Party of the Poor), two guerrilla movements of the late 1960s and early 1970s that mounted political kidnappings and ambushes of military patrols before being crushed by massive counterinsurgency operations.

Aguas Blancas was the site of a brutal massacre of peasants by government forces on June 28, 1995, and as a consequence has become a symbol of the abuse of authority in Mexico. The turn of federal and state administrations toward supply side policies favoring entrenched political players and neglecting social causes has only exacerbated the already intense political climate of this section of the state. The militant Organización Campesina de la Sierra Suriana (OCSS) or Peasant Organization of the Southern Sierra has become the latest incarnation of this persisting agrarian cause. A group of activists on their way to a rally of this organization was mowed down by police agents in Aguas Blancas, and the masked and armed members of the EPR made their first public appearance at a memorial to these slain peasant activists. The police officers who did the shooting are in jail awaiting trial but the participation of higher authorities in the state has yet to be clarified. As is customary in Mexico, it has proved difficult to unmask the "intellectual authors" of the massacre, though word of mouth attributes responsibility to the governor, who was forced to take a leave of absence in March 1996. Corridos about the Aguas Blancas massacre are circulating in Acapulco and on the Costa Grande, with some circumspection due to the politically charged nature of the case.

The EPR rises to combat *el mal gobierno* (the pattern of mis-government), and thus Aguas Blancas is the perfect place to assert its antiestablishment agenda. To a considerable degree, the political violence stems from the unfinished social agenda of the revolution, which promised a realignment of power and wealth but instead largely preserved the status quo. Corridos sung on the Costa Grande recall the lives and deaths of early agrarian leaders such as Juan Escudero and Valente de la Cruz as well as the more recent guerrilla leaders Genaro Vásquez and Lucio Cabañas, assimilating all of them to the paradigm of the bold hero standing up against an abusive government.

The Costa Grande, then, evinces a pattern of grass-roots political opposition to the control of local and state elites—a struggle that predates the revolution, that can be traced clearly in the battles between agrarians and reactionaries in the 1920s, and that persists in ongoing peasant protest movements and in the occasional flare-up of armed resistance. The Costa Chica, a region of greater isolation, less wealth, and a more scattered population, displays a rather different situation. There are echoes of the Costa Grande scenario, for example, in the attempts of indigenous communities in Igualapa, Azoyú, and Huehuetán to recover communal lands appropriated by Costa Chica landlords (de los Angeles Manzano 1991:23). But on the Costa Chica the conflicts between the classes have failed to crystallize into a concerted rivalry between progressive and reactionary forces. Instead, competing economic and political factions have recruited allies and achieved a temporary dominance in a constantly shifting and somewhat chaotic political environment. Whereas the politics on the Costa Grande has been largely framed according to an ideology of class consciousness, the Costa Chica had remained mired to a greater extent in the clash of local, ethnic, and clan loyalties. Violence on the Costa Grande has largely assimilated to the struggle between peasant organizations and state authorities fronting for vested interests. On the Costa Chica, violence appears to derive from rivalries between individuals, extended families, local factions, and business alliances.

It is revealing that afromestizos in Cuajinicuilapa were slow to join the Zapatistas. As María de los Angeles Manzano (1991:88) points out, they had not experienced the massive and violent expropriation of their lands as had the Native American communities, and "they maintained a certain 'liberty' and privilege" as employees and wards of the Miller family, owners of a vast estate encompassing Cuajinicuilapa and its environs. As in the independence period, the mulattos of the Costa Chica played a role that partially defies expectations, a role marked by loyalties to the existing system. De los Angeles Manzano (1991:103) discusses some factors that might have influenced the people of Cuajinicuilapa to steer clear of the Zapatista program: "There are many ways to intimidate the people, and the landlord took advantage of all of them within his reach, from the subtle manipulation of making them think they were breaking the law and were ungrateful to their boss, to the most incisive way, violence." Afromestizo communities of the Costa Chica experienced a split between those who, through coercion or enticement, remained loyal to the landlords of the region and those who joined the cause of revolution and agrarian reform.

Juan Escudero

Acapulco, placed squarely at the junction of these two coastal regions, has played a crucial role in the area's economic and political development. Some idea of the underpinnings of violence on Guerrero's coasts can be gleaned from an inspection of the accumulation of capital there during the *porfiriato* and of challenges presented to this hegemony in the aftermath of the revolution. These issues are encapsulated in the life and death of Juan Escudero, a leader inspired by the rise of socialism who attacked the uneven distribution of wealth in the area. Juan Ranulfo Escudero Reguera was a remarkable man who rose to prominence in the ebb and flow of the populist movements following the initial phase of the revolution. Scion of a leading Spanish family allied with the *gachupín* (Spaniard) oligarchy in Acapulco, he became their scourge as leader of a populist movement uniting workers and *campesinos* on the Guerrero coast in the early 1920s. After attending college in the United States and spending some time in San Francisco (where he may have met Ricardo Flores Magón), Escudero returned to Acapulco and began organizing the workers who loaded and unloaded ships calling at the port. He began publishing a lively and polemical magazine called *Regeneración* after a similar enterprise started by the Flores Magón brothers in exile in the United States. Escudero founded the Partido Obrero de Acapulco (Workers' Party of Acapulco) and was elected *presidente municipal* of Acapulco in 1921, a position he held for two successive years. In this capacity he initiated a set of reforms aimed at improving the lot of the common people and introducing authentic forms of political representation. An assassination attempt in March 1922 left him paralyzed but still active; in December 1923 he was eliminated by his enemies among the local establishment.

At that time the state of Guerrero was largely under the thumb of the *gachupines,* a small set of Spanish families who controlled the commerce moving

Statue of Juan Escudero, port of Acapulco

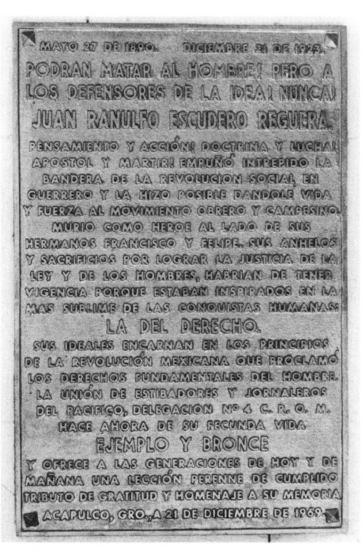

Plaque commemorating Juan Escudero, port of Acapulco

Marciano López Arizmendi, Ejido Nuevo, 1989

through Acapulco. Through alliances with wealthy landowners (and their func-
tionaries) up and down the coast, this clique managed every phase of the regional
economy to their own advantage. Workers and peasants suffered routine and
extreme forms of exploitation under this regime. Juan Escudero tried to break
the economic stranglehold of the *gachupines* by encouraging construction of the
Mexico City–Acapulco highway, by establishing cooperatives that would com-
pete with the Spaniards' enterprises, and by organizing the labor force.

   It is likely that several corridos were written about Escudero, but only two
of them have survived. One of these is a paen to a fallen leader, lamenting his
loss and praising his cause (see Kuri-Aldano and Mendoza Martínez 1987). A
more controversial ballad is remembered by some local singers, and it is this
corrido I recorded from Marciano López Arizmendi in Ejido Nuevo in Feb-
ruary 1989. My good friend and associate Miguel Arizmendi introduced me
to his nephew, Marciano, a lively young man known as "La Coca" for the brown
sheen of his skin. On a sultry afternoon, in the shade of a palm grove Miguel
had planted many years ago, we settled into a rich vein of corridos including
"Juan Escudero," whose text follows:

1. Voy a cantar un corrido
sin agravio y sin disgusto,
el mes de diciembre ha traído
grandes pesares y sustos,
la traición que ha renacido
en el puerto de Acapulco.

[I will sing a corrido
with neither offense nor anger;
the month of December has brought
great sorrows and shocks;
treachery has been reborn
in the port city of Acapulco.

2. Nueva noticia les traigo
de desgracias y millares,
se murió Juan Escudero
el que evitaba los males,
era el que regía las leyes
civiles y militares.

I bring you the fresh news
of mishaps by the thousands;
Juan Escudero has perished—
the one who avoided the ills;
it was he who enforced the laws
of civil and military rule.

3. Triste quedó Acapulco
el palacio entristecido,
de ver a los Escuderos
que los llevaban cautivos,
vendidos en treinta mil pesos
por sus peores enemigos.

Acapulco was left in sadness;
the palace was deeply saddened
to see that the Escuderos
were being led off captives,
sold for thirty thousand pesos
by their worst enemies.

4. Un día viernes por la tarde
Sámano fue a conferencia,
en donde conferenciaron
hicieron firma de apuesta,
Manuel se hallaba sentado
allá por Pie de la Cuesta.

It was a Friday afternoon;
Sámano went to the meeting;
at the place they went to meet
they signed on to the deal;
Manuel found himself seated
there at Pie de la Cuesta.

5. Fernández dió diez mil pesos
al Alzuyeta e Uruñuela,
firmaron los Muñúziri
y también Francisco Vela,
porque ellos tenían recelo
que Juan les hiciera guerra.

Fernández gave ten thousand pesos
to Alzuyeta and Uruñuela;
the Muñúziri signed on,
and also Francisco Vela,
because they were concerned
that Juan might war with them.

6. Sámano le dijo a Flores
ensillando su caballo:
"Matando a los Escuderos
nos vamos a correr gallo."
De gusto que les cabía
que los tenían sujuzgado.

Sámano said to Flores
while saddling his horse:
"When we kill the Escuderos
let's throw ourselves a party."
What pleasure it gave them
having them in their power.

7. El mayor Flores le dijo:
   "Ganaremos el dinero,
   ya la mecha está prendida
   en Iguala de Guerrero,
   ganaremos esa plata
   va decaído el gobierno."

Major Flores told him:
"We will earn the money,
now the wick is lit
in Iguala, state of Guerrero;
we will earn ourselves the money—
the government is down."

8. Luego siguieron su marcha
   rumbo para Chilpancingo,
   pues iban bien escoltados
   por la compañía del gringo,
   que vigilaron las calles
   y vista por los caminos.

Then they continued their journey
on their way to Chilpancingo;
they were very well escorted
by the gringo's company,
who kept an eye on the streets
and watched along the roads.

9. Un día sábado temprano
   alboreando la mañana,
   Escudero estaba vivo
   todavía no se acababa,
   alzó la cabeza y dijo:
   "Ah, cuánta sangre regada."

Early one Saturday morning,
just as dawn was breaking,
Escudero was still alive—
he still wasn't finished;
he raised his head and told them:
"Ah, so much spilled blood."

10. Escudero estaba vivo
    pero con gran desespero,
    de ver a sus dos hermanos
    revolcados en el suelo,
    pero quedan dos caudillo
    que es Vidal y El Ciruelo.

Escudero was still alive
but in a state of despair
on seeing his two brothers
sprawled out on the floor;
but there remain two leaders,
who are Vidal and El Ciruelo.

11. Luego mandaron el parte
    de La Venta a Barrio Nuevo,
    que ahí estaban tres cadáveres
    eran los tres Escuderos,
    que venga el gobierno a juzgarlos
    para determinar de ellos.

Then they sent the report
from La Venta to Barrio Nuevo
that three cadavers were there—
it was the three Escuderos;
the authorities should come inspect
and see what to do with them.

12. Su madre fue a levantarlos
    el cura y señoritas,
    como iban bien escoltados
    porque así es la disciplina,
    el comercio lo ha comprado
    para quitarle la vida.

His mother went to reclaim them
with the priest and the nuns,
as they were well escorted,
because that's as it should be;
business has paid the price
to deprive him of his life.

13. Su muerte fue resonada	His death reverberated
en Costa Chica y Costa Grande,	on the Costa Chica and Costa Grande;
hasta México llegó	word came to Mexico City
y pasó a los imparciales,	and passed to the authorities
a la república indiana	of the sovereign Mexican nation
en nombre de esos cadáveres.	in the name of those three bodies.
14. Los ricos y españoles	The rich folk and the Spaniards,
todos quedaron a gusto,	they all were greatly pleased,
porque quedó esclavo el pobre	for the poor man remained a slave,
de ellos no tenían producto,	from them they got no bounty;
todos en ahogo decían	all were saying in grief,
se murió el dios de Acapulco.	the god of Acapulco is dead.
15. Mas en fin ya me despido	But now I must bid farewell
por lo que el país va anunciando,	to what the nation is saying;
el rico se está vendiendo	the rich are selling themselves,
el extranjero está comprando,	the foreigner is buying;
los hombres más opulentos	the most opulent men
son los que están acabando.	are the ones who are disappearing.]

This corrido is a partisan volley composed apparently out of rage and frustration after Escudero's death. It provides extensive detail on the conspiracy and largely coincides with historical accounts (Vizcaino and Ignacio Taibo II 1983; Ravelo Lecuona 1987; Jacobs 1982). The historical moment is a reactionary wave sweeping across Mexico in 1923 under the banner of a mutinous general, Adolfo de la Huerta. The *delahuertistas* united vested and conservative elements throughout the nation in a desperate attempt to stem the reformist tendencies of the revolution under its emergent power broker, Alvaro Obregón. On the Guerrero coasts, this movement emboldened the enemies of agrarian reform, who organized paramilitary units to eliminate *campesino* leaders. It was at this juncture that the reactionary elements in Acapulco found it convenient to remove their nemesis, Juan Escudero.

The first three stanzas of the corrido introduce the theme—the wicked murder of Juan Escudero—and describe the sadness felt by those who saw him led off captive. Stanzas 4 through 7 depict the planning of the action: the plotting of the murders, the raising of funds to pay the assassins, the anticipation of the men who will do the killing. The fifth stanza names the financial backers of the plot, all wealthy businessmen in Acapulco: Fernández and Alzuyeta ran two of the large Spanish commercial houses, Muñúziri published *El Suri-*

ano, a local newspaper friendly to the *gachupín* cause. Colonel Crispín Sámano was allied with conservative elements behind the *delahuertista* counterrevolution that took off in Guerrero around the end of 1923. He surrendered to Amadeo Vidales with the defeat of this movement in 1925. Major Juan S. Flores was in charge of a paramilitary unit that operated along the coast against civilian supporters of the agrarian cause. He was in charge of the initial attempt on Juan Escudero's life in 1922 and was involved as well in the final capture and murder.

With the advent of the *delahuertista* rebellion, the agrarians found themselves in jeopardy. The *delahuertistas* were led by General Rómulo Figueroa, who commanded a force of salaried soldiers with ample supplies of guns and ammunition. The political advantage of the progressive elements, who counted on support from Obregón, was undermined by contradictory signals from the federal government. Escudero's enemies sensed that the situation was sufficiently disorganized to allow for their mission without fear of legal or military reprisals. Economic interests from the United States apparently played some role in the succession of events, as suggested by the content of stanza 8.

With stanza 9, the scene shifts to Escudero's last hours. According to several accounts, Escudero remained alive and lucid for some twelve hours after he and his brothers were gunned down. He is said to have identified his killers and urged his people to continue the struggle so that "mi sangre no sea estéril" (my blood will not be sterile). The corrido poet mentions two leaders who might carry on the fight. Amadeo Vidales and his brother Baldomero were sons of a famous revolutionary from Tecpan de Galeana, and they found themselves in competition with the Acapulco monopolies. These brothers had made common cause with the Escuderos. Amadeo was elected mayor of Tecpan and remained a progressive force on the Costa Grande for some years. Silvestre Castro, known as El Ciruelo after his hometown on the Costa Grande, was a distinguished figure of the revolution who rose to defend the common people on several occasions until his death in 1927.

The unfortunate doña Irene Reguera, mother of the Escudero boys, played a decisive role in keeping them in Acapulco in the face of dangers from the *delahuertistas.* With assurances from a priest, a family friend, that the Escuderos would not be harmed, she persuaded Juan not to vacate the city in the company of a well-organized force of agrarian fighters. The corrido ends by adducing the final result of the murders. The death of the Escuderos caused quite a sensation and did serve to mobilize a furious *agrarista* response. Still, vested interests were able to weather the storm and persist as a wealthy elite in Acapulco and along the coasts.

There stands today in the heart of Acapulco, where the port meets the city center, a monument to Juan Escudero, hero of the working people. Evidently, the issues contained in his life story are not completely resolved. I was told by the singer, Marciano López Arizmendi, that one had to be careful with this song since it names those who plotted against the life of Juan Escudero, and these families are still influential in the area. Nonetheless, he expressed the wish to sing "Juan Escudero" in the center of Acapulco at a rally of the opposition leftist party.

An Unfinished Revolution

The persistence of powerful families along the Pacific coast of Guerrero is a remarkable feature of the region's history. During the last decades of the nineteenth century, families that had long been prominent on the coast, or newly arrived influential families, established financial empires that have survived the vicissitudes of reformist and revolutionary fervor to emerge as stronger economic and political players. The entire coastal economy was regulated through the wealthy Spanish establishments based in Acapulco, who aligned themselves with prominent landowners on the Costa Grande and Costa Chica. One scholar describes the system operating in the early decades of this century in these words (Illades 1989:280): "a complex monopolistic system that, without owning directly all the goods of the coastal people, strictly controlled industry, commerce, retail business, land transport, maritime transport, activities at the port, the buying and selling of agricultural products, fishing, and the better part of the service sector. . . . The *gachupín* control of the port was accompanied by a kind of aberrant domination that had recourse to violence, racism, economic asphyxiation, fraud, intrigue and crime." The regional cogs in this apparatus were the provincial elites, allied with the Acapulco magnates, who made use of several strategies to advance their local interests. A characteristic move was the seizure of *campesino* holdings through a pretext of land reform, as accomplished by a group of wealthy landlords in Ometepec, on the Costa Chica, in 1873 (Ravelo Lecuona 1987:85–86). The *porfiriato* was friendly to entrenched local interests. During the long years of this dictatorship, seven families boasting of Spanish and other foreign origin took control of the cattle industry on the Costa Chica (Ravelo Lecuona 1987:100). The area around San Marcos became in the early 1900s the region's largest *latifundio* (large landholding), with some 200,000 hectares in the hands of the Guerrero Trading Company, a U.S. enterprise.

These vested interests managed to survive the periodic attacks aimed at them through several maneuvers. One of these was the use of violence to intimidate and remove those thought to be their enemies. Daniel Molina Alvarez (1987:241) notes that wealthy landowners on the Costa Grande employed soldiers, private police forces, hired guns, their own family members, and local political bosses to bring a reign of terror to the Costa Grande during the height of the *delahuertista* reaction. Anyone suspected of agrarian sympathies was in danger of being murdered. Another adaptive strategy to preserve local hegemony was to join in the revolutionary causes when these were in their apogee. In Ometepec, two small-scale ranchers signed on to the revolutionary Plan de Ayala, issued by Emiliano Zapata in late 1911 as a call for returning land to the *campesinos;* this move allowed them to conserve their weapons, which they used in support of the region's large landowners (Ravelo Lecuona 1987:160). Ian Jacobs (1982:167) describes the typical pattern: "On the Costa Chica, the Guilléns, already prominent figures in the days of Porfirio Díaz, were revolutionaries in 1911 and were still making political careers for themselves in the 1940s. Still more long-lived were the dynasties of the Regueras and Añorves of Ometepec, where both families were prominent royalists in the wars of independence, held local political office throughout the nineteenth centry, joined the Maderista revolution, and were still holding political office decades later." Jacobs (1982:168) observes that "the revolution, whether as a matter of policy or merely through some accidental process, absorbed many of the established family dynasties in Guerrero and molded them into the new political system."

Influential families on the Costa Chica were able to openly assert their interests during moments of conservative ascendancy, such as the Carranza reaction in 1918 and the *delahuertista* uprising in the early 1920s. When the political climate did not favor this posture, these elements were sometimes able to camouflage themselves as revolutionaries and preserve in this fashion their privileges. As the full-scale violence of the revolutionary period settled into the deceptive calm under the Partido de la Revolución Institutional (PRI) or Party of the Institutional Revolution, the vested interests on the Costa Chica found ways to stave off efforts to redistribute land and wealth. Tomás Bustamante Alvarez (1987:413–14) describes how the plans of the Cárdenas land reforms were thwarted on the Costa Chica: "In the region of Ometepec, the *campesinos* waited years to cultivate their *ejido* properties . . . because they continued to be invaded by the cattle of the previous owners; those *campesinos* who organized to work the lands were shot by ranchers and hired gunmen." It was during the presidency of Lázaro Cárdenas, especially from 1934 to 1938, that land in the Costa Chica was significantly reallocated.

Large landholders eventually realized that their extensive domains were a fixture of the past. The federal government sought to return land to those who worked it, in the form of *ejidos* (cooperative farms), while the landowners frequently tried to sell selected parcels in the form of small private holdings in *colonias agrarias* (agrarian communities). The most intense period of agrarian reform on the Costa Chica, 1931–55, was also the period of the rise of *gavillas* or *brosas,* whose leaders and deeds are recorded in the repertoire of local and regional corridos. Names like Moisés Colón, Cirilo Hernández (El Culebro), Filadelfo Robles, and Porfirio Pastrana, celebrated in the corridos, belong to this period.

During the heyday of agrarian reform under Lázaro Cárdenas, the indigenous communities on the Costa Chica regained some of their communal lands, and afromestizos gained ownership of lands they had previously used through arrangements with large landholders. In the area around Cuajinicuilapa, for example, several *ejidos* were established and initially received support from the government in the form of loans, planting seed, farming equipment, and transportation to market. However, later administrations moved away from the progressive policies of the Cárdenas period, and the *ejidatarios* were abandoned as the government turned once again toward supporting large-scale capitalist interests.

The Costa Chica remained a Mexican backwater, isolated from centers of cultural and economic development, mired in poverty, lacking educational facilities, and subject to endemic violence. According to María de los Angeles Manzano (1991:113), it was not until the mid-1960s, when the coastal highway was opened, that commerce on the Costa Chica was finally released from the grip of the Spanish monopolies in Acapulco. Baltazar Velasco, my friend in Pinotepa Nacional, assured me that if I had arrived in the 1950s looking for corridos, I would have experienced serious difficulties in the afromestizo communities, which were still mostly inaccessible to outsiders. Progress in the decades since then is most evident in the major towns located on the national highway. Although there is evidence of government investment in schools, factories, and other facilities, one gets the impression that these developments are rather superficial. In San Marcos, Cruz Grande, Marquelia, and Cuajinicuilapa, two-story structures have been recently constructed along both sides of the highway, but venture a block or two away from this narrow thread of vitality and you will find the dirt roads and unimproved adobe houses reminiscent of an earlier period. If the progress in these commercial centers is only skin deep, it goes without saying that the more remote settlements persist virtually unaffected.

Perhaps the persistence of such conditions has allowed the ballad community to survive intact. Unlike the Costa Grande, where one perceives the interpenetration of the local and the national, the Costa Chica remains a region apart, more immersed in its own vernacular culture. Towns like Cruz Grande, Ometepec, Cuajinicuilapa, San Nicolás, Pinotepa Nacional, and Jamiltepec can be said to be major nodes in a modern ballad community or perhaps discrete centers of related ballad communities. Throughout this afromestizo zone, the conditions that foster ballad communities remain: isolation, social homogeneity, prolonged conflict in the absence of a strong central authority. Taurino Hernández Moreno (1996) notes that factional groups of armed men served de facto as the local authority in these communities, and the leaders of the groups have been the primary focus of Costa Chica corridos. But he states that their hold on these communities is slipping: "As the communities have improved and the control of the state has increased in the region, those groups began to lose their power. . . . Today, they only have influence in the small settlements" (1996:24).

There are many signs of change. Schools, with their broadening agendas, are becoming more influential in the cities and towns of the region, and commercialized culture has more of a following among the youth. As one resident of Cuajinicuilapa states, "Ahora Cuaji ya ha desarrollado su comercio, y no tenemos que ir a comprar hasta Ometepec" (Now Cuaji has developed its commerce, and we don't have to go to shop in Ometepec; qtd. in Hernández Moreno 1996:20). A new generation of *costeños* is more educated, cosmopolitan, and prepared to compete in the regional economy. Many people have traveled to the United States in search of the dollars that are so hard to come by locally, and these people inevitably bring back home a range of expansive perspectives. Perhaps the coming generations will gradually shed the local culture, so vibrant yet so tied to poverty, isolation, and violence, and with this sweeping tide of change, the corrido will become an heirloom here as it has in some other regions of Mexico.

But for the moment the ballad community is alive on the Costa Chica, and it still entices the skills of talented young musicians such as Isaac Vargas of Ometepec, who learned the corrido repertoire of his distinguished uncles, Moisés and Juvencio, and continues in their footsteps as a recognized *trovador* of local corridos. Further evidence of a vital tradition can be found in the practice of musicians like Juan Saguilán Peña and his friend, Teódulo García Pastrana, who came of age in the town of Maguey, Oaxaca. They have relocated to Cuajinicuilapa, where they perform at dances and other social events, staving off for the time being the growing tendency to hire canned music for these occasions. Central to the musical life of these young men is the composing and performance of regional corridos.

The next generation: Vargas cousins, Ometepec, 1996

The Costa Chica offers a fascinating historical profile, in some ways distinctive, in some ways typical of other Mexican zones. The persistence of a strong black African heritage is unusual in Mexico, yet the evolution of this population toward a broadly mestizo paradigm connects the region to national trends. The isolation of the Costa Chica, especially the afromestizo enclaves, is striking, yet people from the coast have played an important role in the drama of Mexican history, and for all its inaccessibility, the coast has always been integrated through economic and social structures to regional and national entities. Violence is endemic to the zone, yet, as we shall observe in the next chapter, the Costa Chica could hardly be said to exercise a monopoly on violence in modern Mexico. And finally, the Costa Chica nurtures a living ballad tradition, yet we can point to other Mexican communities and regions where ballads have also flourished.

To gain a handle on this particular ballad community, we must strike a balance between appreciating its distinctive qualities and recognizing its adherence to general historical currents. The Costa Chica is remarkable for its afromestizo population, for its isolation from the mainstream, for the violence it has experienced, and for the presence of a living ballad tradition. All these factors are intertwined in the historical trajectory of the coastal populations. Critical to this study is the existence of a regional ballad community, or perhaps several local ballad communities, on the Costa Chica. How can we account for this phenomenon? Is it the love of verbal art and music in afromestizo culture? The region's comparative isolation from modernizing external influences? The ravages of chronic violence? I submit that each of these elements contributes to a climate conducive to the making and performing of ballads. Yet none of them by itself, nor the whole set of them in concert, requires the existence of a living balladry. After all, there are other places in Mexico that exhibit a similar historical profile, but not a living ballad tradition.

It makes most sense to view the development of ballad community on the Costa Chica as a fortuitous result of several circumstances, prominent among them the factors I have stressed in this chapter. Surveying the sweep of Mexican history, it is clear that ballad communities arise and perish for a variety of reasons. On the Texas-Mexico border, according to Américo Paredes, interethnic strife generated a ballad community at the outset of the twentieth century. In many regions of the interior, the turmoil of the Mexican revolution fostered the custom of composing and singing ballads. Today in the U.S. Southwest and in the northern states of Mexico, the prominence of trafficking in narcotics, and of efforts to put an end to it, sustains a rebirth of the corrido known as the narcocorrido. On the Costa Chica, we will identify clashes deriving from regional economic rivalries, in the absence of a strong central authority, as the stimulus for the ballad process.

Underlying all these manifestations of ballad community is a persisting climate of violence that cannot be resolved through access to conventional legal channels. The *corrido trágico,* devoted to the commemoration of heroic action, thrives in these conflictive settings. Some degree of isolation is inherent in the stipulation that legal authority be slack or, when present, a source of further complication. Yet the performance of corridos, a sign of Mexican identity, also connects people to the national ethos. Perhaps it is impact of *personalized* violence, opening a space for heroic postures and gestures, that lays the foundation for ballad community. Personalized violence, expressed through local networks and local faces, does not guarantee the emergence of a ballad community, but it does establish conditions favorable to this result.

4 Violence on the Costa Chica

Unrest and the will to change or to forcibly prevent change—
above all as regards to land—seethe under the rural life of much
of Mexico, today as in earlier decades. This is part of a complex
universe of interacting structures and energies that range from
sheer hunger and the loyalties of the vendetta to ancient rivalries
between villages, tangled interpretations of agrarian law, and the
use and misuse of government troops.
—Paul Friedrich, *Agrarian Leadership and Violence in Mexico*

Vengeance for personal deaths is common and these deaths are
often the result of maneuvers by those who attempt to retain po-
litical and economic power and who order killings or kill per-
sonally, as a sign of courage and power. In this way they make
themselves respected and feared. The people of Cuajinicuilapa
say: "Joe is the god of Jack," which means that Joe killed Jack.
—María de los Angeles Manzano, *Cuajinicuilapa, Guerrero*

Violence is seen as a troubling feature of the Costa Chica's social landscape. In
this chapter I address its sources, first examining the evidence provided in cor-
ridos and the discourse surrounding them and then exploring in some detail
what I am calling "the Africa thesis," the popular notion that violence can be
attributed to the black African origins of the Costa Chica's population. We will
have to carefully disassemble this nexus of common wisdom linking violence
to the afromestizo. On inspection, such conceptions assume a racist ideology
that harks back to the Spanish colony, with its social hierarchy placing the *ga-
chupín* at the top of the heap and characterizing all slippage from this ideal as
a movement toward degeneration. I will argue that observers of the Costa Chica,
both insiders and outsiders, have tended to reinforce these antiquated habits
of thought by advancing the thesis of the afromestizo's violent nature.

Violence *is* a problem on the coast, and it does require explanation. But it should be abundantly clear that the argument linking violence to the "blood" or "character" of the afromestizo is simply racist thinking. The argument tracing violence on the coast to the residual influence of black African ancestry must be put to rest. A related argument, that this violence derives in part from the fierce demeanor of *cimarrones* (the escaped slaves who settled in the marshes and thickets of the coast), is not so easily disposed of. But, on balance, I find a discussion of the process of capital formation in the region more effective in accounting for violence on the coast and for the roles played by various ethnicities in its exercise.

But let us begin with an assessment of violence on the Costa Chica from the perspective of the corridos, whose poets, in keeping with the tragic and heroic vision of the ballads, feature its more idiosyncratic dimensions.

Evidence from the Corridos

The corridos portray violence as stemming from a series of related sources. Most prominent among them are episodes of gang warfare, featuring the *brosas* in conflict with one another. These gangs are groups of several to a dozen or more armed men, usually based in a particular town or village and often organized around a central leader. Taurino Hernández Moreno (1996:23–24) has written about the *armeros* (armed gangs), as they are called in the area around Cuajinicuilapa; he notes that "generally the nucleus of a faction was an extended family that controlled a specific territory, well defined and recognized by the other groups." He concedes that most of these groups lacked an ideology of social reform; they arose, typically, out of squabbles between rival families and gangs, and to the extent they had a political agenda, it involved stealing from the rich families on the coast. But in some settings, the *brosas* inevitably became associated with *campesinos* seeking access to lands awarded them in the agrarian reform, especially during the Cárdenas era. In the area around Cuajinicuilapa, afromestizo *vaqueros* in the employ of large haciendas sometimes found themselves opposing afromestizos trying to claim redistributed lands.

In the absence of effective state authority, these armed factions became in effect the local power in most Costa Chica towns, according to Hernández Moreno (1996:24): "Even though they were always kept somewhat under control, these factional groups gave rise to a structure of local power that was inserted into the official national structure through their ambiguous relationship with the government and the army." Episodes of gang violence arise from any number of tensions. In the discourse of the corrido, perhaps the major impetus toward violence is the need to avenge the life of a fallen comrade. Gangs can be mobilized when a friend or ally arrives with a request for help. Any serious misunderstanding between individuals allied to separate gangs can become the spark for a general conflagration. In "El Culebro" the point of contention is a piece of land whose ownership is disputed initially by two rivals. In "Agustín Rojas,"[1] it is the theft of some sugarcane stalks. Stealing cattle can result in armed confrontations between rival gangs. Excessive pride and drunken valor are frequently pictured as the source of the mobilization of rival gangs. In some cases gangs are formed in response to a perceived wrong, as when a group of brothers and uncles rally to avenge the death of a family member.

The first encounters in a dispute between rival factions or gangs can degenerate into a blood feud that may persist for years, with each side exacting vengeance on vulnerable members of the enemy clan, normally confined to the pool of adult males. As one corrido singer, Ernesto Gallardo, told me regarding the feud between the Gallardos and the Mejías of Cruz Grande, "Entre ellos había una lucha a muerte" (Between them there was a war to the death). It reached the point that a Mejía killed a Gallardo who was *presidente municipal.* Male relatives of a man blamed for a death may find themselves targeted by relatives of the dead man. These imbroglios may force families to relocate for an extended period to avoid devastation.

If the Costa Chica corridos can be believed, the intervention of the authorities is an invitation to further violence. A good many corridos describe persecution of local heroes by agents of local, state, and federal governments. These officials may take sides in local conflicts because the system is based upon patronage linking the periphery to the center. Government agents are viewed as supporting their clients with guns, ammunition, safe passage, legal cover, and even concealed assassins. But they are presented in the corridos as devious partners, inclined to double-cross their clients whenever they find it convenient to do so. The picture is complicated by the diversity of the government itself: one gang or faction may enjoy the support of one government agent or agency while a rival gang musters support from some other element in the government. It is not unusual in Costa Chica corridos to hear of shootouts between rival governmental or police agencies.

Much of the violence portrayed in Costa Chica corridos stems from outlaws, hired guns, social bandits, and revolutionaries. The expression used when a man turns to violence is "Se echó de malas" (He turned to a life of crime), and it is thought that these individuals remain dedicated to violence until it catches up with them and they are destroyed by the very forces they have released. Distinctions between criminals and revolutionaries are made but they are not always that clearly drawn. The revolutionary is said to be "an idealist," to have reasons for bucking the system, but most corrido heroes share a set of traits: they are *bragados* (ballsy or fearless); they experience relentless persecution from the government; they succeed (for a time) in *burlándose del gobierno* (resisting, evading, making a fool out of the government); and generally they are killed in a violent encounter.

In most cases the corridos do not closely examine the social and political background of the violence they describe. Indeed, many corridos focus exclusively on the personal rivalries brought into the foreground by violent events. Some corridos point to differential class standing as a factor in the violence, and others attest to the inappropriate behavior of government agents. But corrido poets are more interested in the thoughts, words, and deeds of the heroes in the grip of violent encounters than in the underlying causes of the violence. James Greenberg (1989:16–17) discusses the gap between surface and deep analyses of violence in relation to a blood feud in the Chatino district of Oaxaca:

> Although the passions which led to the tragic death of Emiliano and his sons were wrapped in local issues, their deaths were not merely the result of a local blood feud. Their murders were driven by conflicts and social processes that went far beyond the village. In this context, factionalism and blood feuds serve as mechanisms of social control to undermine the effectiveness of consensual politics. Emiliano and his family, like the other casualties of blood feuds, were victims not merely of their enemies, but of a much bigger game, a class struggle, of whose rules they were hardly aware.

The interplay of the local and the global, of the passions and the underlying politics, is much the same just down the mountains from the Chatino homeland, on the Costa Chica. There too the actors in violent episodes may be only dimly aware of the societal factors that have set them in motion. It is also clear that some contingents benefit from the limited space allotted to consensual politics on the coast. Corrido poets may hint at an encompassing environment but it is their job to commemorate violent episodes and not to dissect them.

Corrido poets, on balance, highlight the more personal dimensions of violence and give it a name and a face. Corrido heroes display a variety of character flaws drawing them relentlessly to their demise: a proclivity to drink too much, overweening pride, obsession with a past slight, a lust for women. Moisés Vargas, a canny observer of the local scene, traced much of the violence to *machismo,* by which he meant something like a senseless urge to dominate.

Vargas compared the attitude of corrido heroes to the gunslingers of the American West: "Yo soy hombre, valiente, te mato" (I am a man, a bold man, I'll kill you). Several commentators alerted me to the danger of combining guns and alcohol, and corridos recount many encounters among friends who exchange bullets while under the influence of *aguardiente.* The canny Vargas also spoke to me of "el interés del dinero" (the lure of money), as he rubbed the first three fingers of his right hand together in the Mexican gesture used to signify the avid reception of bills.

Corrido poets make frequent reference to these immediate causes of violence. The protagonists of their narratives are flawed human beings, quick to anger and take offense, prone to excessive drinking and *machismo,* impulsive in their dealings with peers, driven by personal ambition. Many a fallen hero lands in difficulties "por no saberse tantear" (for not knowing how to figure, for not playing it smart). Editorial comments inserted into the narratives convey a common wisdom asserting the importance of exercising good judgment and citing the consequences of showing poor judgment. The framework of the Costa Chica corrido is essentially tragic, exhibiting bold men and women destroyed by their innate flaws of character. But there is another important angle to this story: many a hero commemorated in Costa Chica corridos seeks trial by violence, and even violent death, as a passport to regional fame. In the next chapter we shall explore this drive.

The less personalized, more abstract causes of violence on the Costa Chica are given scant attention in the corridos. Several lines of analysis are intimated in corrido discourse, including the theme of black African ancestry, allegations regarding the inflammatory role of the Mexican government in the affairs of this region, and references to the perennial conflicts between rich and poor. The corrido poets key on these trends of thought only intermittently or indirectly, preferring to focus attention on the more visceral, and immediate, causes of violence. A comprehensive account of Costa Chica violence would have to register and evaluate all of these factors, immediate and remote. We could argue that the remote causes set the stage by defining social categories and placing them in conflict with one another, while the immediate causes shape the thinking of individuals as they respond to situations of conflict.

The Africa Thesis

What are we to do with the common belief that violence on the Costa Chica revolves around the black African ancestry of its population? Efforts to detect black African cultural practices in these communities have focused on a number of elements: round houses, making hollowed canoes from single logs, speech patterns, names evocative of African regions and tribes, the use of medicinal herbs, polygamy, and the custom of bride capture. These leads are suggestive rather than conclusive. On balance it appears that afromestizos have assimilated to a broadly mestizo paradigm. Africans on the Costa Chica no doubt brought with them and retained some practices from their places of origin, but over the centuries they intermarried with Native Americans and mestizos and adapted to the lifeways of the region. The afromestizo communities on the Costa Chica are best seen as a regional variant on the general pattern of cultural blending that characterizes the Mexican people. Gonzalo Aguirre Beltrán (1958:8) was clear on this point: "Even the groups that today could be considered as black . . . are nothing other, in reality, than mestizos." Véronique Flanet (1977:145) draws a similar conclusion: "The strong tendency toward *mestizaje* has as its consequence the disappearance of the black race."

Dispensing with the canard of a "pure" African individual or community on the Costa Chica frees us to address the values assigned to the various permutations of *mestizaje*. Racial calculations being so important in Mexico from the colonial period onward, it is not surprising that residents of the Costa Chica have worked out their own racial typology and invested it with social significance. Much of the Costa Chica population appears to have descended from intermarriage between people of black African origin and Native Americans. This initial base has received some admixture of European ancestry, mostly indirectly through mestizos. The centuries of intermarriage in these combinations have led to a highly diversified population. Aguirre Beltrán (1958) tells us that those mestizo families and individuals with features considered European are known as *los blancos*, a small group confined mostly to the more populated centers and claiming an exalted social status. Until recently, they were the only store owners in the area, and they served as local representatives of the large commercial interests housed in Acapulco. Aguirre Beltrán (1958:68) noted the growing tendency for members of this group to refer to themselves as *la sociedad* (the society) or *alta sociedad* (high society), due to the perceived imprecision of using the term *blanco* for people visually exhibiting black African and Native American ancestry.

Many people on the Costa Chica have physical features that point to some degree of black African ancestry. The segment of the population exhibiting these attributes constitutes the majority of those living in the *cuadrillas* or *bajos*, small settlements along the rivers where contact with the outside world has been less extensive. The racial ideology of the Costa Chica characterizes this social element as "degenerate" and castigates its members as *matones* (killers), holding them responsible for the violence afflicting the region. There is only this much foundation for this stereotype: many of the heroes commemorated in corridos—Moisés Colón, Leonicio Esteban, Mauro Lorenzo, and Juvencio Moreno—came from these isolated settlements and had black African physical features.

The research of Laura Lewis in San Nicolás sheds light on current attitudes toward issues of ethnic identity among members of the Costa Chica's afromestizo communities. Many of her consultants play down the African connection, preferring to stress their linkage to *los indios,* Mexico's Native Americans. They tell her they prefer to call themselves *morenos,* which they consider to be "a conflation of blackness and Indianness" (n.d.:36). Possessing a partially Native American ancestry, and sharing with Mexico's Native Americans an alienation from the dominant "white" power structure, the *morenos* of San Nicolás seek, through their identification with *los indios,* a solid footing in the ideology of the Mexican nation. Although there are many points of tension between *morenos* and *indios,* there are ample grounds for symbolic association as well, as Lewis (2000, n.d.) argues convincingly. It is also the case that in San Nicolás, as elsewhere on the coast, the historical process of intermarriage continues, as Native American women not infrequently take *moreno* husbands.

Another trend is the gradual awakening of a Mexican version of what we might call "black African pride." My friend El Cobarde embraces his African heritage. He attributes his love of music to his mother's people, *la raza negra,* and he celebrates his identity as the product of a father who was of *la raza española* (the Spanish race) of Ometepec and a mother who was from *la negrada* in Cuajinicuilapa: "Mi mamá era negra, negra, cien porciento negra, ya aquí ya hubo un cruce de mi papá con mi mamá; mi papá de raza española, ah, y mi mamá, negra. . . . Aquí está toda mi raza pero por parte de mi padre. Y allá la negrada por parte de mi mamá" (My mother was a black woman, a black woman, 100 percent black, so here there was a crossing of my father and my mother; my father was of the Spanish race, ah, and my mother, black. . . . Here are all my people on my father's side. And there *la negrada* on my mother's side). When I mentioned that he seemed to be comfortable in both settings, he replied in the affirmative: "Ah, sí. Además, yo estoy contento de que hubo una combinación, de, entre mi padre y mi madre. Y yo creo que por eso yo nací compositor, por la mezcla que hubo" (Oh, yes. Also, I am happy that there was a combination, of, between my mother and my father. And I believe that's why I was born a composer, because of the mixing that took place).

I quizzed my companion: Why? "Ah, porque mi padre fue muy letrado. El estudió para sacerdote. Entonces, este, y mi madre analfabeta. Quiere decir que no se sabía nada, nada de escribir, nada nada. Entonces, yo lo poquito que, yo se lo heredé a mi padre. Porque mi padre sí sabía" (Ah, because my father was very lettered. He studied for the priesthood. So, well, and my mother was illiterate. Which means she knew nothing at all about writing, nothing at all. So, the little that I know, I inherited from my father. Because my father really knew it). And I inquired, What came from your mother's side? "Ah, la música, la música. Porque la familia de mi madre es músico, son músicos. Pero ellos no son compositores. No más son músicos. Yo tengo las dos cosas: soy músico y soy compositor" (Ah, the music, the music. Because my mother's family is musical, they are musicians. But they are not composers. They are just musicians. I have both things: I am a musician and I am a composer). El Cobarde claims with pride both components of his ancestry, but clearly differentiates the contributions traceable to each. Significantly, he credits his father's people, whom he labels "Spanish" but are presumably *mestizos,* for his ability to compose music. His mother's people, *la raza negra,* have provided his passion for performing music. In the local value system, both skills are appreciated, but the ability to compose is considered less common, a gift of God.

El Cobarde at work, Ometepec, 1989

El Cobarde's understanding of local history is structured by the play of racial categories: "Cuenta la historia que hace tiempo el indio era el que pobló aquí, pero luego vino el negro y ése lo sacó, y se fue más pa' arriba, ¿sí? Y entonces ése, vinieron a prevalecer los extranjeros, sea como los españoles, los ingleses, todos esos. Pero esos ya llegaron a ser los principales hace tiempo aquí en el pueblo, y esos son los que hacen las divisiones" (History tells us that long ago it was the Indian who settled here, but then the black people came and threw them out, and they went further into the hills, right? And then those, the foreigners came to dominate, such as the Spanish, the English, all those. But those people came to be the main families here in town, and they are the ones who divide things).

When I asked what he meant by "dividing things," El Cobarde replied: "De los bienes y de raza y de todo. De todo hacen división" (Material goods and races and everything. They divide up everything). It is interesting to note the interplay of ideas here. On the one hand, Indians and blacks are recognized as the "natives" of the region, the former with some priority, for all others are characterized as "foreigners." On the other hand, El Cobarde's sketch places the "newcomers" firmly in charge, as those who have the authority to control the material and mental realms and to stipulate the definitions and implications of racial categories.

El Cobarde told me that racial discrimination was less prevalent today than it had been a generation ago, due to the influence of the schools, which bring young people of all races and areas together. But he pointed to a continuing sense of racial superiority in the main families: "Ah sí, sí todavía hay un poco aquí, como ahora por ejemplo, los que se catalogan como los principales de aquí de Ometepec, esos no permiten muy bien que una de sus hijas se venga conmigo, no, para nada" (Ah, yes, yes, there's still something of that here, like for example, those who count themselves among the main families here in Ometepec, they wouldn't allow one of their daughters to go off with me—no, no way). El Cobarde's comments indicate the persistence of traditional ideas about identities even within a positive reformulation that allows for pride in black African roots.

As we have noted, Aguirre Beltrán applies the concept of an aggressive ethos to the afromestizos. What evidence can be mounted to certify this claim? One telling example developed in Aguirre Beltrán's monograph is the custom of bride capture, very active when he was in Cuajinicuilapa and still not entirely eclipsed. Juvencio Vargas, the corrido singer, proudly told me that he had stolen his wife: "Me la robé, pero después me llegó a querer" (I stole her, but later she learned to love me). More than a few corridos deal with problems arising from this custom, dwelling on the anger of the bride's family or the predicament of a woman returned because she was not a virgin. Bride capture, as described by Aguirre Beltrán, is an involved sequence of stylized moves that features at every turn aggressive male tendencies. It begins with an agreement between the young man and woman to meet at the edge of town in the early morning. The young woman appears with one or more of her female associates, and the young man appears, often with a companion or two. He sweeps up his intended bride, apparently by force although the arrangement is in fact consensual, and carries her to a secluded spot. The young couple spends the day there and returns cautiously at dusk to the compound of the groom's family. It is crucial in these early stages to avoid contact with male relatives of the captured woman, for her people experience at the outset shame and anger and a desire to seek revenge.

With the beginning of the next day, in Aguirre Beltrán's account, it is customary to set off fireworks outside the groom's compound to indicate that the young woman "has turned out well," that is, has been found to be a virgin. If the fireworks are not forthcoming, it is a sign that she "has not turned out well" and will be returned to her people. By the middle of the day the two young people appear at the mayor's office, to announce either their intention to marry or that there will be no marriage. If the marriage is on, a reconciliation must be made with the family of the bride. After a few days the groom's family sends an intermediary to the bride's family. When the situation calms, a meeting is arranged at the home of the bride. When the groom arrives, he is subjected to a mock beating by the bride's father, who retains some of his initial anger. In the end, it is normal to transcend this delicate period and arrive at friendly relations.

I cannot say how prevalent bride capture is today in Cuajinicuilapa though I was assured that it still takes place. I think it likely that this method of procuring a bride is still widely practiced in more isolated settlements. Laura Lewis suggests that in San Nicolás people distinguish consensual elopements from forcible extraction of the bride, a distinction that does not feature in Aguirre Beltrán's somewhat romanticized account of bride capture. Lewis notes that the wider presence of authorities and sanctions discourage the practice of forcible abduction. An additional note of caution is sounded in the belief, on the part of some *morenos,* that the practice of bride capture originated with the Spanish (Lewis, personal communication).

Aguirre Beltrán's version of bride capture features at every juncture the aggressive ethos he attributes to the afromestizo: the bravado of the young man and his friends who accomplish the capture; the menacing anger of the bride's male relatives, who must be kept away from the groom's people until the matter cools off; the rage of the father, who literally whips the groom before forgiving him. In all these details, this ritual evinces the masculine bluster and defiance, the aggressive posture that is said to characterize the ethos of the community. I had ample occasion to observe the display of manliness and the caution exercised to avoid misunderstandings among gatherings of men on the Costa Chica. I saw among some *morenos* an exaggerated masculine demeanor, marked by a scowl and a swagger, that discourages any thought of trifling. In visits to Cruz Grande, Ometepec, Cuajinicuilapa, and Pinotepa Nacional, I have always had the good fortune to fall in with friendly associates, men like El Cobarde, Juvencio Vargas, Moisés Vargas, Raul Mayo, and Juvenal Arellanes, who have contributed so much to my project. But I have also noted the presence of tough-looking characters, many of them packing weapons, whose rough visage inspires a certain awe.

Perhaps even more revealing is the strict etiquette displayed when men gather in public settings. In these venues I observed gestures of diffidence, avoidance of eye contact, and a general tendency to preserve zones of personal sanctity. It is as if people are aware that any spark could ignite a fire. Yet I cannot say that this masculine code on the Costa Chica differs remarkably from the generalized code of the Mexican *macho*, marked by a stylized toughness replicated in virtually every population within the nation (Paz 1959; Ramos 1962). In this domain as in others, the Costa Chica is better characterized as a regional expression of a widespread pattern than as a distinctive cultural prototype. There is evidence for Aguirre Beltrán's aggressive ethos on the coast, yet one could hardly maintain that this ethos is unique to the Costa Chica.

The corrido responds to violent situations, and the coasts of Guerrero have been plagued with violence. Throughout Mexico the people of Guerrero are said to be prone to violence; "Son matones" (They are killers) is a common phrase. Many people on the Guerrero coast do not exactly dispute this epithet, but rather turn it into a virtue. One of the *gritos* frequently heard in the heat of a ballad-singing session is "¡Así es Guerrero, puro gallo!" (That's Guerrero, nothing but fighting cocks!). The *gallo bien jugado* (well-played fighting cock) symbolizes one viable solution to the dilemma of achieving manhood in a world defined by the quest for honor. The heroic vision of the corrido accepts violence as a natural response to several situations, and the *costeños* inhabit a world largely shaped by this vision. The honorable man (or woman, in some cases) will meet violence with violence, in self-defense, in defense of the home and family, and in revenge of violence inflicted upon a relative or ally. In the heroic code of honor, violence may be an appropriate response to a grievous and malicious personal slight.

These are the legitimate uses of violence. People also recognize that misguided individuals will perpetrate violence in settings that do not require violent means. And not all *guerrerenses* (people from Guerrero), of course, subscribe to the heroic vision advanced in the corridos. I have heard people exclaim in exasperation, "Somos brutos que nos matamos por nada" (We are brutes who kill each other for nothing), and I have witnessed impassioned pleas for the demise of the corridos, which are seen in some quarters to promote violent tendencies. As Baltazar Velasco cautioned me, "No hay que tirar gasolina al fuego" (No need to throw gasoline on the fire). He told me that he once canceled a Costa Chica corrido contest out of fear that one of the contestants would take advantage of an opportunity "a tirarle a una familia cacique de su tierra" (to trash one of the leading families of his district). This, my friend told me, could cause problems. But the prevailing view, especially among those active in the corrido tradition, exalts the *guerrerense* as a bold defender of what is right, *una persona que no se deja* (a person who does not back down). Again, this attitude is hardly unique to the people of Costa Chica. After all, several of Mexico's most hallowed vernacular expressions play on the root *rajarse,* "to back down, to give up." In virtually every corner of Mexico, men are urged not to back down (*que no se rajen*) or are accused of being *rajados* (cowards). Famously, a mariachi tune, "Guadalajara," implores a whole state, Jalisco, not to back down: "Ay, Jalisco, no te rajes."

Octavio Paz (1959:165) features this locution in his discussion of the Mexican personality. He argues that "the ideal of 'manliness' consists in never backing down." For Paz, "backing down" shows weakness, a fundamental betrayal of male identity: "The Mexican can bend over, humiliate himself, 'stoop down,' but not 'back down,' that is, allow the outside world to penetrate his intimacy. The '*rajado*' is not to be trusted, a traitor or a man of doubtful loyalties, who reveals the secrets and is unable to confront danger as one should." If Paz is correct in isolating this trait as basic to Mexican identity, then the Costa Chica, with its emphasis on resolute manliness, must be judged in this regard as typical rather than as radically distinctive. It seems that every effort to argue a peculiar Costa Chica ethnicity leads instead to recognition of national patterns.

Conflict on the Coast

Is there truth to the attribution of violent tendencies to the people of Guerrero, and specifically to the *costeños?* There is plenty of evidence of violence in Guerrero, but such violence is hardly exclusive to this region. One must recall that much of ancient Mexico was the scene of continuous warfare and extensive human sacrifice. Nueva España was born in the blood and fire of the conquest, and the Spanish colony was a scene of internecine violence between rival elites and institutionalized violence toward the underclass of Native Americans and mulattos (Johns 1995). It was these popular elements, the foot soldiers in the insurgency, who found vindication in the Plan de Iguala, proclaimed by Agustín de Iturbide and Vicente Guerrero in 1821, declaring full citizenship for all social classes in the new nation of Mexico. But the violence had not yet run its course, for the nineteenth century is stained with the blood of Mexicans who fought one another in expelling the French, for or against the liberal agenda during the reformist period, and in a bewildering variety of local and regional struggles. Many of these cleavages achieved a kind of apotheosis in the general conflagration of the Mexican Revolution, starting with the movement to oust the dictator, Porfirio Díaz, in 1910 and continuing unabated into the mid-1920s, with a regional extension of the conflict through the years of the Cristero Rebellion (1926–29). The establishment of the institutionalized revolution in the early 1930s may have brought a tentative peace to the nation, but disagreements continued to be settled through violence.

Against this backdrop, is it possible to isolate the Guerrero coast as a scene of special virulence? The conventional formula traces violence on the coast to the black African heritage of its people, using arguments that may emphasize biology or culture or both. The biological argument holds that black African blood is "savage," not fit for "civilized" life, and to the extent that this blood persists in the the coastal population, it contributes to the disturbing climate of social violence. This argument cites the prevalence of dark-skinned bandits in the region. As we have seen, many of the figures commemorated in the regional ballads were men from poor villages on the Costa Chica, where the *moreno* has persisted.

One observer of the local scene, Baltazar Velasco, schoolteacher, composer of *chilenas,* and student of Costa Chica culture and history, spoke to me at length about ethnicity and violence on the Costa Chica, as seen from his vantage point in Oaxaca. Velasco shares physical attributes with afromestizos, yet as a recognized composer and eduator, he claims a higher niche in the racial taxonomy. He locates his comments, as we shall see, from a position largely (though not entirely) external to the afromestizo population:

> La mayor parte del mestizaje de la costa generalmente está conformado con las tres sangres, ¿no? La negra, la indígena, y la blanca. Porque, por allí . . . se puede notar perfectamente en un negro sus facciones indígenas, y en un blan-

co que de pronto le sale un hijo morenito: dice, "Y este, ¿qué? ¿Que pasó?" [Laughs.]

Y es parte de la cuestión genética, ¿no? Que proviene desde épocas de la colonia.

Entonces ésta tal vez sea la cosa distintiva de esta región. Y que se asemeja mucho a la Costa Chica guerrerense. Costumbrismos, manera de expresión, sus grupos étnicos bien conformados, y un caso muy esencial, la chilena, que quizás sea el rasgo más distintivo de todos, que hace que la Costa Chica conforme como tal, ¿no?

[For the most part, race mixing on the coast is composed of the three races, you see? The black, the Indian, and the white. Because over there . . . you can easily see Indian features in a black man, and a white man might happen to have a black child; he says, "And this one, how come? What happened?" (Laughs.)

And it has to do with genetics, right? Which comes down to us from the epoch of the colony.

So this is perhaps the distinctive thing about this region. And it closely resembles Guerrero's Costa Chica. Local customs, manners of expression, its well-defined ethnic groups, and a very essential case, the *chilena*, which might be the most distinctive trait of all, that makes the Costa Chica the way it is, you see?]

It is clear that this gentle and perceptive man from Pinotepa Nacional is deeply committed to his native region. In addition to a distinctive pattern of *mestizaje*, Velasco argues for the *chilena*, local songs set to a lively dance rhythm, as a defining feature of the vernacular culture.[2]

Velasco, exhibiting an ambivalence that is characteristic in these discussions of violence on the coast, credits the afromestizos for the brusque style of this music and its associated dance: "La influencia del negro fue determinante, definitivamente fueron para mi punto de vista, fueron los negros que la adoptaron primero y que le dieron ya su carácter bravío, su carácter hasta valentón, ¿no? fanfarrón. Ellos lo adoptaron, después los mestizos, y finalmente los indígenas" (The determining influence was that of the blacks. They were definitely, from my point of view, the blacks were the ones who adopted it first and who gave it then its fierce character, its somewhat gallant character, you see, its flashiness. They picked it up first, then the mestizos, and finally the Indians). Velasco is a true *aficionado* of the *chilena*, but his attitude toward the corridos of the Costa Chica is rather different: he admires the corrido as an expression of the popular genius, but he deplores its association with violent deeds and violent individuals:

La mayor parte, quizá un noventa porciento, de los corridos están dedicados a matones. Asesinos viles, ¿no? Que se dieron a balazos por ahí con el otro, con otro mafia, y ganó el mejor. Y el muerto murió como macho.

Y eso sucede generalmente en los pueblos afromestizos. En esta región es más dominado por mestizos, y por indígenas, y por la montaña, es menos la influencia del corrido. Ya de hecho, nada más, su reducto, su último reducto, queda en las zonas costañeras. Pegados en los pueblos negroides.

[Most of the corridos, maybe some 90 percent, are dedicated to killers. Vile murderers, no? Who traded shots over there with the other guy, with the other mafia, and the better of them won. And the dead man died like a macho.

And this happens generally in afromestizo communities. In this region, the mestizos are more prevalent, and the Indians, and in the hills, the corrido's influence is less. Nowadays, for sure, its redoubt, its last redoubt, lies in the coastal zones. Right there in the negroid communities.]

My friend traced his objection to the corrido directly to its link to violence, so I asked him to discuss the problem of violence on the Costa Chica. He expressed a hope to respond not in a racist vein but in a vein that would honestly assess *la idiosincrasia* (the inborn traits) of the Costa Chica population:

Aquí en la región de la costa se nota más la violencia por la cuestión de la gente negra. Porque por su propio índole, por su propia manera de ser, el negro es muy violento.

Es decir, la africanización de nuestra gente, yo lo comparo, malamente, con la vieja africana. Que es otra cosa muy diferente pero de alguna manera su temperamento del negro, este, quedó mezclado en todos nosotros y esa africanización se refleja, no solamente por sangre, por razas, sino por reflejo. Porque, ¿quiénes son los pistoleros en la región? Los negros.

[Here on the coast you notice the violence mostly among black people. Because by his nature, by his way of being, the black is very violent.

That is to say, the Africanization of our people, I compare it, perhaps unfairly, to old Africa. Which is something totally different but in some way the temperament of the black, well, it became mixed into all of us and that Africanization is reflected not only in blood, in race, but in our reflexes. Because, who are the gunmen in the region? The blacks.]

Velasco continues to meditate on the persistence of this "culture of violence," which he says took root when the coast was an isolated region, but seems to resist the impact of modern educational resources. He recognizes the possibility that even he, an educated man, could fall under its spell, given the appropriate circumstances. But his thinking begins to lead him outward from his initial formulation of racial ancestry as the central issue:

Tenemos radiodifusoras. Tenemos canales de televisión, repetidora. Sin embargo, no han logrado quitarse eso, esa cultura de la violencia. Por lo tan ancestral que viene ya. Yo podría decir que hasta atávica, por atavismo.

Y como estamos africanizados, y de alguna manera viviendo en la violencia, uno se empapa de la violencia, sin que uno lo quiera hacerlo. De pronto yo estoy pensando como el cuate aquél a pesar de que yo supuestamente tengo una cultura, o tengo un, ya, estoy cultivado. Soy profesionista.

Pero de pronto veo que me mataron a mi hermano, yo no voy con las autoridades. Porque sé que las autoridades no me van a hacer caso. Y es uno de los factores: la falta de partición de justicia es una de las razones, es uno de los factores más incidentes en la cuestión de los actos violentos. Porque si voy a poner mi denuncia, sencillamente, llega el otro y le dice: "Mira, aquí estoy."

Allí muere. O sencillamente, la misma autoridad dice: "¿Para qué persigo este crimen si ya sé que no me van a decir nada?" Un círculo vicioso que termina cuando venga la venganza. Esa venganza que va creando un engranaje, una cadena, se va concatenando, los hechos violentos. "Tú mataste a mi hermano; yo te mato a ti. A mí me mata tu hermano. Mi primo mata a tu hermano."

El primo de aquél mata al otro. Es una cadena, de violencia, de crimen.

[We have radio stations. We have television stations, relay broadcasts. Even so, this thing has not left us, this culture of violence. Because it is so rooted in our ancestry. I would even say it is atavistic, an atavism.

And since we are Africanized, somehow living in this violence, a person soaks up the violence, even without wanting to. Suddenly I am thinking like that fellow over there despite the fact that I supposedly have an education, that I am a cultivated person. I am a professional.

But it happens that I see they killed my brother, I don't go to the authorities. Because I know the authorities will not listen to me. And that is one of the factors: the lack of the provision of justice is one of the reasons, it's one of the most important factors with regards to violent actions. Because if one goes and files a complaint, simply, the other guy comes and tells him: "Hey, here I am."

There he dies. Or simply, the authorities say: "Why should I pursue this crime if I already know they will tell me nothing?" A vicious circle that concludes when vengeance is done. That vengeance starts creating a mechanism, a chain, they start piling up, the violent deeds: "You killed my brother; I will kill you. Your brother kills me. My cousin kills your brother."

That guy's cousin kills the other guy. It is a chain, of violence, of crime.]

The conversation turns to additional elements implicated in the local violence, and Velasco speaks to me about *machismo* and alcoholism, which are by no means restricted to the coast, and points to economic and political intrigue as an underlying factor.

As we move toward closure, Velasco is concerned that his comments smack of racism: "Para mí los casos que ocasionan más actos violentos es primero la idiosincrasia nuestra, que es mi punto muy particular, podría ser por la africanización. Quién sabe si no caigo en cuestiones racistas, ¿no?" (For me, the cases that bring about the most violent deeds stem first from our idiosyncrasy, which is my own particular notion, it could be due to the Africanization. Who knows if I am falling into racist ideas, no?). He revisits the thesis of Africanization to provide a point of clarification he considers essential:

> Pero la africanización debido al negro cimarrón, no al negro esclavo. El cimarrón fue el hombre, el negro que vivió libre y que creó sus villorios, este, sus escondites por allá. A ese me refiría para ser más exacto; no, no al negro que vivió como esclavo. No, porque si no estaré yo generalizando.
>
> Porque no sé si el negro de los Estados Unidos sea igual de violento que este de acá. O el negro de Jamaica, el negro de Africa, o el del Perú. No lo sé. Pero éste, al menos nuestra gente, de raza afromestizo, descendiente de los cimarrones, en realidad sí, son muy violentos.

> [But Africanization deriving from the black *cimarrón*, not from the black slave. The *cimarrón* was the man, the black who lived in freedom and created his settlements, well, his hiding places over there. That's the one I am referring to, to be more exact. Because otherwise I would be overgeneralizing.
>
> Because I don't know if the black of the United States is as violent as the black here. Or the black of Jamaica, the black of Africa, or the one from Peru. But this one, at least our people, of the afromestizo race, descendent of the *cimarrones*, in reality, yes, they are really violent.]

Baltazar Velasco has delved into his soul in seeking plausible answers to my questions about violence on the Costa Chica. He begins by casting the blame on a persisting black African cultural heritage in the Costa Chica population, but then points to a set of causes that are not directly related to ethnicity, including the quest for justice in the absence of effective legal institutions and the devilish contributions of alcohol consumption and *machismo*. In closing he returns to the theme of ethnic inheritance, but now amended to reflect the historical circumstances of the coast, its role as a refuge for escaped slaves during Spanish colonization.

Aguirre Beltrán, as we have already observed, is the main proponent of a thesis linking violence on the Costa Chica to the formative experience of the *cimarrón,* a thesis familiar to Baltazar Velasco. Noting that some Costa Chica communities have their origin in escaped slave settlements, Aguirre Beltrán argues that people in these communities adopted a fierce demeanor as a means of survival. To the natural protection of thickets and swamps, these *cimarrones* added a cultural deterrent, an aggressive ethos, to discourage the Spanish authorities from attempting their recapture. Aguirre Beltrán tracks the perpetuation of this aggressive ethos into the postcolonial period, when vying financial interests found uses for violence-prone men in the emerging regional economy. He also discusses the *brosa* as the "arma ejecutiva de la negrada" (executive arm of the black population), ready to settle scores in a social and economic system that had largely neglected the needs and interests of the local population. Aguirre Beltrán views the corrido as a summons to action that models and reinforces the aggressive ethos typical of the community. This argument skirts the mention of biological proclivities by concentrating on cultural attributes originating in the *cimarrón* experience and persisting from the colonial period to the present as a cultural inheritance.

Violence on the Coast Reconsidered

The Costa Chica has been and continues to be a violent place, but it is not unique in the Mexican context. It is interesting to note that just up the mountain trails beyond the riverine plains of the coast, Native Americans have experienced a comparable plague of violence. According to James Greenberg (1989), the Chatino people in Oaxaca's Juquila district evince "astounding" homicide rates. Further afield, in the Tarascan communities of Michoacán, Paul Friedrich (1981) describes a devastating pattern of local violence. Are we to resurrect the stereotype of "cruel Indian blood" to account for these observations? This option revives the reigning social paradigm of the colony, in which Spanish "blood" (or Spanish culture) was held to be "pure" (or correct) and all deviations from this baseline were measured, sometimes finely calibrated, as "contaminations." Or shall we bring in a hypothesis about cultural forms and attitudes derived from the harrowing experience of the conquest?

Grand theories allocating violence to race, ethnicity, or formative experiences lose much of their force once we inspect local conditions with an eye toward the distribution of power and wealth along racially determined lines. For the Chatino, Greenberg shows that the trend toward excessive violence began in the 1920s and 1930s with the introduction of the coffee economy. This capitalist expansion into what had been a communally organized economy laid the foundation for the assertion of economic control on the part of mestizos who provided the trees and bought the crop and for rivalry between local factions allied with one mestizo entrepreneur or another. In a similar vein, violence on the Costa Chica derives from social and economic considerations rather than from blood, though Aguirre Beltrán's (and Velasco's) stipulations about the impact of history on attitude may contain an important kernel of truth. The most plausible account features the intrigue of agents who have found it convenient to mobilize the most alienated social element, the poverty-struck *morenos* of the coastal villages, in fighting regional economic battles. Corridos on Guerrero's coasts make constant reference to the recruitment of *pistoleros* in the process of capital formation and economic competition along the coast. Struggles among local factions for government indulgence, and the continuous intervention of state and federal authorities in regional and local squabbles, have contributed to mobilization of the outcast elements of the area.

This analysis finds support in a striking account of violence and its sources by the French anthropologist Véronique Flanet, who visited Jamiltepec, a town on the Costa Chica near Pinotepa Nacional, in the 1970s. Not unlike the area around Ometepec and other Guerrero sites, Jamiltepec is the center of a multiethnic region ranging from the coast to the foothills of the Sierra Madre. Here Flanet discerns the hand of *los principales* (the leading mestizo families) behind much of the violence associated with *morenos* or afromestizos. Noting that "almost all the murderous gunmen are black," Flanet (1977:37) highlights their link to local elites: "The on-going conflicts arising between mestizo landowners are settled through the intervention of gunmen who, to retain impunity, make use of their black helpers." According to Flanet (1977:146), a significant portion of the afromestizo population in the vicinity of Jamiltepec works on the lands of prominent local families: "They work as helpers, peons, or cowboys for the mestizo landowners; they are 'the people' of these landlords." She portrays the afromestizo in this capacity as "a trusted employee," whose work involves helping and protecting the boss: "He is a 'guardian angel' who can turn into a gunman if necessary."

Flanet (1977:135–36) creates a vivid portrait of a mestizo patron securing the deadly assistance of his afromestizo peon, initially situating us in a cantina where this dialogue takes place between patron and peon. I include the Spanish original along with my translation to convey the flavor of this speech:

> —Ya sabes, compa, si tienes algún problema, me lo dices con confianza.
> —Sí . . . fíjate que . . . ¡ándale, tómate otra copa! Ya sabes que hay varias veces que este pinche Juan me dice palabras. Entonces, si podrías ir a su rancho una noche. . . . Pero antes tienes que ver un poco la onda: espíalo dos, tres noches seguidas. . . . Pero, con confianza, si te agarran, si tienes un problema, no dices nada; no te preocupes, yo te saco de la cárcel.
> —No te preocupes, compa, ya sabes, soy tu amigo.
> —Andale, aquí está la botella, para después.

[—You know, *compa,* if you have a problem, you can talk straight to me.
—Yes . . . you know what . . . hey, have another drink! You already know that several times that damned Juan has had words with me. Well, if you could go to his ranch one night. . . . But first you have to test the waters: spy on him two, three nights in a row. . . . But, trust me, if they get you, if you have a problem, don't say anything, don't worry, I'll get you out of jail.
—Don't worry, compa, as you know, I am your friend.
—That's fine, here's the bottle, for later.]

The sequel to this initial chat comes some three days later, when Juan is surprised as he relaxes in his hammock:

—¡Hola, tú! ¿Qué andas haciendo por acá?
—¡Vengo a matarte!
—¿Cómo? ¿Estás loco? ¡No tenemos problemas! Somos amigos ¿¡No es verdad!?
—Sí, pero andas chingando a mi compadre Luis, entonces te vengo a matar . . .

[—Hey, you! What are you doing here?
—I have come to kill you!
—What? Are you crazy? We don't have any problems! We're friends, right!?
—Yes, but you've been messing with my *compadre* Luis, so I'm going to kill you . . .]

As Flanet (1977:136) states in concluding this pair of dialogues, "neither seen nor heard . . . the mestizo has not dirtied his hands." Flanet has captured nicely the tonalities of these voices, reproducing scenes that are enacted and indexed repeatedly in the corridos.

On the basis of these intrigues, Flanet (1977:148) finds the mestizos' tendency to detect a violent nature in afromestizos rather disingenuous: "Nonetheless, the mestizos, who shout so much against the aggressivity of the blacks, know how to take advantage of it: not only do they purchase at low cost their labor, using them as peons, but they also purchase their violence and opportunism, employing them as gunmen." Flanet, present on the Costa Chica during the turbulent 1970s, describes a social distribution of violence that tallies with my more recent soundings in Ometepec and Cuajinicuilapa. This violence is by no means restricted to afromestizos, though it is prominent among them. More importantly, afromestizo hired guns commemorated in local and regional corridos are deeply implicated in the ambitions and feuds of local elites.

The participation of *morenos* in the schemes of Costa Chica's leading families certainly goes a long way toward accounting for the violence in this region. But a range of additional social and political factors must be assessed to gain a comprehensive vantage point on the matter. If we view the flow of history as experienced in Guerrero's communities, we can discern several flash points contributing to a prevailing climate of violence. Ian Jacobs (1982), writing about the aftermath of the revolution in northern Guerrero, discusses social tensions affecting rural zones. One source of conflict was the constant struggle between the large landholders and the *agraristas,* who sought access to their own plots and recovery of communal lands. As on the Costa Chica, the wealthy elites used multiple strategies to preserve their estates, some of them nonviolent, including legal maneuvers—often overseen by friendly judges—and harassment in the form of cutting off water supplies and allowing cattle to roam through planted fields. When these tactics failed, large landholders could always resort to violence or the threat of violence, usually administered by their agents, the *guardia blanca,* a private armed force. As noted above, often the estates' *vaqueros,* many of them afromestizos, were recruited for these labors on the Costa Chica (Flanet 1977; de los Angeles Manzano 1991; Bustamante Alvarez 1987).

The end product of these maneuvers was retardation or frustration of the federal government's intentions during its most active reform phases. Tomás Bustamante Alvarez (1987:418) recalls the violence unleashed by private armies and paramilitary squads on the Costa Chica, which at some times seemed little short of a reign of terror: "In each region gangs of hired killers sprung up, who were used by the large landholders against agrarian leaders and cores. For example, in the area around Ometepec, the gang directed by Alfredo Añorve created both fame and terror." Bustamante Alvarez (1987:413–14) judges that these efforts achieved their sinister purpose: "In the area around Ometepec, Costa Chica, the *campesinos* waited years to cultivate their *ejido* lands . . . because these were continuously invaded by the cattle of the former landowners; those *campesinos* who organized to work the land were shot by *vaqueros* and hired guns."

According to Jacobs (1982:160), *rancheros* (smaller landholders) could be especially ruthless, and they played an active role in stifling the impact of agrarian reform on the Costa Chica. But social tensions in northern Guerrero, as in the south, were not confined to class-oriented disputes. There were also many sources of conflict between different groups of *campesinos,* and these tensions were artfully fanned by the enemies of land reform. Competition between those who were benefiting from the policies of the postrevolutionary government and those who were not caused tremendous strife in the Mexican countryside, and this helps explain the social alignments that emerged during the Cristero rebellion (McDowell 1975; Meyer 1976). On the Costa Chica, indigenous communities and afromestizo communities often recognized different priorities and responded differently to the agrarian cause. In afromestizo communities, a friction arose between those who received *ejido* grants and those who purchased plots in *colonias agrarias*.

In the north, as on the coast, agrarian communities suffered from internal conflicts as well. Rivalries erupted between adjacent communities and disputes within the *ejidos* over control of resources and access to lands. Jacobs (1982:162) notes that "at the municipal and village level the reform provided ample opportunities for factionalism, political intrigue, and manipulation." Outside political elements often sought alliances with political factions in the agrarian communities, touching off additional rounds of disputation and violence. All these sources of conflict have contributed to the waves of violence sweeping across the state of Guerrero, condemning the population to relentless social unrest.

A variety of irritants in Costa Chica society foster a social climate favoring the resolution of conflict through violent means. These same fault lines are evident throughout Mexico, particularly in rural areas. The Costa Chica is unusual in Mexico for its large and visible population with black African roots; only the coastal portion of Veracruz has a comparable profile. But it makes little sense to construe the afromestizo as the source and cause of the violence on the Costa Chica. I contend that the origins of this violence reside in structures of social relations linking the afromestizos to other ethnic populations on the coast and linking the Costa Chica to Acapulco, Mexico City, and the global economy. As in several other Mexican regions, a class of dispossessed citizens is available to serve the interests of elites, and, it must be admitted, the habit of resolving disagreements through violence seeps into the very fabric of community life.

Notes

1. "Agustín Rojas," one of the better-known corridos on the Costa Chica, tells of a mysterious shooting evidently involving two rival gangs. One interesting detail is the use of a wooden statue of El Niño de Atocha to locate the body of the drowned man. This version is from the singing of Juvencio Vargas, in Acapulco, on different occasions.

2. It might come as a surprise that the *chilena*, by its name apparently a "foreign" element, serves as a marker of local identity on the Costa Chica. This dance, with its characteristic 6/8 rhythm, evidently traveled to Mexico from its points of origin in Chile and Peru. Was it sailors from these South American regions, temporarily at port in

Acapulco and Huatulco, who taught it to the local musicians? Américo Paredes, suspicious that such slight contact could produce such dramatic results, advanced in conversation with me the idea that a taste for the *cueca chilena,* once the rage among elites throughout Latin America, spread to the Costa Chica, where it became entrenched and has persisted as a definitive element in the local ethos.

5 Poetry Celebrates Violence

There is less focus on "being a good man" than on "*being* good *at* being a man"—a stance that stresses *performative excellence,* the ability to foreground manhood by means of deeds that strikingly "speak for themselves." Actions that occur at a conventional pace are not noticeable. . . . There must be an *acceleration* or *stylistic transformation* of action.
—Michael Herzfeld, *The Poetics of Manhood*

The celebratory thesis holds that poetry about violence celebrates the deeds of the heroes who initiate and sustain violent encounters. Celebration here entails the rehashing of violent episodes in public narratives designed to exalt the noble qualities of story protagonists. These episodes are defined and shaped to highlight adherence to an idealized code of behavior or deviation from its strictures. Celebration implies a community of cohorts surrounding heroes, who realize in some measure the collective ideal. Poetry arises in this setting as a song of praise for heroes, as recapitulation of the values they represent, and as exhortation to follow their example. The commemorative force of heroic poetry lends it a special efficacy, above and beyond the more practical efficacy of other narrative forms. Recitation of heroic poetry can serve the ritual function of elevating heroes as archetypes of community prowess.

The celebratory thesis has been quite influential in scholarship on traditional poetry. H. M. Chadwick formalized in 1912 the concept of *heroic* poetry tied to the *heroic* age, conceived as a formative moment in the evolution of societies. The heroic age was a somewhat fanciful concept, located in a penumbra at the dawn of history, before literacy and before agriculture, when nomadic groups wandered the land and engaged in struggles with rival clans. The husband-and-wife team H. M. Chadwick and Nora Chadwick pursued these ideas in a three-volume compendium, *On the Growth of Literature,* published during the 1930s. Their text is richly illustrated with materials from antiquity and from all quarters of the then-extant British Empire. If the notion of a herioc age strikes our modern ears as a bit contrived, there is still plenty of sharp commentary in these volumes on the content, style, and social themes in this vast body of oral literature.

For the Chadwicks, as for their distinguished follower C. M. Bowra, heroic poetry flourished in settings of armed conflict between opposing bands prior to the establishment of nation-states. Heroes of these bands were men, and sometimes women, skilled in the arts of combat and prepared to sacrifice their lives in defense of their honor and the honor of their peers. A staple feature of these settings is the court poet, retained by local leaders, who keeps company with the heroes and sings their feats. As Bowra (1952:3) has it, "An age which believes in the pursuit of honor will naturally wish to express its admiration in a poetry of action and adventure, of bold endeavours and noble examples." The Chadwicks and Bowra see this drive to express admiration for heroes as the impetus behind the world's oral epic traditions.

The poets who create and perform heroic poetry are often portrayed as minstrels attached to royal courts, where they sing the praises of the ruler's retinue. One famous instance of this arrangement is Homer's harper and sing-er, Demódokos, retained by the Phaiákian lord Alkínoös and skilled in per-forming dance music as well as amorous and heroic poetry. In one of the most moving scenes in *The Odyssey,* Demódokos, apparently unaware of his guest's identity, brings Odysseus to furtive tears by reciting the tale of the clash be-tween Odysseus and Akhilleus. This scene, and several others like it, show the central role of heroic poetry in the feasts and entertainments of the period Homer celebrates. Another instance is the Anglo-Saxon *scop,* who sat close to the ring-givers and was much appreciated for an ability to transform action into narrative. One paradigmatic case mentioned repeatedly by the Chadwicks is the king's squire in *Beowulf,* "a man full of grandiloquent phrases and in-tent upon poetry, who remembered a very great number of stories from the past" and who composed, on the day after the killing of Grendel, "a well-con-structed narrative" describing Beowulf's adventure "in skillful style" (see Chadwick and Chadwick 1932:574).

The composer of heroic poetry is a valued member of the entourage, knowledgeable of traditional verse, and able to compose on the spot or in short order verses celebrating the deeds of the local heroes. This bardic figure attached to the military camp recalls the corrido poets and musicians who traveled with commanders during the Mexican Revolution, creating ballads in the evening about the day's events. The dean of corrido scholarship in

Mexico, Vicente T. Mendoza (1954:20–21), stresses the role of *corridistas* in the armies of the revolution:

> The poets of the people, mixed in among the soldiers, who are also from the people, covered the fields of battle, and whether they dealt with disaster or victory, they felt they had an inescapable mission to inform the other men of their class about the truth they themselves had witnessed, about the suffering of the humble ones, about the self-sacrifice and self-denial they revealed, whether they were digging trenches, defending moats, attacking barricades, receiving treatments in the hospitals of blood, witnessing the death throes of the wounded, or listening to the funeral tones as they buried some leader fallen that day.

Many photographs and testimonies confirm the presence of *corridistas* in various revolutionary bands (see, for example, Avitia Hernández 1989:441). Among the most famous accounts are those rendered by John Reed, a journalist and radical leftist from the United States, who spent four months in Mexico in 1913–14, much of this time with Pancho Villa's army. In his book relating his experiences, *Insurgent Mexico,* Reed takes notice on several occasions of ballads sung to the heroes of the troop. In one such passage, Reed (1914:88) recounts the spontaneous singing of a corrido around a campfire one evening: "One of them began to sing that extraordinary ballad, 'The Morning Song to Francisco Villa.' He sang one verse, and then the next man sang a verse, and so on around, each man composing a dramatic account of the deeds of the great captain. For half an hour I lay there watching them, as they squatted between their knees, sarapes draped loosely from their shoulders, the firelight red on their simple, dark faces." "The Morning Song" is almost certainly a translation of *las mañanitas,* a corrido lamenting the death of a hero who has been executed, normally at the first light of dawn. In Mexico as elsewhere, the strains of heroic song rise in manly company to celebrate the deeds of the retinue, of bold men admired and often known to the singers.

Ruth Finnegan (1977:247) describes the heroic society as one "characterized by an aristocratic and military ethos, itself reinforced by the existence of court minstrels who praise the dominant warrior princes." Conceding that scenarios of this sort have existed from time to time, she rightly challenges the necessity of this construction, arguing that forms of literary expression are too "free-floating" to be pinned down to specific social contexts. But the notion of a poetry that celebrates heroic deeds, and of poets who specialize in this task, transcends the limitations of a theory of heroic society to broadly inform the discussion of poetry about violent encounters. Mexico's Costa Chica could be· said to exhibit some features of the heroic society though it exists as an isolated enclave within a modern nation-state. But more important for our purposes, its corrido tradition provides ample evidence to confirm and refine the celebratory thesis.

The copious literature devoted to heroic poetry stresses reciprocity between poetry and action. In the formulations of the Chadwicks and Bowra and the summation of this literature by Jan De Vries, heroic poetry is seen as both derivative of the actions of the heroes and a kind of precondition for their displays of heroism. The poets are on hand to celebrate what the heroes do, but the heroes do not act in a vacuum. Instead, they are strongly influenced by the paradigms for violent action celebrated in heroic poetry. This point comes out clearly in a discussion of poetry used in preparation for battle. De Vries (1963) devotes several pages to poets brought to the edge of the field of battle to recite stanzas meant to inspire the warriors. He mentions the *juglares* in Castilla of medieval Spain "who sang heroic songs in the army to rouse the courage of the soldiers" (1963:168). One striking case is the ancient Irish *file*, the traditional poet-reciter, who De Vries (1963:168) portrays in these terms: "He went to the head of the troop, dressed in a white garment, the glittering harp in his hand, and surrounded by musicians. As long as the battle was raging, the poet stood aside. His person was so sacred that his life was not in danger. He followed the whole battle and, in order to celebrate them in his songs after the victory, noted all the brave deeds his lord performed." De Vries (1963) points to banquets and feasts among the noble assembly, in addition, as occasions given over to the performances of the court minstrels. In a similar vein, men on the Costa Chica gather at social events known as *bohemios* to partake of food and drink and to share romantic and heroic songs.

Many themes present in Mexico's corrido tradition are reminiscent of epic poetry in the heroic age. The protagonists of corridos are mindful of heroic prototypes celebrated in the corridos of their regions. On the Costa Chica, men of action have been raised in the corrido tradition. They know, sometimes perform, and often solicit from musicians the ballads about the most famous heroes in their districts. Not only that, they find inspiration in these narratives and in some cases seek to emulate the example of the heroes as recorded in the corridos. There is a spiral of mutual receptivity, wherein the actions of the heroes inspire the poets and the heroes in turn are inspired to action by the words of the poets. The evidence suggests the activation of a social drama in which institutionalized forms of expression recapitulate, but also promote, institutionalized forms of behavior.

The celebratory thesis, as I have framed it here, lies at the heart of Aguirre Beltrán's (1958) discussion of the Costa Chica corridos. In a masterful work of Mexican anthropology, he fashions a portrait of this regional ethos using fragments of corridos as reflections of attitudes central to the local culture. He pictures the corrido as a vehicle for reinforcing an aggressive ethos developed as a posture of self-defense by a community plagued with hostile enemies. The corrido, "always truthful," holds up as exemplary the defiant actions of the heroes, portraying them as "the ideal of the macho," as "the prototype of the personality desired by the culture" (1958:130). Aguirre Beltrán saw the regional corrido as a mirror of Costa Chica identity, preserving an ethos developed over the long sweep of history and deeply embedded in the local psyche.

The centerpiece of this vision is the social category known variously as *la brosa, la gallada, la gavilla, el armero,* or *la palomilla* (the band or gang of armed associates). The literature on the heroic age and its poetry insists on a particular social environment, the assembly of heroes in a rough company of fighters and their companions. This literature points to these gatherings, what De Vries (1963), drawing on Tacitus, calls the *comitatus,* "the retinue . . . of princes and dukes," as the locus where epic poets find their primary audiences. There are many prominent examples of heroic poetry composed and performed in assemblies of warriors and former warriors. Medieval epic, including the poetry about El Cid, is thought to have flourished in the monasteries, where aging fighters would settle among peers into their dotage. As Richard Fletcher (1989:67) states: "Historians of medieval literature are steadily more inclined to stress the role of monastic communities in the formation of heroic epic: against this background of old soldiers re-fighting the campaigns and feuds of the past, how right they are!" In settings like this, the celebratory intent of the poetry can hardly be doubted. Naturally, it is not possible to stipulate this social environment as the sine qua non for all heroic poetry, but it seems reasonable to suppose that the heroic ethos, as well as the origins of much epicial poetry, can be traced to these arenas of manly association. Gangs of armed men have played a critical role in the recent history of the Costa Chica, and they merit careful examination here.

Armed Gangs on the Costa Chica

Aguirre Beltrán (1958:128) flagged the *brosas* as the natural habitat of the local corrido. He portrays them as "the association of all those individuals who, for one reason or another, have entered into conflict with the law or with the community." He exhibits some ambivalence about these gangs. On the one hand, he characterizes them as gatherings in which "oral, physical, and sexual aggression is not only permitted but even required and cheered." These tough characters are "feared for their aggressive behavior." He goes on to say that "they live, generally, in the outlying areas, suspicious of their neighbors, armed with rifles and pistols, carefully watched by everyone, but especially by the principal families or rich people of the towns" (1958:129). On the other hand, Aguirre Beltrán attributes to them a vital role in providing justice to a social class and a rural population that is systematically exploited by the regional establishment. He tells us that these gangs "carry out justice by their own hand" (1958:130). They constitute "the executive arm of the black population," by which he means a militia without charter that advances rough justice in the countryside.

A similar ambivalence prevails when residents of the Costa Chica discuss the *brosas* and the general pattern of armed resistance toward the authorities. The semantic core of the word *brosa*, for the *costeños*, resides in a derogatory vision of the common herd, the unwashed classes, similar to the more widely used Spanish term *la plebe*, according to Alejandro Gómez Maganda (1960:304). From this core the meaning is readily extended to denote armed gangs along the coast. People readily judge the leaders of violent gangs and their followers as criminals, in the words of Moisés Vargas, "men who rise above the law in pursuit of money." But they simultaneously celebrate the heroes of Mexican history who stood their ground against the *mal gobierno* (misgovernment), starting with the Spanish colonizers and continuing to the present-day authorities. In moments of introspection, people draw a clear distinction between criminals and revolutionaries on the basis of what Onofre Contreras calls "un ideal" (an ideal), that is, an unselfish commitment to a program of social reform. But this distinction palls in the heroic vision of the corrido, which assimilates all bold action to the ideal of the *macho*, the real man meeting his obligations to self, family, friends, community, and allies. It is worth noting, in this regard, that corridos about recent *guerrilleros* of the region, such as Genaro Vásquez and Lucio Cabañas, often connect these rebels to the male heroic image. For example, the composer of "Lucio Cabañas"[1] refers to this rebel commander, the idealistic leader of El Partido de los Pobres (the Party of the Poor), as "un hombre bragado" (a ballsy man), an epithet normally bestowed on local strongmen. It is worth noting that Cabañas's abstemious nature, not relevant to the heroic archetype, receives no mention in the corridos about him.

The *brosa* is a group of armed men, as few as a handful or as many as a dozen or more, usually based in a specific locale and held together by loyalty to a central leader. Most of them include a nucleus of men related to one another through blood or marriage or as *compadres*, a form of ritual kinship. *Brosas* may be identified by their leader, as in *la brosa de Moisés Colón* (Moisés Colón's gang) or by their place of origin, as in *mi brosa de Maguey* (my gang from Maguey). The *brosa* may be loosely formed or it may cohere more tightly as a quasi-military outfit. Typically, its members pursue their lives independently of one another and assemble only when there is a call to action. Some *brosas* maintain a fairly constant presence, as militialike entities regularly involved in combat situations. Others come into existence around a particular grievance and disperse once that cause has been settled. In earlier days the *brosas* were groups of armed men on horseback; nowadays they are more likely to travel by automobile. But mobility continues to be an essential trait: the *brosa* is a group of determined men who are disposed to move away from their base and engage in violent actions in nearby locations.

The social structure of the *brosa* pivots around the central leadership, in most cases a single man respected (and feared) for his decisive responses to threatening circumstances. The leader is a tough character, *un gallo bien jugado*, who has proven himself in mortal combat and has also managed to elude or face-down the authorities. These men attract a following of other men who have run afoul of the law or who are bound to them by kinship or other ties. Within these groups, the leaders, known as *jefes, fuertes,* or *cuartos,* exercise control through toughness and distribution of resources. Frequently, the leader achieves a fruitful alliance with some outside element, a general in the army, a well-placed politician, a wealthy merchant who bankrolls his activities, supplies him with guns and ammunition, and provides cover with the authorities. Ambitious entrepreneurs and politicians have found uses for these gangs in a setting marked by the absence of a reliable central authority. Through these vertical alliances, the Costa Chica *brosas* have exerted considerable influence on the economic and political life of the region, often entering into conflicts between rival financial interests and opposing political factions. These *brosas* have sometimes found employment as a paramilitary force used to intimidate grass-roots political movements and secure the financial empires of the elite.

The *brosa* of Moisés Colón, perhaps the most famous of the Costa Chica bands, is in many ways representative of the general pattern. The older generations conserve a good deal of legendry about the leader of this well-known *brosa,* who even surfaces from time to time in the printed record, for example in a dictionary of regional names compiled by Epigmenio López Barroso (1967:249). Additionally, Moisés Colón makes several appearances in the store of local corridos, and his death is the topic of a corrido that has become standard in the regional repertoire. Taurino Colón, a singer of corridos in Cuajinicuilapa, claimed Moisés Colón as an uncle. He knew something about his family tree and told me that Moisés Colón Esteves (one rarely hears his mother's family name) was a *primo hermano* (first cousin) of another famous outlaw of the region, Leonicio Esteves, whom he characterized as "un perro rabioso" (a rabid dog), who would kill even children. Taurino concluded his reminiscences with this disclaimer: "Sí hay malos, hasta los tíos de uno" (Yes, there are bad men, even one's own uncles).

Juvencio Vargas told me that Moisés Colón had worked breaking horses, and that when his father was killed, he set about avenging his death until everyone involved in the murder had been killed. Vargas's friend Enrique Mares presents a slightly different story, but one that leads to the same conclusion:

> Ese muchacho su papá fue revolucionario. Cuando el estaba de chiquillo, su papá venía jalando una vaca y él venía arriándola. . . . Entonces éste tenía unos trece años, por ahí. Mataron a su papá; él en vez de que corriera, agarró un rifle de su papá y peleó con ellos, mató a tres.
>
> Entonces, después su mamá lo mandó a otro lado, a cortar una yerba para remedio, ¿no? Pa' allá, ¿no? Estaba así sacando a la yerba cuando llega otro con machete, pero hizo la pistola así, BRUM. Mató a uno, luego mató a otros tres. Porque, cuando los primeros muertos, no lo castigaron porque estaba chamaco. Pero ya cuando pasó esos otros tres, entonces sí, ya es que peleaba contra el gobierno.
>
> [That boy, his father was a revolutionary. When he was a youngster, his father came leading a cow, he came along herding it. . . . That fellow was about thirteen years old then, just about. They killed his father; he, instead of running, grabbed his father's rifle and fought with them, he killed three men.
>
> Then, later his mother sent him to another place, to cut some herbs for remedies, you see? Over there, you see? He was getting the herbs when a guy came with a machete, but he went like this with the pistol, BRUM. He killed one, then he killed three more. Because, with the first killings they didn't punish him since he was a child. But then when those other three happened, then yes, that's when he fought against the government.]

Most corrido heroes on the Costa Chica have an initial phase in their biographies telling how they first became outlaws, and often enough they are presented as blameless in their first brush with violence. In Enrique's version, Moisés Colón at thirteen years of age is helping his father move an animal when enemies set upon them and kill the father. Young Colón responds courageously to avenge his father's death, but after that his recurrent violence sends him down the road to life as an outlaw. In the legend of every Costa

Chica strongman, there is this point of no return, a decisive moment when the hero *se echa de malas* (turns to a life of crime). These accounts implicate both the social climate of lawlessness and the hero's inclination toward violence as the causative factors.

We do not have a systematic account of Moisés Colón's life, but rather a series of brief glimpses capped by the narrative of his death. He appears at the head of his *brosa* in several Costa Chica corridos. For instance, his *brosa* puts an end to Rubén Ramos, son of the agrarian leader Rodrigo Ramos Añorve and mayor of Ometepec in 1939 (see López Barroso 1967). In "Rubén Ramos," Ramos is set upon by his enemies, people from Tacubaya and Buena Vista, two afromestizo strongholds. One stanza mentions Moisés Colón:

A los primeros balazos	[With the first shots fired
gritaba Moisés Colón,	Moisés Colón shouted.
estaba lloviendo balas	It was raining bullets
como fruta de algodón.	like tiny puffs of cotton.]

López Barroso (1967:248–49) tells us that Moisés Colón killed Rubén Ramos in 1940.

My musician friends Juvencio Vargas and Enrique Mares discussed the events leading to the death of Moisés Colón. Vargas remembered that Colón had married the daughter of a military man, General Diego Avila, and Mares added that the Avilas were among the rich families in the Costa Chica town of Cayaco, near Acapulco. Both Vargas and Mares recalled that when Colón was killed, he was no longer wanted by the government. Instead, he was caught in a power struggle between two factions or perhaps some past grievance came home to roost. My companions told me that Colón was killed for money by one of his own gunmen, and a cousin of his wife to boot:

> Vargas: Pero cuando lo mataron, ya estaba indultado.
> Mares: Lo supimos aquí, fuimos a ver. Estaba indultado, o sea el gobierno ya no lo buscaba a Moisés. Lo mató un contrario de él, pagó aquél, en ese tiempo pagó treinta mil pesos, pero que es equivalente a treinta millones de pesos. Lo mató, ese muchacho que lo mató era su pistolero de él, y primo de su esposa.

> [Vargas: But when they killed him, he was already pardoned.
> Mares: We heard about it here, we went to see. He had a pardon, that is, the government was no longer looking for Moisés. He was killed by one of his enemies. That man paid, in those times he paid thirty thousand pesos which would come to thirty million pesos. He killed him, that boy who killed him was one of his own gunmen, and a cousin of his wife.]

Juvencio Vargas, Acapulco, 1990

If there is a common pattern to the hero's immersion in the outlaw life, there is also a standard arrival at closure, typically in a moment of carelessness at the hands of a hired gun working for the hero's enemies.

"Moisés Colón" paints the canvass of this bold man's demise. Here are the traditional stanzas, as sung by Tomás Navarrete in Acapulco on February 12, 1996:

1. Voy a cantar un corrido permiso pido atención, en el pueblo de Cayaco se murió Moisés Colón, lo mató Antelmo Castillo y Amado Palma el Pelón.[2]	[I will sing a corrido; if you please, I ask your attention; in the town of Cayaco Moisés Colón has died; Antelmo Castillo killed him with Amado Palma El Pelón.
2. Antelmo traía una super y Amado su parabelo, conferenciaron con Sierra y se pusieron de acuerdo, hay que matar a Colón para que se enojara Diego.	Antelmo carried his thirty-eight and Amado his nine millimeter; they got together with Sierra and they came to an understanding— they would have to kill Colón in order to anger Diego.

3. Sierra se puso a pensar
y vió que le tenía cuenta:
"Si bien lo pueden matar
saben que conmigo cuentan,
contra el gobierno no hay nada
soy jefe de la defensa."

Sierra started to think
and he saw that they were right:
"If you are able to kill him
know you can count on me;
don't worry about the government—
I am a chief of defense."

4. Amado le dijo a Antelmo:
"Es peligroso ese amigo,
si tantito le haces sombra
ése se mata contigo,
para poderlo matar
se necesita el bolido."

Amado said to Antelmo:
"That friend is a dangerous guy;
if you cast a slight shadow on him
he will shoot it out with you;
in order to be able to kill him
you must catch him by surprise."

5. Moisés Colón se paseaba
de Soto hasta Tacubaya,
en el pueblo de Cayaco
allí terminó su raya,
lo mató Antelmo Castillo
con una super escuadra.

Moisés Colón went about
from Soto to Tacubaya;
in the village of Cayaco,
there his race was run;
Antelmo Castillo killed him
with his thirty-eight.

6. Estaba Moisés Colón
en casa de Pablo Galeana,
llegaron unos amigos
con las pistolas fajadas,
como no tenían cuestión
Colón no se fijó en nada.

Moisés Colón found himself
in the home of Pablo Galeana;
some friends came to the place
with their pistols strapped on;
since they didn't have a quarrel
Colón paid them little heed.

7. Colón se metió pa' adentro
y unos cigarros pidió,
al darse la media vuelta
Castillo lo aseguró,
y al pegársele a la puerta
seis balazos le metió.

Colón went inside the house
and asked for cigarettes;
when he went to turn around
Castillo made sure he got him;
when he fell against the door
he sank in all six bullets.

8. Antelmo mató a Colón
sin haber ningún motivo,
se veían como compañeros
no se veían como enemigos,
el culpable de esa muerte
fue ese mentado pajarillo.

Antelmo killed Colón
without really having a motive;
they appeared to be companions—
they didn't seem to be enemies;
the one to blame for this death
was that notorious little bird.

9. Ya me voy a despedir   Now I will bid you farewell—
   mil gracias por su atención,   many thanks for your attention;
   en el pueblo de Cayaco   in the village of Cayaco
   se murió Moisés Colón,   Moisés Colón has died;
   lo mató Antelmo Castillo   Antelmo Castillo killed him
   y Amado Palma el Pelón   with Amado Palma El Pelón.]

This corrido, like many others, has three thematic sections. The first of them, after the formulaic opening, sketches the prelude to the assassination: we learn of a convoluted plot whereby Colón must be eliminated to annoy his patron, Diego, whom we know from Vargas's comments to be General Diego Avila, Colón's father-in-law. As in many Costa Chica corridos, the events played out at the local level have much deeper roots, often extending to the very center of Mexico's power structure. A well-placed conspirator, a man named Sierra, promises to smooth things over with the authorities. He also warns the assassins to move with caution, using a traditional expression: "If you cast even the slightest shadow on him, he will shoot it out with you," implying that Colón is not a person to take lightly. Sierra recommends *el bolido*, a slang term meaning "to catch somebody by surprise."

With the sixth stanza we cut to the action sequence. Colón is visiting with friends, innocent of the plot that has been hatched. He sees armed men arrive but thinks nothing of it as he has no quarrel with them. He goes inside a house to ask for cigarettes, but instead receives a flurry of bullets from his assassins. The stanza that describes the actual killing is rather graphic: as Colón turns to leave, a bullet knocks him against the door, and while frozen in this position, his killers sink six more bullets into him. The corrido finishes with a brief assessment in the aftermath of the killing, in which the corrido poet expresses puzzlement at the involvement of Antelmo Castillo, who seemed to have no personal motive, and lays the blame on *ese mentado pajarillo*, evidently a behind-scenes player, possibly Sierra or one of his influential associates. Details like this one illustrate the degree of local knowledge presupposed in most Costa Chica corridos. The final stanza offers the customary farewell in the voice of the corrido poet and singer.

Additional commentaries I extracted from old-timers confirm the main themes in this ballad narrative. For example, Benito Hernández, a musician and retired teacher with a firm grasp on local history, verified the role played by Antelmo Castillo in these events. He knew Castillo personally and thinks of him as a hard-working farmer, not a bad man: "Era buena gente, pero quién sabe qué tenía con Moisés Colón" (He was a good person, but who knows what he had going with Moisés Colón). Castillo's participation in the killing of Moisés Colón is undisputed; what remains opaque are his motives. Did he have a quarrel of some sort with Colón, his cousin's husband? Was it out of loyalty to a political faction? Or was money the motive, as Enrique Mares suggests?

María de los Angeles Manzano (1991) spoke to senior citizens in Cuajini- cuilapa and obtained information quite similar to the skeletal biography of Moisés Colón presented here. De los Angeles Manzano (1991:115) includes excerpts from Francisco Vásquez Añorve's reminiscence about life on the coast, in which he attributes to Moisés Colón "an agitated life." Vásquez Añorve praises Colón for the courage that brought him fame: "When they pursued him with rural troops in Oaxaca and Guerrero, he fought with them all; pur- sued unto death by the rural defenses and the Guerrero authorities, he had to move about constantly. With his courage he worried those who pursued him and his name was repeated all over the place."

He stresses another attribute of this hero, his human decency:

> He didn't kill those he defeated or prisoners who fell into his power; he respected the poor, their property and their families; for the authorities it wasn't easy to know where he was, because everyone denied seeing him until he would appear to them in combat form. He set prisoners free, women found protection with him, even if they were alone in the country; he forced no one and didn't use threats to extract loans of money and other things, and since he knew the rich people in the region, only from them did he take what he needed for his men.

The portrait here is close to the image of a Robin Hood—taking from the rich to give to the poor and fighting bravely against an abusive authority—show- ing once again the remarkable kinship between heroes from different times and places in the popular imagination.

And so we have the trajectory of a hero's life, from the moment of entry into the outlaw life through a series of memorable violent actions to a denoue- ment in a violent death at the hands of enemies or government forces. In the interval between the first and final events, Moisés Colón stood tall as the leader of a well-organized and well-connected *brosa*. His stature was sufficiently high to attract the notice of Aguirre Beltrán (1958:219), who visited the area in late 1948 and early 1949 and mentions *la brosa de Moisés Colón* as one formed "por reservas agrarias" (by fighters who had been active in the agrarian cause in the wake of the Mexican Revolution). This *brosa*, like many others, thrived in a climate of social chaos in the aftermath of the revolution, a period marked by intense local rivalries fanned by the consolidation and expansion of state capitalism into the isolated reaches of the Costa Chica. These gangs found ample opportunities for employment in the battles between cattle barons and other magnates, in the repression of grass-roots organizers, in the bitter quarrels between *campesinos* and vested interests, and in the struggles between rival factions that developed among rural agricultural workers as they fought over access to land distributed through agrarian reform policies of the federal government (Jacobs 1982; Greenberg 1989; de los Angeles Manzano 1991).

The Celebratory Intent

In the light of this portrait of Moisés Colón, a typical case, it might be asked: What is so glamorous about the life of the *brosa?* In what sense does the corrido "Moisés Colón" celebrate this life? On the surface of things, it seems to be a difficult proposition, this life of violence culminating in a violent death. To understand its attraction, and to appreciate the celebratory intent of the narrative poetry that addresses the hero's life, we will need to immerse ourselves in the mentality of the coastal population, at least that portion of it drawn to the traditional value system. Among this element, there is no fairer fortune than to be remembered in a corrido, and specific nuances in corrido poetry are seen to convey the measure of the heroic man.

Alvaro Guillén Bracamontes, known widely as El Cobarde, an astute observer of the local scene, surveys the world about him from the door of his barbershop in Ometepec. He possesses an excellent vantage point on the *brosas,* for a number of relatives on his mother's side of the family have participated in their activities. He portrays the *brosa* as a quasi-military unit with a leadership contingent, the *cabecillas* (gang leaders) who position themselves at the front of the group, for as he says, "Ya ve que para enfrentarse a balazos, no cualquiera quiere ir adelante" (You see, to face the bullets, not just anybody wants to go out in front). The leaders gather a group of followers, whom he describes as men who have killed and therefore cannot risk taking an ordinary job for fear of exposing themselves to retaliation. Men may join a *brosa* in search of protection from their enemies and in search of a living that they cannot pursue through ordinary channels. As El Cobarde says, "Una persona que está trabajando bien, como ahora yo, ¿por qué me voy a meter con ellos?" (A person who has a good job, as I do now, why would I get involved with them?).

According to El Cobarde, most *brosas* are formed for a revenge killing. As he tells it:

Siempre empieza por la muerte de un familiar. Como ahora, por ejemplo, matan a mi hermano; entonces vengo yo y mato al que mató a mi hermano. Luego viene el otro y me mata a mí. [Laughs]. Así empieza.

Y luego uno de los, de los contrarios pues, busca palomilla, busca hombres, busca armas. Ya andan armados, pues dicen, anda fulano con tantos hombres. Entonces viene el otro y también hace lo mismo. Ya tal vez busca su palomilla.

[It always begins with the death of a relative. Like now, for example, they kill my brother; then I come and kill the one who killed my brother. Then another comes and kills me. (Laughs.) That's how it begins.

And later one of the rivals, well, he looks for a gang, he looks for men, he looks for weapons. Now they are armed, so they say, so-and-so has so many men. Then the other guy comes and does the same thing. Now perhaps he looks for his gang.]

Once a *palomilla* (gang) is formed, it comes to be seen as a resource disposable in other causes. Thus, a person with a grievance may approach gang leaders and ask for assistance, a type of encounter that is frequently depicted in corridos. El Cobarde states it like this:

Ya se dedican a andar así, ya no trabajan, este, honradadmente, ¿no? ya se dedican a andar nada más así. Y ya si hay alguien que dice: "Oye, quiero que me mates a fulano; ése está peligroso pa' matarlo."

Entonces dice el mero de la palomilla, dice: "Si me das tanto, yo le caigo con mi gente," y lo matan. [Laughs.]

[Now they just go around like that, they no longer do honest work, you see? Now they just go around like that. And if there's someone who says: "Listen, I want you to kill someone for me, that one is not going to be easy to kill."

Then says the main man of the gang, he says: "If you give me this much money, I'll fall on him with my people," and they kill him. (Laughs.)]

El Cobarde pictures the dynamic between leaders and followers in a *brosa* in terms of *confianza* (having confidence or trust in a person). The leader of the *brosa* knows who are the dependable fighters in his gang, the ones who will not shy away from the action, the ones who are ready to die, and these are the men he prefers to have at his side when he leaves his safe haven. The corridos display many professions of loyalty unto death, and in their narratives sometimes the promise is kept and sometimes it is not. In "Leonicio Esteves," the hero's companion assures him of his loyalty: "'Leonicio, yo soy tu amigo / donde te mueras, me muero'" ("Leonicio, I am your friend; / where you die, I will die"). This prompts Leonicio to exclaim, "'Ay, no me otorgues tanto'"

("Hey, don't flatter me so much"). And in many instances, when the shooting is done, the two heroes are laid out side-by-side, as the poets say, *bien aparea-ditos.* In others, the gang disperses, leaving the hero to fend for himself, perhaps complaining of *una brosa regada* (a scattered gang). Like the hero in "Filadelfo," who had many friends in life but was left to die alone, an unfortunate *cabecilla* may find that his erstwhile loyal companions have deserted him in his moment of need.

One factor that militates toward the fulfillment of obligations within the *brosa* is the stress placed on honor in the local ethos. Men live for their reputations, and in some instances would rather die than surrender their honor. This element comes to the surface in the many corridos featuring attempts by the authorities to disarm the local gunmen. In one case after another, the hero is portrayed as unwilling to hand over his revolver or rifle, even when he is vastly outnumbered by the representatives of the law. El Cobarde points to the familiar situation in which the hero tells his adversaries, "'Sólo que me maten me rindo'" ("Only if you kill me will I surrender"). Indeed, in one of the most famous corridos of the Costa Chica, La Gallinita (the Little Hen) refuses to hand over his weapon, telling the commander, "'No me rindo ni a mi padre'" ("I won't surrender even to my father").[3]

El Cobarde is very clear about the importance of a proud death duly celebrated in a corrido. Referring to the young men attracted to the lifestyle of the *brosa,* he affirms with passion in his voice: "Para ellos es la gloria que se mueran y les compongan un corrido, sí, es la gloria. . . . Ellos lo que quieren es que su nombre se ande oyendo en distintas partes" (For them it is glorious to die and have a corrido made about you, yes, it is glorious. . . . What they want is that their name can be heard all over the place). Another commentator, the composer, musician, and teacher of social sciences Baltazar Velasco of Pinotepa Nacional, Oaxaca, makes a similar point in conversation with me. Velasco is drawn to the corrido as a manifestation of the popular voice, but repelled by what he sees as its tendency to promote violence. When I ask him to consider what I am calling the regulatory thesis, he recognizes the concept that the corrido might argue against certain forms of violent behavior but he assesses its social impact as being in the opposite direction, especially for "la gente que está acostumbrada a manejar armas y a vivir en un mundo de mucha violencia" (people who are accustomed to use arms and to live in a world of much violence). Velasco told me that these people view the corridos as a celebration of their lifestyle. He dramatized their thought process in this way: "'Yo me tengo que ganar un espacio, que me mencionen, en algo, y solamente matando a otro voy a ser famoso. . . . Como fulano de tal es famoso, lo canta fulano y lo canta sutano, yo también voy a seguir el mismo ejemplo. Me voy a matar con los soldados; voy a matar a mis enemigos, me doy a la mala vida, cuando me matan yo voy a ser famoso porque me van a mencionar en un corrido. . . . Me van a matar pero voy a ser famoso. Me van a mencionar en toda la región'" ("I have to earn a place for myself, so they will mention me, in something, and only by killing someone will I be famous. . . . Since so-and-so is famous, this one and that one sings about him, I also want to follow the same example. I'm going to shoot it out with the soldiers, I will kill my enemies, I'll take up the outlaw life, when they kill me I will be famous because they will mention me in a corrido. . . . They will kill me but I'll be famous. They will mention me all over the region").

Velasco summarizes his objection to the corrido in these terms: "Porque se enaltece la violencia, se enaltece a individuos que debían haber sido borrados de la historia de la región, ¿no? Y sin embargo quedaron, pues ya como si le hubierah hecho un monumento" (Because it praises violence, it praises individuals who should have been blotted out of the history of the region, you see? And instead they remained, as if they had made them a monument).

Another commentary on the celebratory role of Costa Chica corridos came from Onofre Contreras, a composer and performer in Acapulco. Contreras, active in the corrido tradition, expresses some ambivalence about the social impact of the corrido, which he recognizes "viene a incrementar muchas ocasiones la violencia" (often works to increase the violence). He notes that in small towns, in isolated settlements, and even in some barrios of the city, people are influenced by the messages they hear in the corridos. He continues his analysis, focusing on the link between the corrido and violence:

> Entonces, OK, al igual en las provincias, en los pueblos, en los ranchos, se andan en ocasiones quitando la vida, cuando entra una discusión por un corrido; o que alguien se quiere sentir aquel héroe, pero no se pusieron a pensar, no se están poniéndose a pensar que ese héroe murió por lo mismo.
>
> Creo yo que en muchas ocasiones perjudica, la verdad, aunque le duela uno darse cuenta, pero sí tiene uno un poquito de brutalidad, de inconciencia, falta de preparación. Eso es lo que viene y concierne a todos. Porque usted, o quién sabe quién más por allá, escucha un corrido, y escuchó un corrido simple y sencillamente; nada más. Lo escuchó, oye que bonitos versos, ¿no? Hasta allí, nada más. Pero otras personas, no; otras personas agarran la copa y le dan el sorbo. Aproximan más rápido, la copa la terminan, se embrutecen más rápido, con más facilidad, y quién sabe quién en la barra donde estén, y ya quiere ser aquél.
>
> [So then, OK, just as in the provinces, in the towns, on the ranches, they sometimes go about killing people, when they get into an argument about a corrido;

or it may be that someone wants to feel like that hero, but they didn't stop to think, they aren't stopping to think that the hero died for the same thing. I believe that often it is harmful, though a person hates to admit it, but yes, it does contain a little brutality, a lack of awareness, a lack of education. This is what it brings and is of concern to all of us.

Because you, or someone else out there, hears a corrido, and they simply heard a corrido; nothing more. They heard it, listen, what fine verse, no? Just so much, no more. But other people, no; other people grab hold of their drink and they take a gulp. They get to it more quickly, they finish their drink, they get drunk more quickly, more easily, and who knows who in the bar where they might be, and now they want to be like that hero.]

Contreras presents the resulting situation as an imaginary movie scene: "Sí, sí, sí. Están mirando un héroe. Y al rato en las provincias se suben al caballo, y ya con la pistola en la cintura, con cargadores acá [points to waist], y quién sabe quién, haga de cuentas que está detrás ellos, la cámara filmando, desafortunadamente, es así" (Yes, yes, yes. They are looking at a hero. And soon, in the provinces, they get on their horse, and already with the pistol around the waist, the bullets here [points to waist], and who knows with whom, imagine you are behind them, the camera filming it all, unfortunately, that's how it is).

These testimonies by three persons in close proximity to the Costa Chica's culture of violence demonstrate the currency of one fixture in the celebratory thesis, the inspiration drawn by some men in the appropriate social categories from stories told by corrido poets. For these men, the existence of a poetry about violence is a spur to a violent life (and death). Such men are motivated to engage in violent action by the prospect of gaining fame, albeit posthumously, as the hero of a corrido. They hope in this way to emulate the heroes of the ballads and transcend the anonymity of a life played out in the provincial backwaters of the nation.

Chante Luna: The Archetype

This drive toward celebrity status through the office of a commemorative ballad can be exemplified in one salient case, that of Chante Luna, a gunman who operated on Guerrero's coasts into the early 1950s. The Mexican writer Ricardo Garibay (1978) presents testimony from Luna's uncle, who laments that despite his own best efforts to gain notoriety, it is still his nephew that they sing about. Garibay (1978:35) attributes these words to this fellow: "All the glory was Chante's, and oneself here in obscurity." After "Simón Blanco," the tale of a man in Tres Palos done in by his *compadre*, "Chante Luna" is probably the most often performed corrido on the Guerrero coast. It has enjoyed a prominence in singers' repertoires since at least the early 1970s, when I first heard it in Chilpancingo and Acapulco. A fixture in the repertoires of singers specializing in corridos, it is one of the few local corridos performed even by those who prefer romantic songs. It has become the archetype of the corrido celebrating the deeds and death of a hero, and its verses display the range of effects employed by corrido poets in that endeavor. Based on the currency of this song, and especially its popularity in the cantinas, it is safe to say that men operating at the margins of the law find in it a celebration of the hero's idealized life and death.

Let's examine one version of this ballad, as performed for me by Juvencio Vargas and his friend from Ometepec, Enrique Mares, in March 1990:

1. Voy a cantar un corrido
   a los que me están oyendo,
   diré de lo que pasó
   en el estado de Guerrero,
   mataron al Chante Luna
   por órdenes del gobierno.

   [I will sing a corrido
   for those who are listening to me;
   I'll tell about what happened
   in the state of Guerrero;
   they killed Chante Luna
   on orders from the government.

2. Era Celestino Luna
   hombre de resolución,
   por las costas de Guerrero
   rifaba su gran valor,
   sus amigos le decían
   el Chante de corazón.

   He was Celestino Luna,
   a man of great resolve;
   along the coasts of Guerrero
   word flew of his great valor;
   his friends would call him
   Chante, heartfelt friend.

3. Por las calles de Acapulco
   Celestino se paseaba,
   le tocó la mala suerte
   que mataron a Baraja,
   la muerte se la cargaron
   porque el gobierno lo odiaba.

   On the streets of Acapulco
   Celestino strolled about;
   it was to his misfortune
   that they killed Baraja—
   they charged him with that death,
   as the government hated him.

4. Estaban en el palacio
   y el Chante a Manuel le dijo:
   "Me llama el gobernador
   quiero que vayas conmigo."
   Pero jamás comprendía
   que lo llevaban cautivo.

   They were in the city hall
   when Chante said to Manuel:
   "The governor has called me;
   I want you to come along."
   But he never would have thought
   they were taking him prisoner.

5. Lo sacaron del palacio
   lo quisieron disarmar,
   le pidieron la pistola
   él no se la quiso dar,
   le dice Mario Martínez:
   "Nada te puede pasar."

   They removed him from city hall;
   they wanted to take his weapons—
   they asked him for his pistol;
   he did not want to hand it over;
   Mario Martínez tells him:
   "Nothing will happen to you."

6. Agarraron la calle real
   rumbo pa' la capital,
   Marquito Luna su padre
   ahí se los quiso quitar,
   en el pueblo de Las Cruces
   no lo dejaron pasar.

   They took the main highway
   on their way to the capital;
   Marquito Luna, his father,
   wanted to recover him there;
   in the town of Las Cruces
   they wouldn't let him through.

7. El comandante le dice
   con un profundo dolor:
   "Marquito, yo soy tu amigo
   lo digo de corazón,
   las órdenes que traemos
   las dictó el gobernador."

   The commanding officer tells him
   with a deep sense of pain:
   "Marquito, I am your friend;
   I tell you straight from the heart,
   but the orders that we have
   were given by the governor."

8. Marcos Luna le contesta:
   "Soy hombre particular,
   has dicho que eres mi amigo
   hombre, déjame pasar,
   llevan a mi hijo cautivo
   lo pueden asesinar."

   Marcos Luna answers him:
   "I am a private citizen;
   you have said you are my friend;
   come on, man, let me through;
   they have taken prisoner my son—
   they might even murder him."

9. Marcos no quiso seguir
   y de allí se regresó,
   entonces le dice a Félix:
   "Esto lo presiento yo,
   el señor Mario Martínez
   a mi hijo lo traicionó."

   Marcos just let it go;
   from there he returned to town;
   after that he says to Félix:
   "This is what I sense—
   Mr. Mario Martínez
   has betrayed my son."

10. Marquito Luna dudaba
    y el Chante iba caminando,
    en el pueblo de Mazatlán
    ya lo estaban esperando,
    setenta y dos federales
    allí lo estaban disputando.

    Marquito Luna was doubtful
    and Chante was on his way;
    in the town of Mazatlán
    they were already waiting for him—
    seventy-two federal soldiers—
    there, they were blocking his way.

11. Le dice Mario Martínez:
"Aquí los voy a dejar,
las órdenes que yo traigo
que aquí se han de quedar,
'ora son los federales
los que los van a llevar."

Mario Martínez tells him:
"Here I will drop you off;
the orders that I carry
are that you should remain here;
now it is the soldiers
who will take you from this point."

12. El Chante se hizo pa' atrás
y la pistola sacó,
del cuello agarró a Martínez
cinco balazos le dio,
también a Nico González
la cara le atravesó.

Chante moved to the back
and he took out his pistol;
he grabbed Martínez by the neck;
he gave him five bullets,
also for Nico González—
he managed to graze his face.

13. Sonó la metralladora
el Chante se le enfrentó,
peleándoles desde el coche
donde el Patotas cayó,
también al Chante mataron
porque el parque le falló.

The machine gun blasted out;
Chante turned to face it,
fighting them from the car
where El Patotas fell dead;
Chante they also killed,
as he ran out of bullets.

14. Mataron al Chante Luna
lo deben de recordar,
pero les queda un amigo
que le dicen el Chacal,
cuídate, Nico González
no se te vaya a olvidar.

They killed Chante Luna,
you all should recall,
but there he has a friend,
the one they call El Chacal;
watch yourself, Nico González—
don't you forget about him.

15. Maganda y Riva Palacio
se encuentran muy afligidos,
por la muerte de Martínez
y Nico que estaba herido,
la culpa no fue del Chante
porque ellos la habían querido.

Maganda and Riva Palacio
are in a state of distress;
for the death of Martínez
and Nico who was wounded—
it was not Chante's fault
since they had asked for it.

16. Ya me voy a despedir
por las leyes que derogan,
mataron al Chante Luna
porque les hacía malogra,[4]
de esos hombres pocos nacen
y el que nace no se logra.

Now I will bid you farewell;
by the laws that are in effect,
they killed Chante Luna
because he caused them trouble;
few men like these are born
and the one born doesn't last.]

The first three stanzas sketch in the initial situation: Celestino Luna, known affectionately as Chante, is presented as a man of resolution and valor who liked to go out on the town in the company of his friends. The corrido poet attributes to Chante Luna qualities that define him, by local standards, as a complete man: he is brave, affable, and sociable. But, we are told, he has run into trouble with the government, which has come to hate him. The next two and a half stanzas set the plot in motion: Luna is told that the governor wants to see him, so he agrees to travel from Acapulco to Chilpancingo, the capital of Guerrero, not realizing that he has in fact been taken prisoner. But he refuses to yield his pistol to companions who are masquerading as friends. Throughout the Costa Chica balladry, the hero must not set aside or surrender his weapons, on penalty of relinquishing his status as hero.

The next four and a half stanzas, beginning with stanza 6, present the touching interlude of Marcos Luna, Chante's father, attempting to follow his son along the highway but being deterred by the federal forces, in the guise of a friend who is sympathetic but powerless to help him. This interlude argues for the humanity of Chante, who is dear to his father, and it manifests a theme running throughout these corridos—the importance of family ties. In one corrido after another, immediate kin fight and die for one another, and this corrido depicts a strong sentimental attachment between father and son that speaks well for both of them.

The next three stanzas, starting with stanza 10, narrate the violent encounter. In a small town just south of Chilpancingo, a large contingent of soldiers are waiting to apprehend Chante Luna. His false friend, Mario Martínez, delivers Luna to the *federales*. But Luna does not go peacefully: he pulls out the pistol he would not surrender, pumps several bullets into Martínez, and even manages to graze the face of the other traitor in the car, Nico González. Then Luna and his true companion, El Patotas, turn to face the machine-gun fire of the *federales*, a futile but courageous stance. At last Luna is killed, but not until he has run out of ammunition. The defiance shown by Luna in this unequal fight, his willingness to die rather than to be captured, and that he was killed only after he ran out of bullets confirm his heroic character. A defiant death against superior odds is the trademark of the corrido hero.

The final three stanzas sketch in the aftermath of the action. Nico González is warned to be on the lookout for El Chacal (the Jackal), who will surely avenge his friend's death. Maganda, the governor, and his police chief, Riva Palacio, are pictured as troubled by the outcome of this violent episode. But the corrido poet states that it was not Luna's fault, for he had not sought this encounter. Indeed, the final stanza pulls out all the stops, using a traditional formula to portray Luna as one of those remarkable men who do not last long in this world. The version of this ballad performed by Francisco Arroyo in 1972 contains another stanza:

El Chante ya está en el cielo	[Chante is already in heaven
dándole cuenta al creador,	giving account to the Creator;
y Nico está en la cárcel	and Nico is in the prison
consignado por traidor,	assigned there for being a traitor;
también quedó desterrado	also sent into exile
Maganda el gobernador.	was Maganda, the governor.]

The formula of the fallen hero giving account to the Creator is conventional in the corrido tradition. The details about González and Maganda have the ring of historical truth to them: Alejandro Gómez Maganda was removed from office shortly after this killing in a swirl of controversy about his connections to *pistoleros* (hired guns) active in Guerrero politics. But in other respects this corrido can be seen to present a rather skewed perspective on the life and times of Chante Luna. The corrido offers a sympathetic portrait of a man who by all accounts was a hardened killer.

Chante Luna was a presence in Acapulco and on the coast during Gómez Maganda's term as governor in the early 1950s. A glance at the newspapers of the period reveals much concern with *pistolerismo*, and Luna was among the more visible—and ruthless—of these tough characters. The corrido alludes to the death of a man named Barajas as the pretext for Luna's suppression, and the newspaper account in the main Mexico City daily, *El Excelsior*, on Monday, August 25, 1952, substantiates this linkage. The story is given front-page, banner-headline coverage: "The Murderers of Dr. Barajas Were Planning a Massacre of the Police." Smaller headings claim that "his death put an end to a frightful band of outlaws" and that "they had on their account numerous murders in the state of Guerrero." Ignacio Barajas Lozano is identified as the director of public health services in Acapulco. The article identifies Mario Martínez as an agent for the Dirección Federal de Seguridad (Federal Security Administration), and Nicolás González as the chief of Guerrero's secret police, active in antinarcotics work. Although the newspaper account corroborates the events in the corrido, it offers a rather different interpretation of the protagonists' roles and motives. The journalist, presenting what one assumes is the official story, takes as a given Luna's involvement in the murder of Barajas, which the corrido poet frames as a pretext invented by the government to go after Luna. Throughout the newspaper account, Luna and his friend El Patón (the Big Foot, not El Patotas, the Big Feet, as in the corrido) are painted as leaders of a gang of hired assassins. The corrido poet, in contrast, stresses the human side of Luna, appreciated as a true friend and beloved son. In the corrido, we encounter a hero betrayed by an iniquitous government rising to the cause of self-defense. In the midst of agreement over the essential facts, two very different stories emerge.

As it happens, a third story line is available in the recollections of those who lived through the period and encountered Luna and his associates. Our two performers, Enrique Mares and Juvencio Vargas, spoke of personal connections to the principals in this story and offered yet another interpretation. Vargas recalled Barajas as a good man, a doctor who would go out of his way to help people. Both Vargas and Mares remember Chante Luna as a bold and dangerous man. Mares tells of a friend who was shot and severely wounded by Luna over a capricious exchange of looks. But Vargas and Mares remain essentially friendly to Luna's cause and construe him, in line with the take of the corrido poet, as a victim of government intrigue. Their rationale presents the government as running illegal drugs, and Luna as an accomplice who became too knowledgeable about the operation:

Vargas: A Barajas yo lo conocí pues, era buen doctor, chaparrito, y buen amigo.
Mares: Pero estaba metido en eso, en la mafia . . .
Vargas: A Barajas lo mataron pues . . .
Mares: La mafia pues del narcotraficante.
Vargas: Traficaban en marijuana y cocaína.
Mares: Entonces le echaron la culpa de esa muerte de ese muchacho, pero él no era. El les sabía su movida, todo lo del gobernador. No le convenía al gobierno.
Vargas: El gobernador dice: "Mejor debemos matarlo, porque él se sabe todo." El sabía toda la política de ellos.

[Vargas: I knew Barajas, he was a good doctor, a little guy, and a good friend.
Mares: But he was mixed up in that, in the mafia . . .
Vargas: So they killed Barajas . . .
Mares: The mafia of drug dealers.
Vargas: They were trafficking in marijuana and cocaine.
Mares: So they put the blame for that death on that boy, but it wasn't him. He knew what they were up to, everything about the governor. The government didn't like that.
Vargas: The governor says: "It's better if we kill him, because he knows too much." He knew all the political dealings of those guys.]

In the midst of these conflicting reports, it is difficult to sort out the truth about Chante Luna. Was he a cut-throat killer who would blast somebody at the drop of a hat? A mafia-style gangster who moved in a circle of organized crime? A rakish man who fell afoul of corrupt government officials? A good son and friend who was used by the politicians and then discarded when no longer needed? For our purposes, what counts most in this tangle of interpretations is that Chante Luna persists as a hero to those people, like Vargas and Mares, who are drawn to the romance of the hero's life. The corrido celebrates this man and his insistence on meeting a heroic death. The civic sector of Guerrero society, as represented in the newspaper accounts, might condemn him as a cold-blooded killer, but to the marginalized sectors of society he remains a hero—indeed, the archetype of the bold man who stands proudly against the force of a corrupt and ruthless government. Where the central government lacks credibility and the revolution is widely thought to be unfinished business, a tale of defying the government unto death resounds.

Whether singing the deeds and death of Moisés Colón, Chante Luna, or any other tough character on the coast, the corrido poet fashions a narrative readily interpreted as a celebration of a hero's life. The very mention of a man's name in a regional corrido and that performances of this ballad carry the name from town to town are strong incentives for those who seek fame and glory through engagement in bold actions. But the corridos do not merely mention heroes' names. In addition, they assimilate these persons to a master narrative stressing the virtues of unbounded courage and manly companionship as embodied in the lives of these individuals. These heroes are pictured as almost invincible; they "cast a heavy shadow" and must be approached through *el bolido*. Typically, they can be eliminated only when they have run out of bullets or when they have momentarily dropped their caution. With luck, a fallen hero will receive the corrido poet's most coveted accolade: "De esos hombres pocos nacen / y el que nace no se logra" (Few men like these are born / and he who is born, doesn't last). Véronique Flanet (1977:207) formulates the irony in this situation: "Death will have to give him what life did not know how to give him." Through the agency of ballad poetry, heroes are fashioned out of the flux of events, celebrated in their apogee, and glorified after they have met their fates. For those who tune into the celebratory themes in corridos, "es la gloria" (it is glorious), as El Cobarde reminds us, to die a death worthy of notice in a corrido.

On Guerrero's Costa Chica the ballad poets make use of formulaic phrases to signify heroic scale, intimating that heroes stood their ground in the face of danger, responded in kind when accosted with aggressive words or actions, and succumbed to the superior force of adversaries only when their supply of bullets was expended. These poetic conventions lift men and women from the realm of the ordinary and place around their heads the laurel of a true hero.

This celebratory verse serves first as inspiration and later as epitaph to the bold actors who take up the corrido's challenge.

Notes

1. Several corridos about Lucio Cabañas were composed and performed on the coast and in other Guerrero locations. A few of them, including one composed by José Luis M. Ramírez, whom I interviewed and recorded in the early 1970s, have made their way into oral tradition. I was able to record versions of two ballads about Cabañas from the Morales brothers in Zihuatanejo in March 1996.

2. "El Pelón," a nickname formed from the root "to peel," designates a bald man or a man with closely cut hair and, by extension, the young army recruits exhibiting this type of haircut.

3. "La Gallina" or "La Gallinita" is one of the best-known ballads of the coast. It tells of a bold man (ironically nicknamed "the Hen") who seeks out the police for fatal combat. Amazingly, he survives and lives to fight another day.

4. *Malogra* is apparently a shortening of the word *malogramiento,* meaning "frustration, trouble."

6 poetry Regulates violence

The man who says to another "Let's kill each other" adopts a
clearly suicidal attitude. . . . He wants, in a way, to take for him-
self the courage he recognizes in the other: if he kills that coura-
geous man, he will acquire his courage; if that one kills him he
still delivers to him his courage.
—Véronique Flanet, *Viviré, si Dios Quiere*

Inspired by the threat of political anarchy, the ceremonial narra-
tor was preoccupied with a wish for a moral authority as he con-
sidered the chief's construction of a secure domain of peace. As
the ceremonial narrator pursued such a project, he relied upon
two central concepts—one within the sphere of human relation-
ships and another more awesome one beyond this sphere.
—Michael Meeker, *Literature and Violence in North Arabia*

If the notion that heroic poetry celebrates heroes' deeds comes readily to mind,
the idea that this poetry might censure, evaluate, and at last *regulate* the em-
ployment of violence emerges only upon reflection. It would seem that these
two theses must be in conflict with one another, for how can poetry simulta-
neously celebrate and censure the violence it addresses? Yet inspection of cor-
ridos in Costa Chica reveals that these approaches, though opposed in prin-
ciple to one another, may be operative in a community and within the mind
of a single individual. It appears that each thesis highlights a legitimate hear-
ing of the poetry, a response rooted in formulas and themes in the song lyrics
and supported by patterns of thought habitual to members of the ballad com-
munity. The regulatory thesis moves in the direction of what we might call a
more mature hearing of the poetry, a hearing that places emphasis on the vi-
tality of community rather than on the individual's quest for glory. Among
members of the ballad community, frequently the older people, or those more

inclined to reflect on their lives, most readily perceive the regulatory messages embedded in narratives.

The regulatory thesis emerges within an interpretive framework that ascribes to poetry a commemorative tendency. In this view, whereas narrating events is an essential component of a poetry addressing violent action, that is not its only—or perhaps even its primary—role. In addition, this poetry is seen to interpret these events, to find in them a meaning that resonates with the core values of the community. Every act of commemoration leads from the surface material to an appreciation of its underlying significance. Details in the mundane world are assimilated to a timeless charter intertwined with the history and identity of the group. The brash deeds of the hero, exemplary in the celebratory thesis, are now subjected to a more careful scrutiny in the light of communal wisdom. In this framework, a hero's bold actions are measured against a set of principles whose scope is moral and religious rather than factional or partisan. Based on my conversations with people on the Costa Chica, it is quite possible to admire the courage of a hero celebrated in local corridos while at the same time question the aptness of his behavior. In short, the celebratory thesis can co-exist with the regulatory thesis, in a mental process that first recognizes the heroic quality of narrated deeds but then moves to assess their meaning.

The corrido poet does not exclusively celebrate and glorify violence, although these motives are surely present. Importantly, the poet also tracks the effects of violence, distinguishes good violence from bad, and allocates to God the final word on the affairs of men and women. In the approach developed by Miguel Angel Gutiérrez Avila (1988), the corrido poet is a social critic who praises violent action when it is justified and condemns it when it is not. Gutiérrez Avila (1988:15), it will be recalled, attributes to Costa Chica corridos the "indispensable and major function of ideological *regulator* of the violence." Aguirre Beltrán, who had emphasized the celebratory features of corridos, appears to recognize their contribution to critical thinking in the concluding passage of his monograph. Drawing attention to the corrido's important role as an instrument of social control, he recommends a close look at phrases from the corridos, such as "No se crean de los amigos, porque son los más traidores" (Don't ever trust your friends, as they are the worst of traitors), and proposes the outlines of a regulatory thesis: "The protracted telling of robberies, assaults, murders and other unusual happenings, involves the corrido poet in exalting or condemning those who intervened in the event and on occasions extracts, from those value judgments, norms and principles he imposes on the listeners through the reiteration of the song and the expressive esthetic of the verse"

(1958:213–14). This suggestion of a regulatory function is made explicit in the formulations of his disciple, Gutiérrez Avila.

Viewing the Costa Chica balladry as a whole, it is not difficult to discern the moral universe imposed by corrido poets on the events they narrate. The poets recognize the presence of violence in the community and they accept it as a necessary and sometimes laudable response to human predicaments. Though people are generally good, some are wicked, and even a good person can be driven to violent action in the grip of a strong emotion such as fear, shame, or anger. Further, the poets recognize that people are inevitably thrown into conflict with one another as they pursue their self-interest and their obligations to family and friends. Moreover, a general climate of social chaos prevails in the absence of fair and efficient legal authorities. In this climate, people are often obliged to take action for themselves if they expect to achieve satisfaction for wrongs. The potential for discord and violence is ubiquitous in the human realm. In presenting this orientation, the poets index a moral philosophy shared by members of the broader community.

The corridos evince a grudging respect for any assertive act that exposes the actor to mortal danger, especially when the actor is working within an embattled situation. If human nature makes us prone to experience moments of conflict, it also leads us to advance our positions and defend our rights through bold and aggressive means. The male of our species, so goes the common wisdom in the corrido, is inclined to respond aggressively to challenges. Not all men display this trait in equal proportions, but the most remarkable men have in them a wide streak of the *macho,* the aggressive male animal. Like the rooster, ram, and bull, his counterparts in the nearby animal world, the aggressive man will not shy away from altercation. Instead, when his life or honor is threatened, he will engage in battle without regard for the wounds he may deliver or sustain. The standard corrido formula "aunque me cueste la vida" (though it may cost me my life) expresses the stance of the aggressive male roused to violent action. A related formula has the hero lose his love for life, his wish to continue living: "perdió el amor a su vida."

Once the hero is aroused and has decided upon violent action, he turns all his resources of wit and muscle to the task. The most common theme in these narratives is that of exacting revenge for a slight to one's honor or for the killing or mistreatment of one's relative or friend. The corridos propose a code of honor that entails a disregard for personal discomfort, a willing embrace of death, an unstinting loyalty to companions, a tough resolve in the face of all adversity. If, as he displays these qualities, the hero can also taunt his adversaries with a round of defiant and derisive speech, all the better. The corri-

do poets express an ideal of the free-fight, with each party having a reason-
able chance to prevail. This sentiment is palpable in these words addressed by
the hero in "Lalo Reyes" to the men firing on him from the protection of a
field of boulders:

"Hombres viles y cobardes	["Cowardly and vile men
¿por qué en las piedras se esconden?	why do you hide in the rocks?
Sálganse a campo razo	Come out into open country—
que así se mueren los hombres."	that's how real men die."]

The concept of the *hombre*, the "real man," is pervasive in the corridos as an
ideal of forceful but fair conduct. Still, the poets recognize that few men real-
ize this ideal, and the courageous hero is likely to find himself penned in by
rivals who have minimized their exposure to danger.

In the actual violent encounter, the code of honor stipulates that the hero
must respond without hesitation to every challenge. If he is fated to die, he
must go down fighting, preferably taking with him as many of his assailants
as he possibly can. The ambushed hero may receive a mortal wound before
he has the opportunity to inflict damage on his killers. Still, any gesture of
defiance he can muster sits well upon him. In some corridos the hero mana-
ges to draw his gun and fire into the air, into the ground, or into one of his
assailants. In others, he is limited to having the last word, but gains at least a
verbal mastery over the situation. These last words are a fixture in the Costa
Chica corridos. The hero may use them to warn his adversaries of an avenger,
to insult them as cowards, to call for a corrido in his name, or to express ac-
ceptance of his fate. Whether by deed or by word, the dying hero retains his
posture of rigid defiance to his final moment of consciousness.

This code of honor governs the hero's actions as he performs in the arena
of violence. But the hero's efforts are subject to a higher power, a destiny that
is ultimately enforced by an almighty God. It is important to be very clear about
this fountain of destiny controlling people's lives. The coastal population is
predominantly Catholic, and local culture features many elements of a Cath-
olic worldview. It is not surprising to encounter in corrido poetry numerous
references to God, the Virgin, and the saints in heaven. But much of this ap-
parently religious content is somewhat formulaic and habitual. For example,
many a speech contains routine exclamations such as *por Dios,* or *válgame Dios,*
phrases that do not necessarily intend an invocation of the deity.

More weighted with religious content are occasional pronouncements by
corrido poets and protagonists that echo church litany. Corrido poets some-
times begin and end invoking the name of God:

En el nombre sea de Dios	[May it be in the name of God—
voy a empezar a cantar.	I am going to begin to sing.]
(from "Antonio Veles")	

Pues en fin ya me despido	[So at last I bid you farewell,
y que sea en nombre de Dios.	and let it be in God's name.]
(from "Emiliano Radilla")[1]	

These formulaic openings and closings seem to be fairly automatic, yet they may intend a blessing on the performance occasion. Corrido poets sometimes insert phrases with a religious flavoring into the main body of their narratives, for example, by asking God to keep the hero "in his glory" or requesting for him a divine pardon. The protagonists in corrido narratives will also on occasion give voice to religious phrases, alerting people that they should "commend their souls to God" and asking for "a blessing" at the moment of violent confrontation. Phrases associated with Catholic worship endow the Costa Chica corridos with a broadly religious aura that is reinforced by periodic allusion to rosaries, wakes, masses, and blessings.

At the same time, corrido poets express an indifference, at times bordering on contempt, for the emissaries of organized religion. Priests, for example, are not highly appreciated in the ballads. They may sound rather ineffectual, as in "Silvano Ramos":[2]

Al lanzar el machetazo	[When he slashed with the machete
hasta el cura se espantó:	even the priest took fright:
"Hijitos, no sean tan malos	"My children, don't be so wicked;
miren que hay un solo Dios."	look, there's one God for us all."]

In others, they provide moments of amusement, as in this episode from "Chautengo":[3]

Bernardo salió corriendo	[Bernardo came out running;
de ver lo que sucedió,	when he saw what was going on,
se iba a meter a la iglesia	he went inside the church
y hasta el curita sacó.	and even chased out the priest.]

On balance, it could be said that Costa Chica corridos harbor an internalized folk Catholicism rather than a deeply religious sentiment. But one religious factor is taken very seriously indeed in the corridos, and that is the existence of a remote but influential deity who does not so much watch after human affairs as provide the final guarantee of such order as can be expected in this tempestuous world. Terms like *Dios* (God), *tata Dios* (God the Father), and *el Eterno* (the Eternal One) are used to identify an entity portrayed as so detached and impersonal as to practically correspond to *el destino* (fate). In one Costa Chica corrido after another, this remote deity is brought into play as the final arbiter of human affairs. The equation between God and destiny is suggested in this stanza from "Mingo Martínez":[4]

Mingo no se quería ir	[Mingo didn't want to leave
por el valor que tenía,	due to the courage that he had;
estaría de Dios que pagara	it would be God's will he pay
o su destino quería.	or what his fate required.]

The typical reference attributes the final cause or explanation of a hero's demise to the will of God, as in "Nacho Carmona":[5]

Preciliano y don Carnuto	[Preciliano with Don Carnuto
salieron a sabanear,	went out to round up cattle,
pero ya estaba de Dios	but it was already God's will
que allí se habían de matar.	that there they would shoot it out.]

This formula, based on the expression "estar de Dios" (to be according to God's will), recurs frequently in the Costa Chica corpus and expresses confidence in the final judge of human conduct.

At this level of abstraction, God becomes virtually identical to *el destino*. More precisely, we could say that God is in charge of applying or enforcing the objective designs of fate. In "Jesús Díaz" that matter is stated quite directly: "a todo hombre valiente / Dios llevará su destino" (to every valiant man / God will send him his fate). *El destino* is often "marked," that is, shaped in advance as a fate awaiting the story protagonist. Human beings may be the carriers of destiny, though not its source, and several Costa Chica corridos contain the expression "le voy a dar su destino," literally, "I'm going to give him his destiny," but equivalent in meaning to "I am going to kill him." *Destino*, used with the possessive pronoun, often denotes a person's dying time. The idea of an implacable fate is conveyed in this stanza from "Sidonio":[6]

Prisco Soto se murió	[Prisco Soto died—
según ya eso era su siño,	it seems his time was at hand;
no le tiraron a ella	they didn't shoot at her,
le tiraron al marido,	they shot at her husband instead;
según no quería morir	it seems he didn't want to die,
pero ya eso era su siño,	but his time was already at hand;]

Here the word *siño*—evidently a vernacular fusing of *seño* (sign) and *destino*—brings two concepts together to indicate the relentless approach of death. With the corrido's implicit code of honor and the security of a world constructed of fate and controlled by God, the narratives move beyond celebrating violence to reflecting on it. Corrido poets are surely social commentators, distilling the wisdom of the community in assessing the effects of violent maneuvers and casting doubt on inappropriate uses of violent means. These judgments take place within a worldview that favors decisive action in the face of provocation—in keeping with the celebratory impulse—so the expressed hesitations are not always granted center stage. But they are there, sometimes embedded in speeches attributed to story protagonists, sometimes floating as editorial segments that accompany or qualify the action. One common theme is the intercession of God in response to a violent deed that has seriously breached the moral code. We can observe this theme in the most famous of the Costa Chica corridos, "Simón Blanco."

"Simón Blanco": Offense to the Eternal One

"Simón Blanco," a ballad that has migrated from its point of origin on the Costa Chica to become a national standard, tells the story of an unfortunate resident of Tres Palos, a town on the edge of Acapulco, now essentially integrated into the larger metropolitan area. It is a classic narrative theme: the protagonist ignores his mother's warning and meets his death at a social gathering. But the tale has a fateful twist: Blanco has been killed by his *compadre* Onésimo Martínez in violation of a sacred bond uniting the two men. Aguirre Beltrán (1958:126) emphasizes the importance of this form of ritual kinship in the Costa Chica settlements he visited as "an instrument for avoiding aggression." He describes the formal rules of conduct that mark the interactions among the parties of a baptism. A baptized child enters into a relationship of *hermano de pila* (brother of the font) with the children of the godfather and godmother, a relationship that defines them as siblings and consequently precludes intermarriage, in spite of the absence of a familial relationship. In general, these *compadres* adopt a posture of formal reserve toward one another, and it is expected that they will come to each other's aid in times of difficulty.

It is perhaps not surprising that a number of corridos deal with shocking violations of this pact. The Costa Chica corridos document vendettas that pitch *compadre* against *compadre* and rifts between *hermanos de pila*. These situations, contrary to the norm and therefore especially troubling, make excellent material for corrido narratives. "Simón Blanco" unfolds as a morality tale in which the corrido poet reveals at several moments in the narrative an editorial stance questioning the violence he is depicting.

I have evidence of a longer original version of "Simón Blanco" that has largely been supplanted by a standardized version promulgated through commercial recordings and now fixed in the repertoires of Costa Chica performers. Let us inspect this standard text for evidence of the regulatory function of poetry:

1. Voy a cantar un corrido
sin agravio y sin disgusto,
lo que sucedió en Tres Palos
municipio de Acapulco,
mataron a Simón Blanco
más grande fue su resulto.

[I will sing a corrido,
with neither offense nor anger,
about events in Tres Palos
in the township of Acapulco;
they killed Simón Blanco—
the outcome was even bigger.

2. Su mamá se lo decía:
"Simón, no vayas al baile."
Y Simón le contestó:
"Madre, no seas tan cobarde,
¿para qué es cuidarse tanto
de una vez lo que sea tarde?"

His mother said to him:
"Simón, don't go to the dance."
And Simón answered her:
"Mother, don't be such a coward;
why should we take such care
when right away would be too late?"

3. Cuando Simón llegó al baile
se dirigió a la reunión,
toditos lo saludaron
como era gente de honor,
se dijeron los Martínez:
"Cayó a las redes el león."

When Simón arrived at the dance
he went where the people were gathered;
all of them greeted him,
as he was a person of honor;
The Martínez boys said to each other:
"The lion fell into the net."

4. Como a las tres de la tarde
dio principio la cuestión,
cuando con pistola en mano
Adrián Bailón lo cazó,
Onésimo su compadre
vilmente lo asesinó.

Around three in the afternoon
the dispute got underway
when, with pistol in hand,
Adrián Bailón came to get him;
Onésimo, his *compadre,*
wickedly murdered him.

5. A los primeros balazos
Simón habló con violencia:
"Adrián, dame mi pistola
¿no ves que esa es mi defensa?"

When the first shots were fired
Simón spoke with great force:
"Adrián, give me my pistol—
can't you see it's my defense?"

Quiso lograr a Martínez	He wanted to get at Martínez
le falló la resistencia.	but he ran out of strength.

6. Como a las tres días de muerto   Some three days after his death
los Martínez fallecieron,   the Martínez boys passed away;
decían en su novenario   they were saying at their wake
que eso encerraba un misterio,   that this thing held a mystery,
porque matar a un compadre   because to kill a *compadre*
era ofender al Eterno.   was to offend the Eternal.

7. Mataron a Simón Blanco   They killed Simón Blanco,
que era un gallo de traba,   who was a well-played cock;
era un gallito muy fino   he was a fine fighting cock
que el gobierno respetaba,   that the government respected;
él con su treinta en la mano   with his thirty in his hands
Simón Blanco se llamaba.   he was known as Simón Blanco.]

What evidence do we find in this text of a moral consciousness, of reflection on the proper uses of violence? A hint of things to come is given in the first stanza with the line "más grande fue su resulto," referring to larger consequences of this initial act of violence. Corrido poets frequently allude to the catastrophic results of violent acts that unleash a chain reaction of retaliations before the violence finally subsides. It is well known in the towns and villages of the Costa Chica that one act of violence begets another. Corrido poets remind their listeners of the complications that are likely to flow from the employment of violent means and implicitly (and sometimes explicitly) call for a tempered response. As we shall see in the next chapter, composers will take calculated steps to avoid inciting violence.

The second stanza delivers a customary warning. The headstrong hero is usually advised to avoid a particular event, setting, or encounter, most often by his mother, wife, or another female relative. Typically this advice is sound and the hero pays with his life for disregarding it. This feature of corrido plots carries the suggestion that the tragedies they record could have been prevented with the exercise of better judgment. Simón's flip response to his mother, in stanza 2, that death can hardly come too soon, catches the stubborn attitude that leads many a corrido hero to an early death. To an extent this posture of indifference toward the blessings of life is portrayed as admirable. Yet it is hard to miss the implication that the hero is drawn to his death by a flaw in his character, an overweening pride that will not permit him to make reasonable decisions about his conduct. A recurrent corrido formula conveys the common wisdom here: the hero will die "por no saberse tantear" (for not playing it smart).

Skipping to the last line of the fourth stanza, we encounter another juncture at which the corrido poet has tipped his hand. Ballad composers are rightly famous for their objectivity in narrating a story, but they are not incapable of taking sides or presenting a subjective point of view. Here we have the adverb *vilmente* (wickedly) applied to Onésimo's act of killing his *compadre*, Simón Blanco. The poet registers his distaste for a man who kills his *compadre*, and who does so in a cowardly manner, leaving his victim no opportunity to defend himself. Many Costa Chica corridos reproach those who participate in ambushes and preemptive strikes on their enemies, though some laud such tactics as necessary under the circumstances. "Simón Blanco" combines the slaughter of an unarmed victim with the detail of *compadre* murder, which makes things far worse.

This untenable situation is resolved by *el destino* as deployed by God. The Martínez boys, presumably including Onésimo, are themselves struck down shortly after their action against Simón Blanco. The rationale presented by the corrido poet is the moral argument that to kill a *compadre* is to incur the wrath of God. The entire business is shrouded in mystery, according to the poet, but the explanation appears to lie in swift retribution arranged by God in response to the vile killing of a defenseless *compadre*.

The original, longer version of "Simón Blanco," still known to some of the old-timers, contains two additional stanzas of particular importance in assessing the regulatory aspects of this corrido. One of these stanzas extends the condemnation of the Martínez boys:

Tres Palos está en conflicto	[Tres Palos is in conflict,
las madres entristecidas,	the mothers are all saddened;
se murieron los Martínez	the Martínez boys died,
siendo de fama crecida,	being of rising fame;
por creerse superiores	for thinking they were better,
se fueron a la otra vida.	they went on to the other life.]

Here we learn that the Martínez boys were becoming famous but overstepped the boundaries of good sense and died as a consequence. This stanza also alludes to the devastating impact of this killing, which has left the town in a state of conflict and brought tears to the eyes of many a mother.

The other stanza frames a more general caution to the man of action:

Señores, no hay que confiar	[Gentlemen, do not have faith
entre compadres y armas,	when *compadres* and weapons mix;
todo el que cargue su cuestión	whoever carries a grudge

que no se ande por la rama,	should not go out on a limb;
así mueren bonitos hombres	in this way fine men die
aunque sean de grande fama.	even if they are widely famous.]

This stanza is presented as a commentary on the sudden death of the Martí-
nez brothers, but it puts forward a proposition that would seem to challenge
the headstrong, careless employment of violent means. Men may be famous,
and even fine, but if they "go out on a limb" with their weapons in hand, they
should expect to die. All this is stated in the context of a warning about rela-
tionships of mutual trust. These evaluative stanzas are sacrificed in the stan-
dard version, which places emphasis on the action sequences, suggesting one
significant facet of the marketplace's influence on the corrido tradition.

A careful look at "Simón Blanco" reveals a strong undercurrent opposing
the celebratory impulse and requiring a different hearing of the song. The
details I have isolated in this discussion raise questions about the violence that
brought about the death of Blanco. Character flaws in both parties—Blanco
would not listen to the good counsel of his mother, the Martínez brothers
believed they were invincible—lay at the source of the violence. If these atti-
tudes could have been adjusted, the poet implies, the killing and its aftermath
could have been avoided. The corrido poet takes note of the disruptive effect
of this violent deed on the welfare of the community, which is thrown into
great turmoil. Violence can be a seductive option, but its consequences may
be devastating, not only for the principals, but also for the community. The
corrido poet does not come right out and say so, but he implies that decisions
taken by Blanco and by his adversaries led to an unnecessary round of violence
and that this development was such a moral offense that it required the direct
intercession of God to set things right.

"Simón Blanco" can be heard as a skeptical meditation on violence as much
as a celebration of violent behavior. Based on my conversations with Costa
Chica residents, I would say that both hearings are accessible to them. Some
of the younger men cited Simón Blanco as a hero to be emulated, much like
Chante Luna. They were inspired by Blanco's bold statement to his mother and
by his daring effort to secure a weapon so that he could respond to the attack.
In fact, a cult has spread on the Costa Chica and beyond raising Simón Blan-
co to the status of a legendary hero. Stories are told about his participation in
the Mexican Revolution and about the witchcraft his mother used to secure
the death of his killers. In perhaps his final apotheosis, Simón Blanco became
a bold and generous adventurer in a movie with the popular actor and singer
Antonio Aguilar playing the leading role. When I spoke of all this with Benito

Hernández, a canny old fellow who knew Blanco's family, he replied wistful-ly: "Ni modo, si era un muchacho del pueblo no más" (No way, if he was just a kid from the village).

In "Simón Blanco" as in many other corridos of the coast, the regulatory function surfaces in direct editorial comments inserted between narrative seg-ments, in loaded words and phrases, and in twists of the plot as presented by the corrido poet. The death of Simón Blanco emerges as a morality tale in the corrido written about it, a classic story of pride instigating a cycle of violence that ultimately destroys those who set it in motion. It is, nonetheless, a strik-ing fact that people on the coast respond first to the celebratory content and only grudgingly acknowledge the argument regarding regulatory content. My discussion of this point with El Cobarde is typical. When I asked him if the corrido might help to contain violence, he responded emphatically: "No, no, no se puede, no se puede, no. Porque ellos mismos la propician, ellos mismos la hacen reproducir, porque también quieren salir, quieren sobresaltar. Quieren también ellos que les compongan otro corrido [laughs]" (No, no, you can't do it, you can't do it, no. Because they themselves bring it on, they themselves cause it to reproduce, because they also want to shine, they want to stand out. They also want people to compose another corrido about them [laughs]). I persisted: But some of the corridos must illustrate the harmful impact of vio-lence, both to individuals and to the community.

> Ah, como quien dice, allí se les está haciendo entender, se les está haciendo entender que no es bueno, que no es bueno, sobre todo, muchas de las veces, que se maten simplemente por la pura borrachera o porque le compongan un corrido. No están peleando una cosa que tenga mérito, no están peleando una cosa que lo amerite. Y aunque en los corridos también se le hace ver que esos modos no están bien. Pero ellos no, ¿cómo que van a estar comprendiendo eso? Ellos lo que quieren es, es de que su nombre se ande oyendo en distintas partes.

> [Ah, as they say, there they are showing them, they are showing them that it is not good, that it is not good, especially, most often, to kill each other just for being drunk or so they will compose them a corrido. They aren't fighting for anything of real value, they aren't fighting for something worthwhile. But those people, no, how are they going to understand that? What they want is, is that people will hear their name all over the place.]

In a similar vein, most of the people I spoke to on the Costa Chica recognized the validity of the regulatory thesis, but tended to see it as secondary to the celebratory thesis. These reactions by members of the ballad community do not diminish the significance of the regulatory thesis, which, after all, is demonstrably active in corrido texts. They suggest instead that this thesis operates in a subtle manner, perhaps beneath the level of immediate consciousness.

Sermons and Editorials

In view of expectations about the ballad's impersonality and objectivity, it is surprising to find so much commentary in Costa Chica corrido texts. How have the poets managed to preserve the flavor of objectivity in their narratives while interspersing significant doses of opinion and judgment? What are the principal arguments conveyed in these interpolations? These questions arise in confronting a remarkable dimension of corrido poetry, the sermonizing or editorializing poet. Corrido poets are obliged to relate the event sequences in some detail and accurately, but this proviso does not rule out the possibility of introducing commentary. Corridos are composed of propositional as well as narrative content (McDowell 1981). The trick is to move the plot forward while including editorial statements drawn from the common wisdom of the people. It seems that corrido poets are obliged to deliver not only stories well told but also a stream of sensible commentary.

We have inspected the ample editorial apparatus in "Simón Blanco." Corridos on the Guerrero coast provide abundant evidence of stances adopted toward the action narrated. I have mentioned the recurring formula in which the hero is said to perish "por no saberse tantear." Underlying concepts of "figuring" and "feeling" are active in this regional usage of the verb *tantear*, which includes notions of "figuring the score" and "feeling one's way," and perhaps amounts to something like "knowing where you stand." The hero who does not know where he stands has lost his orientation to the central facts of the situation. In a dangerous world, one can hardly afford to lose track of these essential features. The ubiquitous presence of this formula indicates a prevailing thesis that men often enter into violent settings through miscalculation on their part, through lack of awareness of the details. This editorial kernel may be expanded into a complete proposition, as in "Chano Tavares,"[7] which includes this statement: "Así mueren los hombres / por no pensar bien las cosas" (That's how men die— / for not thinking things through). The corrido describes a flawed raid in which a man attacks his adversary who is at that moment "en medio de su gallada" (in the middle of his gang), a mistake that costs the assailant his life. The corrido poet fashions from this incident a general proposition about the extreme consequences of careless acts of violence.

It is difficult to determine whether these attributions of poor thinking on the hero's part indicate a practical or a moral critique of the actions they address. They appear to throw into question the necessity or wisdom of violent action. The corrido poet implies that the hero might have avoided disaster had he played it smarter, had he known where he stood. In this light, this formula and its expansions can be seen to implicate the regulatory function of poetry, casting a cold eye on inept applications of violence. But do these expressions really activate a moral consciousness? After all, the message may be that the hero should have been more clever about planning his violent deed, not that he should have avoided violence altogether.

The argument becomes clearer in a closely related scenario appearing throughout the ballad corpus, attributing the hero's rash behavior to the effects of alcohol consumption. In the final stanza of "Melito Chegue,"[8] the *despedida* (leave-taking), the poet editorializes about the causes of the violence narrated in the corrido:

Ya me voy a despedir	[Now I will bid you farewell;
aquí lo tienen presente,	here you have it before you—
se mataron esos hombres	these men killed each other
por causa del aguardiente.	for the drinking of alcohol.]

The perception of senseless violence is stronger here.

The poet of "Miguel Dorantes" is even more emphatic about the harmful effects of drinking. I reproduce here a text of this corrido as performed by "La Coca," Marciano López Arizmendi, in 1989 in Ejido Nuevo:

1. Escuchen señores la historia de aquellos	[Listen, gentlemen, to the story of those
que en El Treinta se mataron,	who killed each other in El Treinta;
no eran enemigos ni tenían cuestiones	they were not enemies and had no quarrels—
se culpa el maldito trago.	blame goes to the cursed drink.
2. En casa de Cleta estaban tomando	In Cleta's house they were having some drinks,
Cirilo con Efraín,	Cirilo with Efraín;
Miguel en su casa estaba dormido	Miguel in his house was fast asleep
no sabía que iba a morir.	not knowing he was going to die.
3. Un domingo en la mañana	It was on a Sunday morning
esta desgracia pasó,	this tragic event took place;
la colonia Plan de Ayutla	the barrio Plan de Ayutla
en duelo se transformó.	entered into mourning.

4. Cirilo tomado empezó a faltar
como faltan los borrachos,
le dijo Efraín: "Ahí trae tu
    pistola,
por eso te crees muy macho."
	Cirilo, who was drinking, began to err,
	as drinking men will err;
	Efraín said to him: "You have your
	    pistol—
	that's why you think you're so tough."

5. Se fue pa' su casa a traer la suya pa' poderle contestar, le dijo Miguel: "Déjamelo a mí conmigo se va a matar."	He went to his house to get his own gun so that he could respond to him; Miguel told him: "Leave him to me; I will shoot it out with him."
6. Se agarraron a balazos no les importó la vida, así acabaron dos hombres por causa de la bebida.	They started shooting bullets— life meant nothing to them; like that two men came to an end on account of too much drink.]

Here the poet clothes his narrative in a virtual sermon on the evils of hard drinking. He condemns drink in the opening stanza, using a strong expletive, *maldito,* literally "damned" or "cursed." The fourth stanza notes that one man "empezó a faltar" (began to err) and defines this behavior as typical of drunks. The verb *faltar,* in this usage, indicates a failure to observe proper forms of respect toward others. When Miguel is roused to settle matters, the two men lose their affection for living and meet their senseless deaths.

It is hardly possible to ignore the voicing of censure in corridos like "Miguel Dorantes." Notably, all the routine signals of heroism are played down in this narrative, leaving the sermon against heavy drinking the most salient aspect of the poet's message. The insertion of the word *macho* in Efraín's statement in the fourth stanza is significant. According to the common wisdom, much of the violence on the Costa Chica derives from a fatal combination of *machismo* and alcohol, an inhibitor of normal caution that can easily deprive a person of his bearings, of knowing where he stands. The mix of guns, drink, and *machismo* is recognized as fatal in discussions of Guerrero's problems. Baltazar Velasco, distressed by the social climate on the Costa Chica, notes the devastating interplay of drink and *machismo* but adds one factor: "Y luego el alcoholismo. La mayor parte de los actos violentos se realizan cuando anda tomado uno, se surge por allá el machismo, y pues la falta de justicia" (And then the alcoholism. The majority of violent acts take place when a person has been drinking, there his *machismo* comes out, but also, the lack of justice). Alcohol, *machismo,* and the absence of justice from the legal institutions: these are the ingredients, according to the common wisdom, in a recipe for violence on the Costa Chica.

The Vocabulary of Manhood

In my travels on the Costa Chica I have heard many say that the quota of violence in Mexico, and on the Costa Chica in particular, would be far lower if the government provided protection against violent crime and prosecution of those who commit it. There is a widespread dissatisfaction with state and federal authorities, especially the judicial police, the branch charged with maintaining social order. As one musician told me, "Que la cárcel tiene un noventa porciento de inocentes y un diez porciento de culpables. Y el culpable anda en la calle. Y agarran a otro inocente" (The jails have 90 percent innocent people and 10 percent guilty. And the guilty people are out on the street. And they grab some other innocent person). The general perception is conveyed in the closing stanzas of "Tiene Lumbre el Comal" (The Hearth Has Live Embers), a corrido composed by Lucio Arizmendi and made famous throughout Guerrero by Los Hermanos Arizmendi:

Así quedó demostrado	[So it was revealed
que la justicia en Guerrero,	that justice in Guerrero
es pa' el que está en el poder	is for those who are in power
o de el que tiene dinero.	or for those who have the money.]

The pattern of revenge killing and vendetta flourishes in an environment devoid of any reliable central authority, as people on the coast are only too aware.

But the crux of the matter, in renderings of the common wisdom, lies in the heart of a man, in the passions and ambitions that guide and sometimes rule him. The repeated assertion that the hero is driven by his *machismo* suggests that a theory of human nature underlies the moral system proposed in the corridos. At the core of this theory are common epithets given to the hero in corridos, such as *macho, valiente, gallo,* and *bragado.* This vocabulary is mostly affirmative and laudatory, and thus operative in the celebratory thesis, but it has its darker side—an impulse toward willful destruction (and self-destruction). In the moral universe of the corrido, a man must be forceful and fearless to be a man. But when these qualities are carried to an extreme, he enters a realm of caprice and becomes a threat to himself and to others around him. The epithets of the hero turn out to be, on inspection, ambivalent markers whose moral valency is determined by details of setting and degree. Indicative of this ambivalence are the referents used in nicknames, which often feature fearsome or renegade animals such as *la mula bronca* (the angry mule), *el animal* (the animal), *el culebro* (the snake), and *el tigre de la sierra* (the highland jaguar).

Sabino Nava, a hero in "Tiene Lumbre el Comal," Ejido Nuevo, 1996

An extensive and revealing vocabulary refers to the corrido hero. The word *machismo* is an abstraction that occurs in talk about the corridos but rarely if ever in actual corrido texts. Moisés Vargas depicts *machismo* as an aberration that causes a person to think himself superior to another person and to hastily demonstrate the truth of this sentiment by recourse to violent means: "Quiere uno ser superior a otra persona. . . . El machismo, que dice: 'Yo soy hombre, te mato'" (One person wants to be superior to another. . . . *Machismo* says: "I am a man, I will kill you"). He characterizes the corrido hero as a man governed by *machismo*, "dedicados a la violencia" (dedicated to violence). Onofre Contreras presents the *macho* as a man who drinks and becomes aggressive at social events: "'No, no, no, ¿por qué? No, es que sí vas a bailar conmigo.' Por decirlo así, ¿no? En el rancho, en la provincia, inclusive a veces aquí. 'Esta muchacha está preciosa y va a bailar conmigo'" ("No, no, no, what's the deal? No, the fact is that you're going to dance with me." To put it this way, you see? On the ranches, in the provinces, sometimes even here: "This girl is beautiful and she will dance with me").

But the idea of the *macho* has positive associations as well as these negative ones. The term *macho* appears in the corridos most often in the expression "a lo macho" (like a man), in phrases such as "hablándole a lo macho" (speaking to him like a man, that is, telling the truth). In other settings, *macho* stands as a tribute to the quality of raw courage or blind determination that carries the hero into a vortex of dangerous situations. In "Marino y Sus Vaqueros,"[9] a man rises up with a machete against a group of men armed with pistols. According to the corrido poet, the man with the machete "se portaba muy macho" (was being very manly). Américo Paredes (1971) discusses an exaggerated *machismo* seemingly rooted in a nostalgia for bygone days. But he also recognizes in the heroes of his beloved border country a legitimate *machismo*, surging in the man who places his life in jeopardy to defend his life, his family, and his community. Paredes (1971:37) notes that this impulse, which can be associated with foolish excess, can also lead "toward a more perfect realization of the potentialities of man."

The primary term in the corridos for referring to the hero is *valiente*. The root is the verb *valer* and its nominal form, *valor*, is from the Latin word for "worth." Several derivations of this root are found in Costa Chica corridos. The term *valiente*, used as both a noun and an adjective, occurs throughout the corpus. In addition, the hero is said to possess *valor* and to show his *valentía* (bravery). The *valiente* is *un hombre de resolución* (a man of resolve), a forceful individual, possessed of an indomitable spirit, who imposes his will on any person or situation, regardless of the consequences. He is *bragado* (ballsy), and like *el gallo bien jugado* (the well-played fighting cock), he will not shy away from a hostile encounter. In classic Mexican vernacular, the hero will never *rajarse* (back down from an encounter). This terminology suggests that the valiant man thrives on conflict and relishes the opportunity to assert himself. He is typically armed and practiced in the arts of violent combat. At one extreme, he is a hardened character all too ready to initiate violence.

Valiente in essence denotes a man resolved to use whatever means necessary to protect or advance his interests. Such a person is heedless of physical deprivation and fearless in the face of death. Strength of character is manifest to an extraordinary degree. A sign of *valentía* in the corridos is the capacity to maintain one's focus in the midst of adversity. For example, the hero in "Janilcio con Colón"[10] is not silenced by a wound to the knee:

A los primeros balazos   [When the first shots were fired
le dieron en la sangría,   they hit him in the kneecap;
Colón como era valiente   as Colón was a valiant man,
les hablaba todavía.   he continued speaking to them.]

The valiant man defends right and honor at whatever cost. In some instances, this dedication to honor seems excessive, as when two men fight to the death over a trifle such as a stray glance or a few coins. But the corridos tend to associate *valor* and *valentía* with nobility of character.

In the common usage in Guerrero, *un valiente* is a man known to carry and use a gun. Frequently, these men are considered armed and dangerous, and they may be thought of as hired guns or common criminals. The association with the weapon is stressed in many comments. For example, Teódulo García Pastrana, an accordion player and singer raised in Maguey and now living in Cuajinicuilapa, mentioned the shooting skills of the corrido hero Antonio Zarate: "Pues él también era valiente y bueno para tirar. 'Onde ponía el ojo, ponía la bala" (Now he too was a valiant man and a good shot. Where he put his eye, there he put the bullet). The *valiente* lives and dies by the gun, and if he ever surrenders his weapon, he ceases to be a *valiente*. García Pastrana stressed this point when we talked about attempts to disarm the hero:: "Porque dice, entonces se acabó lo valiente, porque no, entregó la pistola, es cobarde. Dice: 'No, yo, voy a morirme peleando.' Y entonces se queda en alto su honor, pues, ¿verdad? de hombre valiente. Porque si se deja desarmar, ya no es valiente. Ya es cobarde" (Because he says, his courage left him, because, no, he handed over his pistol, he's a coward. He says: "No, I'm going to die fighting." And then his honor remains high, right?, as a valiant man. Because if he lets them disarm him, he is no longer valiant. Now he is a coward).

In one manifestation the *valiente* merges with another social category, the *pistolero* (hired gun). One of the musicians I worked with in Acapulco defined the *valiente* in these words: "Ese era un valiente, acostumbrado a usar el arma, pues. O sea, tenía relaciones con gente del gobierno, pistolero pues" (That one was a *valiente*, accustomed to using the gun, see. Or you could say, he had relations with government people, a hired gun, see).

Guerrero, and many other regions of Mexico, has suffered from the mixing of politics and hired guns. It becomes apparent from scanning the newspapers published in Acapulco during the 1960s and 1970s that concerned citizens rose up in protest against this unholy alliance of *políticos* and *pistoleros*. Editors and columnists sounded the alarm over *pistolerismo* in Guerrero. From this angle the *valientes* were seen as the scourge of the period, a violent element that precluded the conduct of civil society. This viewpoint is largely alien to the Costa Chica corrido, which as we have seen is more likely to celebrate the heroic qualities of the *valiente*. Nonetheless, the ambivalence inherent in the term, also expressed in conversation and newspaper editorials, seeps into the corrido. Corrido poets urge young men to think carefully about the costs of their actions, as in "El Famoso de Morelos":[11] "Cuando el hombre quiere ser valiente / desde muy joven lo debe de pensar" (When a man wants to be valiant / from a young age he should think it over).

Another poet sends a sterner warning, in the *despedida* of "Jesús Díaz," concerning a gentleman who has unwisely elected to seek revenge for his brother. I reproduce the full text of this ballad, performed by Ernesto Gallardo and Alejandro Mejía in Cruz Grande in January 1989, as it encapsulates a number of pertinent themes:

1. Voy a cantar un corrido
señores le pido al día,
le daré lo contenido
la muerte de Jesús Díaz,
por seguir esa cuestión
lo cual que no convenía.

[I will sing a corrido;
gentlemen, I ask for your time;
I will give to you the news
of the death of Jesús Díaz,
for pursuing that argument
which wasn't a good idea.

2. Era un domingo por cierto
Juvenal se emborrachó,
en casa de Jorge López
con Antonín se encontró,
con una pistola super
Antonín lo terminó.

It was on a Sunday for sure
when Juvenal got drunk;
in the home of Jorge López
he ran into Antonín;
with a super pistol
Antonín finished him off.

3. Su hermano de Juvenal
con ansias locas le hablaba:
"Ya mataste a mi hermano
lo cual que no traiga nada,
está bien Antonín González
lo que se debe se paga."

The brother of Juvenal,
in a fury, he spoke to him:
"Now you have killed my brother—
may it bring no good to you;
that's fine, Antonín González,
what is owed must be paid."

4. Juchitán y Ometepec
y Cuaji no lo quería,
San Nicolás y Maldonado
Tapextla también decía
que pa' allá no se arrimara
aunque de allá era la cría.

Juchitán and Ometepec
and Cuaji didn't want him;
San Nicolás and Maldonado,
Tapextla also was saying
that he could not settle there,
though that's where he was raised.

5. Del distrito de Abasolo
se dirigió a Chilpancingo,
le dice al gobernador
que le prestara auxilio,

From the district of Abasolo
he made his way to Chilpancingo;
he says to the governor
that he should lend him a hand,

que el pueblo de Juchitán no podía vivir tranquilo.	since the town of Juchitán could not live in peace.
6. "Les voy a prestar auxilio." Fue un gobierno militar: "Porque sé que el Macho Pinto se anda portando muy mal, de la gente campesina no la deja trabajar."	"I am going to give you a hand." It was a military government: "I know that the Macho Pinto is behaving very bad, for the people in the country, he will not let them work."
7. Se dice que Blas Salinas treinta mil pesos pagó, es mentira de la gente porque ninguno lo vió, la muerte de Efraín Pastrana fue la que lo condenó.	They say that Blas Salinas paid thirty thousand pesos; it's a lie among the people, as nobody saw it happen; the death of Efraín Pastrana is what brought about his death.
8. A todo el hombre valiente Dios llevará su destino, con la muerte de su primo como se porta ese amigo, se aventaba en el comercio explotando al campesino.	To every valiant man God will bring him his fate; with the death of his cousin how this friend carries on; he got ahead in his business exploiting the working man.
9. Ya me voy a despedir de todos los que estén presente, ya les canté el corrido pa' el que quiere ser valiente y si sigue la cuestión a ver si no se arrepiente.	Now I will bid farewell to those who may be present; now I've sung you the corrido for the one who wants to be valiant, and if you pursue the matter be careful you don't regret it.]

As in several corridos we have examined, it is easier to see the regulatory than the celebratory function of poetry in "Jesús Díaz." The entire sequence of events is triggered by the antics of a drunken man, Juvenal, who perishes at the hands of Antonín. At that point Juvenal's brother Jesús decides to avenge his death, a project the corrido poet marks as flawed from the outset, as a cause "que no convenía." This corrido shows the interpenetration of personal disputes and political intrigue, as the governor of Guerrero is persuaded to weigh in on the side of one faction in what has apparently grown into a larger conflagration, tipping the balance of power toward one side and away from the other. References are made to additional players as the web expands, and we hear of exploitation of the *campesino* (rural workers), indicating a political stance of the corrido poet. But for our purposes here, the key elements are the editorial bits framing the initial violence and its sequel as misguided and a final caution that one may come to regret adopting the posture of the *valiente*. One of the most insightful portraits I have seen of the *valiente* is Véronique Flanet's discussion of the men involved in violence around Jamiltepec, on Oaxaca's Costa Chica. The centerpiece of her discussion is *el hombre comprometido* (the committed or compromised man), a man who has been drawn into violent action and now must live the consequences of that initiation. Such a man is in a constant state of anxiety: *se cuida* (he takes care of himself). Flanet (1977:203–4) describes his situation as follows:

> When a man has a mortal enemy, he adopts a mode of behavior that is determined by fear that they will catch him by surprise. . . . He trusts in his pistol, he seeks protection or he surrounds himself with gunmen to inspire fear. From then on, the fiestas, the cantinas, the solitary evening excursions are prohibited; the man on the defense closes himself inside his house as early as possible and scrupulously shuts his doors, avoiding taking a seat where he might be exposed: he fears his shadow and the sound of his own footsteps.

Flanet discerns a duplicity to this life brought into focus by the disparity between fearing and embracing death. She writes of "the tragedy" of "a terrible double life" which she pictures in these words (1977:204): "To conserve the image of valor that protects him and suddenly find himself face-to-face with death hidden very close by. It is customary to say that the *valiente* has no fear of death, but that doesn't say which death: the *valiente* lives in such anguish at the thought of an unknown, arbitrary death, that he lives definitively in search of his death that should glorify and immortalize his existence within his community." Flanet, unlike Aguirre Beltrán, is not drawn to the corrido as the single most revealing expression of the Costa Chica ethos, but she does recognize the important part played by the corridos of the coast in perpetuating the role of the *valiente* (1977:204): "That death will form a part of historical record; without a doubt he will have his corrido; the dead man will be converted into a hero, he will have a posthumous life."

According to Flanet (1977:206), the essential posture of the *valiente* is "to defend his personal valor." But she views this hero, beset by the threat of a sudden death yet anxious to die honorably, as something of a sacrificial victim. With the death of the *valiente,* says Flanet, the community experiences a release of accumulated tension (1977:205): "The group has freed itself of its tensions with that death. The group will require on a cyclic basis, then, a death to revitalize itself. . . . We are almost at ritual sacrifice, founding violence. . . .

The victims of violent death in a way could be said to be pushed by the group to die in this fashion; it is the group that causes them to be *valientes.*" This twist of the argument takes us deep into a realm of conjecture, indicated by the conditionals in Flanet's prose. Can we take the *valiente* as a sacrificial victim, offered to soothe frictions arising in the community? There does appear to be a kind of purging when a family releases its pent-up anxiety by extracting vengeance on those who have wronged it. But I find this notion of ritual sacrifice a bit far-fetched here, asserting levels of integration that are not apparent in this system. I prefer Victor Turner's model of social dramas, which seek resolution through redressive action and reintegration, as a template for the cycles of violence afflicting the Costa Chica. Still, Flanet's discussion of the *valiente*'s predicament, caught between fear of an ignoble death and desire for a bold one, coincides with evidence I have gathered from corridos and from conversations with observers of the Costa Chica scene. She captures nuances in the hero's progress as he moves from his initial landing in the life of violence to the moment of his premature death, as sketched so poignantly in the corridos of the region.

Most corrido poets in Costa Chica balladry are neither sentimental moralizers nor hard-hitting critics of the social arena. They take as their main object the creation of historical narrative, and this charge they pursue most assiduously, as we shall observe in the next chapter. The corrido is not often a melodrama, with overblown blasts of raw sentiment, nor is it a sermon masquerading as a narrative. Guerrero has political activists who have composed ideological corridos, but the popular corrido is first and foremost a heroic narrative. We have seen that even the popular corrido allows space for editorial commentary, and it is in these propositional interstices that the regulatory function is most prominent. The poets insert at appropriate moments in their narratives renderings of a broadly shared social wisdom that attributes violent deeds to two kinds of factors, those that lie within the human heart and mind and those that derive from social and political conditions.

Working within the essential rhetoric of the genre and sustaining the heroic discourse of the celebratory code, these poets offer glimpses of a more detached vision, a vision locating the works of people within a larger political and cosmic framework. If at first we admire Simón Blanco for his courage in the face of mortal danger, on a closer hearing of "Simón Blanco" we may come to see him as a victim of pointless violence. The tragic corrido, grounded in the heroic worldview, could never completely repudiate violence. But in passages calling into question the advisability of particular instances of violence, the corridos argue for a critical perspective on the matter. Corrido poets periodically retreat from the excitement of the fray to convey a nuanced understanding of violent action.

This analysis points to a central ambivalence in corrido discourse, which simultaneously celebrates and censures the employment of violent means. We have seen that a single corrido may contain passages that beckon in these two different directions, and listeners may attend to either or both of these options. Conversations on the Costa Chica indicate that the celebratory code may be primary, the code that initially attracts and captures an audience. If this is so, the corrido can be thought of as a kind of Trojan horse constructed to win acceptance through the thrill of heroic narrative, but nurturing a hidden mission, that of questioning and ultimately discouraging the indiscriminate use of violence.

Notes

1. "Emiliano Radilla" is a corrido from the Costa Grande; it tells of a killing and a call for revenge against *los ricos de Tecpan* (the rich people of Tecpan). I have a version of it sung by Enrique Mares in Acapulco in March 1989.

2. "Silvano Ramos" is in the repertoire of Juvencio Vargas and his daughter, Meche. It tells of a fatal quarrel between rivals in the Cuajinicuilapa district of the Costa Chica. When the action is over, one is buried in San Nicolás, the other in Maldonado.

3. "Chautengo" was performed in Cruz Grande in 1972 at the Gallardo home; it tells of a series of battles between rival *brosas,* leaving *los indios de Jalapa* (the Indians of Jalapa) temporarily in control of the situation. Chautengo and Jalapa are two settlements in the area around Cruz Grande.

4. "Mingo Martínez" was sung for me by Enrique Mares at the home of Juvencio Vargas in Acapulco in March 1989. It deals with the betrayal of a hero by agents of the government in the area around San Nicolás. The poet draws the conclusion that even those working for the government can be *de cabrón* (traitorous sons of bitches).

5. "Nacho Carmona" is an older corrido, sung for for me by Enrique Mares at the home of Juvencio Vargas in Acapulco in March 1989. It tells of two rivals who are brought low, one for pride in his position of local authority, the other for pride in his rifle.

6. "Sidonio" was performed by Ernesto Gallardo and Alejandro Mejía in Cruz Grande in January 1989. It tells of a rivalry between two *brosas* over possession of a woman, leading to several deaths.

7. "Chano Tavares" was composed by José Albines Mendoza and performed by him in the company of Juvencio Vargas in Acapulco in February 1989. It tells of a vendetta in which the singer was allegedly directly involved.

8. "Melito Chegue" is a famous corrido associated with the Costa Chica town of Huehuetán. It tells of the shooting of Chegue and the futile attempt to save his life after he is mortally wounded.

9. "Marino y Sus Vaqueros" is surely one of the most interesting corridos I collected on the coast. Composed and performed by El Cobarde, it conveys something of the homosexual subculture in the area around Ometepec. It proceeds in heroic fashion, but its male protagonists have husbands and address each other as *comrade* instead of *compadre*.

10. "Janilcio con Colón" was sung by Juvencio Vargas in Acapulco in February 1989. It tells of an unsuccessful action by a man named Colón who may or may not be Moisés Colón.

11. "El Famoso de Morelos" (The Famous Man of Morelos) is evidently about Emiliano Zapata, although he is not named in the corrido. I have recorded a version by Ernesto Gallardo and Alejandro Mejías in Cruz Grande in January 1989.

7 ρoeτηy Heals violence

Thus we can see that the actual events concerning the train rob-
bery at Loma Trozada have been transmuted into folksong in a
very special way. . . . An outlaw ballad is made into a border-
conflict ballad by excision of some details and by the arrange-
ment of what is left into the pattern typical of the *corrido* of bor-
der conflict. We have here an example of the way that folklore
adapts all kinds of materials into generic patterns dominant in a
tradition.

—Américo Paredes, "José Mosqueda and the Folklorization of
    Actual Events"

Poetry and violence appear to be odd companions, but there is a logic for their
conjunction in the world's oral and written traditions. The formal perfection
of song, and its evocation of deeply rooted values, could be expected to acti-
vate a therapeutic process. There are many valid scenarios here. Aristotle's
notion of *catharsis,* a purging or cleansing effected through pity and fear, is
applicable to the corrido. Costa Chica corridos have the flavor of tragedy, with
heroes brought low partly through flaws in their own character. Literary crit-
icism holds several discussions of grief and rage transformed into reconcilia-
tion through elegy, dirge, and lament, and these forms share a commemora-
tive intent with the corrido. Using the terminology of T. S. Eliot (1934), we can
portray the corrido as a communal "objective correlative," a poetry mediat-
ing emotions aroused in the wake of violent conflict. It seems incontrovert-
ible that poetry addressing violence might provide, in the right circumstances,
a release from the despair that is a natural consequence of experiencing such
difficult situations.

    If we take as established the capacity of poetry to assuage the troubled soul
after a violent event, we might yet wonder about the impact of this poetry on

the larger community embracing the conflicting parties. Corrido performances are able to trigger a cathartic release, evident in the sometimes dramatic responses observed in their audiences. I have already recounted a corrido evening in Cruz Grande marked by ecstatic shouts of approval from the audience, shouts asserting a fierce pride in local identity: "¡Así es la Costa, puro gallo!" (That's how it is on the coast, nothing but fighting cocks!). Corridos, with their tragic themes, transform the sentiments of those who witness their performance, and like the elegies of learned poets, corridos no doubt help people transmute their feelings of sadness and anger.

The object of this chapter is to explore the crafting of Costa Chica corridos to understand their healing mission, especially at the community level. We will enter the minds of the composers as they set about creating and launching a new corrido. The thesis that Costa Chica corridos possess a healing function is not self-evident. If the poets are celebrating the deeds of the heroes, what place can be found for a healing mission? How can the losers in violent encounters find solace in corridos that portray the triumphs of their rivals? In addition, the textual markers for this thesis are more subtle than the clues sustaining the celebratory thesis, which shines forth on the surface of corrido texts, and the regulatory thesis, which resides in editorial comments inserted into the poetry. Textual evidence for the healing effect of corrido poetry is difficult to detect without knowledge of circumstances and strategies underlying their composition.

Inspection of the composer's role in the ballad process reveals a pair of related issues, both deriving from the volatile mood in settings where violence has shaken a community. First, corrido poets face the possibility of exposing themselves to violence as the ripple effects of the initial action move outward. Tied to this concern with immediate personal safety is a larger consideration, the risk of inflaming an already tense social climate. Corrido poets operate in a delicate situation because they are expected to produce a true account of events, yet must avoid making statements that might rebound upon them or endanger others. Corrido texts are carefully crafted objects, responding to the imperative to shape history in a responsible manner while skirting the hazards of throwing fuel on a smoldering fire. We shall discover that the healing effect of Costa Chica corridos is bound up in tactics employed by composers and performers to contain the possible damage of these narratives.

The delicacy of the composer's position helps explain the bounding of corrido narratives. It is the norm to open a corrido with a deferential nod to the audience and to close it with a respectful farewell. These courteous gestures frame the performance as a convivial event and mitigate against offending audience members as the narrative progresses. Opening and closing gambits often contain expressions of vulnerability, couched in the form of a request for the indulgence, permission, or pardon of the audience, along the lines of the ubiquitous "Señores, perdonarán" (Gentlemen, you will forgive me). The audience may be requested to remain calm, as in a formula commonly found in the first stanzas of corridos, "no se vayan a enojar" (do not become angry). At the close of the performance, this plea for indulgence may be reinforced with expressions such as "dispensen lo mal trovado" (forgive me my poor verse). Audiences are courted in these framing segments by singers who present the performance occasion as a friendly convocation and thereby claim for themselves a degree of what we might call "performance" immunity.

It seems that this plea for indulgence is effective, for in combination with good sense shown by performers in selecting material appropriate to specific settings, it keeps corrido performers on the Costa Chica largely safe from the anger of aggrieved parties. Community members seem to have an understanding that corrido performances should not be treated as contributions to factional struggles. Naturally, performers are careful not to select ballads that would clearly be offensive in a given setting, but even their exercise of good judgment cannot guarantee their safety.

In fact, stories are told of occasions when audience members objected to the content of a corrido narrative. Gabriel Moedano (1988:126), a Mexican folklorist, describes a scene he witnessed in an afromestizo settlement:

> On one occasion when I was recording in Estancia Grande, Oaxaca, there were several people who requested insistently that the singer perform the corrido "Los Domínguez y los Herrera," and this fellow replied: "No, why should I sing that corrido? Do you want them to kill me?" Later he sang it, in the offices of the municipal authorities and in rather soft voice. The next day they complained: "Please don't sing that corrido when they request it, because it hurts me." It was the aunt of one of the dead men.

Américo Paredes told me that singers of corridos sometimes found themselves in hot water on the Texas-Mexico border, and Juvencio Vargas told me a comparable tale: once, when he sang "Elyria Carmona," a corrido about a young woman who lands "in the good life," he was confronted afterward by an audience member who introduced himself as the protagonist's cousin. This gentleman apparently did not much appreciate the corrido, but he did not take offense at the performance of it.

In the accounts I have from the Costa Chica, the censure falls most heavily on the originator of the ballad. The composer's vulnerability was driven home

Juvencio Vargas and friends, cantina, Pinotepa Nacional, 1989

to me when I sought corridos about the Aguas Blancas massacre of June 1995, when agents of the government gunned down a busload of unarmed activists with the opposition political party. To a man, these composers were reluctant to perform corridos they had composed on this episode. They were clearly drawn to the topic, and one of them assured me that in time a corrido about Aguas Blancas would be a sensation throughout the state. But when I spoke with these composers, a year after the massacre, the dust had not yet settled. High government officials were suspected of complicity in the killings and the situation remained very touchy. I asked them who would bear the brunt of the government's anger should a corrido on this topic find its way to public notice. Without hesitation they declared that it would be the composers, not the performers. As one of them told me: "Yo no puedo decir que el gobernador autorizó la masacre; si digo eso hoy, yo no amanezco mañana" (I can't say that the governor authorized the massacre; if I say that today, I won't wake up tomorrow). He clarified his point to this effect: "They will ask where they got that corrido, and then come after me."

There is a hierarchy of linkage to a corrido and responsibility for its content. People on the Costa Chica refer to the protagonist and immediate family as the *dueños* (owners of the song). Owners are granted a special level of respect, and close relatives of a song's protagonist will often receive appreciative gestures as musicians perform their corrido. As we have seen, performers enjoy a degree of artistic license that frees them from blame for the content of their songs provided they exercise sensitivity in selecting ballads appropriate to a particular gathering. The corrido poets are held accountable for the content of the songs, and the knowledge of this accountability weighs on their shoulders. For corrido poets, the tension between telling the truth and protecting themselves and their communities from further repercussions can be strong. They strive to produce a narrative text striking an acceptable balance between these two imperatives, pursuing each as far as circumstances permit. The end product is a corrido text compromised in some degree by the desire to preserve the social fabric, in part as a means of self-preservation. Corrido poets occupy a sensitive niche with respect to the violence they witness and record, and they make use of several strategies to reconcile the sometimes conflicting demands of their enterprise.

The Composer's Dilemma

The corrido is a genre enmeshed in history, and corrido poets take very seriously their calling as recorders of historical events. Although they lack academic training, they perceive themselves as grass-roots historians, a role constantly reinforced by expectations of their publics. In Guerrero and other corrido-rich locations in Mexico, the common wisdom is that the corrido tells the truth. When I arrived in Acapulco during a time of social unrest, I was advised to disregard the newspapers and to wait to hear the corridos: "Esos cuentan las cosas como son" (They tell things as they are). The newspapers, in contrast, were said to be under the control of the government, allegedly a party to misdeeds affecting the general public, and journalists were thought to be unable to reveal the true circumstances underlying current events. Time and time again I have heard people insist on the truth value of the corridos, in phrases like this one: "Son puros verídicos" (They are completely true).

Corrido poets make every effort to fulfill these expectations by providing factually accurate accounts. We have seen that they conduct research to assemble information and sift from it the most likely path of occurrences. In the aftermath of violent episodes many different stories will circulate, some through local authorities, some through the news media, others through first- and secondhand accounts. The corrido poet typically consults all these narrative streams in the effort to fashion a plausible rendering of the event. Part of the perceived veracity of the genre stems from the attention paid to specific dates, times, places, names of key participants, and story sequences, and the composer makes every effort to ensure their accuracy. True enough, as a corrido enters oral tradition and passes from singer to singer in the chain of what Phillips Barry (1933) aptly termed "communal recreation," it may stray from its moorings and lose contact with these markers of concrete reality. But by this point its audience is no longer comprised of persons familiar with the events it narrates, and the tale may be in transition from history to legend.

What then are the impediments to telling the truth and how does this issue connect to the thesis that poetry about violence might exercise a healing function? The corrido poet must address the sometimes incompatible imperatives to tell the truth and to preserve the calm. The latter imperative is particularly vital to the poet's own well-being. In several cases that have come to my attention, corrido poets were aware of relevant information that they believed to be true but found inappropriate to include in their ballads. There is, it appears, a practical limit on the truth value of the corrido, formed by the composer's estimation of danger.

Onofre Contreras was very clear about the composer's need to exercise caution, presenting the scenario of a bold corrido that causes problems for its composer:

> Así es que la gente va a decir: "Ese corrido es picoso." Pero el compositor no se ha protegido, y lo acaban con él, diciendo: "¿Por qué escribiste eso?"
>
> Claro, la Constitución dice que tenemos derecho de expresarnos, pero hay que fijarse en la realidad, eso [makes gesture of pointing a pistol] no le proteja de eso.
>
> [So people will say: "That's a spicy corrido." But the composer didn't protect himself, and they got rid of him, saying: "Why did you write that?"
>
> Sure, the Constitution says we have the right to express ourselves, but you have to look at the reality, it (makes gesture of pointing a pistol) won't protect you from that.]

The composer may win the respect of his audience, but what good is that if he loses his life? Contreras told me of a corrido he wrote and released that characterized one protagonist as un asesino (a murderer). Perhaps the man's family would agree, but Contreras was nervous about this case. He told me he is more careful about his language now.

To make matters even more interesting, it appears that the composer's self-preservation often dovetails with a larger concern to preserve the community. In the tense aftermath of a violent episode, the community will often mobilize a range of social resources in an effort to prevent escalation of the violence. Emissaries will travel from one clique to another, close relatives of participants in the violence will declare themselves uninterested in seeking revenge, and local and external authorities will be asked to intervene to defuse the situation. These efforts are required because there is a countervailing movement toward escalation. James Greenberg (1989) has given a striking portrait of the pattern of revenge killing affecting the Chatino communities residing in the mountains just inland from the Costa Chica, and much of what he describes coincides with testimony I have received from people on the coast. In the Chatino communities, one killing can quickly beget another, as factions coalesce around the two parties in conflict, and peremptory strikes are carried out by one or both factions in an effort to gain the upper hand. Greenberg (1989:211) notes that "each murder forces everyone to sort out a tangle of loyalties to kinsmen, friends, and compadres." In these exchanges among the Chatino, "people may be killed simply because they cannot be trusted to stay out of the conflict" (1989:218). As on the Costa Chica, "what starts out as a personal dispute widens, as others are drawn in, to include important leaders, regional political movements, state political parties, and government bureaucracies" (1989:222). The dynamic of blood feuds among the Chatino, as described by Greenberg, matches the swirl of events documented in Costa Chica corridos. But a detail distinguishing the coastal population is their penchant to create in song a chronicle of local conflict, for Greenberg makes no mention of corridos in the Chatino world.

Corrido poets are fully aware that their words are often released into these explosive contexts. They know their narratives might feed into the escalation or containment of the violence. Inopportune elements in a corrido might contribute to a wave of violence that could sweep away the corrido poet and the community. The Costa Chica poets I have talked to care about truth and justice, but they give top priority to the preservation of self and community. They spoke to me articulately about the folly of pursuing truth without any regard for personal and social consequences. All the poets I interviewed saw themselves as socially responsible agents, dedicated to recording the truth about events affecting their communities but concerned with issues of personal and collective well-being.

I was struck by the disparity between pronouncements from the man and woman on the street and the composers' more cautious claims regarding the absolute truth of corrido narratives. But in no instance did I hear from a corrido poet that outright lies or untruths might be included in a composition. Instead, the poets revealed to me their conviction that truth is a matter of degree rather than an absolute and offered a set of techniques for skirting controversial details and incorporating specific elements likely to placate an aggrieved party. Without these features of the composer's craft, it is hard to imagine how the corrido could exist in such intimacy to the events it depicts and commemorates, and without that intimacy it would lack the emotional power of a living balladry.

Strategies of Appeasement

The corrido poets I spoke with are alert and candid about the dangers they face. They are well aware that one misstep, such as the untimely release of a new ballad or the inclusion of a provocative detail, might have dire consequences. In delicate cases, they make use of several strategies to mitigate against these dangers. They may refrain from composing a corrido or withhold from the public a new corrido until the climate is judged to be sufficiently calm. Especially in cases involving allegations of misconduct by government agents, corrido makers exercise caution in releasing their corridos to the public. A subterfuge of some utility in these instances is to arrange for an anonymous initial presentation of the corrido and assert authorship once it appears safe to do so. Currently, one may purchase in the marketplaces in Acapulco and along the Costa Chica audio tapes with corridos about controversial government actions, tapes with neither composers nor performers specified. The source of these materials may be a guarded secret, though no doubt accurate projections could be made by those in the know.

But concern for the government's response is only one factor and, on balance, not the most significant factor in assessing danger. Even when the government is not a player or only a minor player, the corrido poet must anticipate responses from the parties to the violence. The winning faction is likely to take pleasure in a fitting commemoration of its triumph, but the losing faction must be satisfied that their disgrace or sadness is not being flaunted.

More than once I have been told by individuals connected to the losing side in an exchange that they do not like the corrido in circulation about that event. Yet many corridos emerging during tense moments in the life of the community receive at least a grudging acceptance from the aggrieved party. How is this possible? The solution resides in a strategic manipulation of the heroic code to grant even the fallen victim a modicum of posthumous respect and honor, thereby preserving the dignity of family and associates.

The composers were forthcoming on this issue. Onofre Contreras, whose corridos about contemporary events in Acapulco and the surrounding region are well known and admired, has evidently given plenty of thought to the composer's dilemma. He tries to write corridos that will be acceptable to both sides in a dispute: "Eh, hago lo siguiente. Si estoy haciendo el corrido trato de no afectar ni a unas familias ni a otras. Y entonces el corrido da el resultado que yo espero. Lo pueden escuchar de los dos bandos, de una familia y de otra, y no hay duelo, no hay duelo" (Oh, this is what I do. If I am writing a corrido I try not to bother one set of families or another. And then the corrido comes out the way I hoped. Both sides can listen to it, from one family or the other, and there is no sadness, there is no sadness).

Notice that Contreras couches his comments in terms of "sets of families," the social unit corresponding to an extended family or a group of allied families that could become involved in a dispute. He continues his commentary, clarifying his thoughts about the corrido's role in these difficult settings:

> Siguen con su duelo, sí, porque, dicen: "Sucedió eso, ¿no?" Pero no porque yo esté todavía echándole más lumbrita al asunto, no, en ningún momento. Trato de que nada más se escuche el corrido, se oyó, pero dentro de lo normal, dentro de lo que sucedió, y que yo en ningún momento podría evitarlo: esto sucedió porque sucedió.
>
> Y de eso están concientes los familiares. "Bueno, sucedió. Y además, contamos con el corrido que queda de recuerdo."
>
> [They still have their sadness, yes, because they say: "This happened, no?" But not because I am throwing more fire on the matter, no, not for a moment. I try to have them just hear the corrido, they listened to it, but in a normal way, along with the thing that happened, and so that I could in no way avoid it: "This happened because it happened."
>
> And the relatives know this: "True, it happened. And in addition, we now have the corrido as a memorial."]

Contreras recognizes that the sadness of the losing side is not going to disappear, but he alleges that a corrido about the event, if it is done properly, can provide them some compensation by constructing a verbal memorial to their relative or comrade. "Probablemente sea un recuerdo pues triste. Pero dicen: 'Bueno, bueno. También mi hijo quería un corrido.' Ahora, si le digo: 'Trataron de defenderse, quisieron también mas no le dieron tiempo,' que de una manera les estoy dando también un pequeño realce, ¿no? De que no hubo que correr alguien, ah, se murieron en la raya: son gallos" (It will most likely be a sad memory. But they say: "Well, well. My son did want a corrido." Now, if I say: "They tried to defend themselves, they wanted to but they weren't given a chance," then in a way I am giving them a little luster, you see? In that nobody had to run away, ah, they died standing pat: they are fighting cocks). Here

Contreras explores the psychology of bereaved relatives. Although their memory is a sad one, they can take comfort in the fact that their relative hoped to figure one day in a corrido on the lips of people, and now that has come to pass. And what is more, if the composer can throw in a few salutary phrases assimilating the fallen man to the heroic paradigm, the family might take even more comfort in the corrido. In accessing this heroic realm, Contreras indexes its most pervasive root metaphor, the well-played fighting cock, standing firm by the the line in the sand.

Contreras delves deeper into the matter:

> Es importante porque se imagina usted que dicen fulano, ahora, si yo como compositor digo: "Fulano corrió, lo mataron corriendo." Desde allí ya caí mal. Porque, ¿por qué voy a decir que yo vi que corrió? Yo no vi que corriera.
>
> Que entonces, es, de alguna manera, parece que no, pero es una satisfación para la familia decir: "Bueno, murió porque tenía que morirse, pero no demostró cobardía." No como cobarde. Trató de defenderse. Trató también de por lo menos emparejar, de que no fuera solo él que muriera, o bien, por lo menos, no corrió. Pero no agredir ni a una familia ni a otra.
>
> [This is important because imagine if they say that this fellow, now, if I as a composer say: "This fellow ran, they killed him as he ran." Right there I made a mistake. Because, why should I say that I saw him run? I didn't see if he ran.
>
> So then, it is, in some ways, it seems to be wrong, but it is a satisfaction for the family to say: "Well, he died because he had to die, but he didn't show cowardice." Not like a coward. He tried to defend himself. He tried also to at least get even, so that he wouldn't be the only one to die, or else, at least, he didn't run. But without insulting one family or the other.]

In this portion of the commentary, Contreras is wrestling with the composer's imperatives to tell the truth and to avoid offense. He reveals some of the devices composers use when confronted with conflict, and he intimates that compromises are sometimes required. But he stresses the subjective nature of truth as a mitigating factor: if he did not witness a cowardly act, then why should he feel obliged to make reference to it in his corrido? It is easy enough to state that the victim tried to defend himself, or would have done so, and even if there is no explicit evidence for this proposition in some cases, it is clearly the politic thing to do.

Onofre Contreras summarizes his argument by affirming that the best result is for families on both sides of the dispute to find pleasure in his corridos. But this result is not easy or automatic; instead, it comes from a calculation:

Para eso hay que tener una poquita táctica, un poquito de, este, manera, de cómo ir haciéndolo. Ser cuidadoso. Ya hice este verso, y no estoy agrediendo, estoy hablando de aquella familia, y no lo estoy agrediendo.

Ahora, OK, hago un verso donde menciono estos, también no estoy agrediendo, no estoy diciendo nada mal. A lo contrario, si le puede poner un tantito de buena alimentación, perfecto.

[For that you have to use a bit of strategy, a bit of, well, style, as to how you go about doing things. You have to be careful. Now I did this verse, and I'm not insulting them, I am speaking about that family, and I'm not insulting them.

Now, OK, I do a verse where I mention those people, and again I am not insulting them, I'm not saying anything bad. On the contrary, if you can add in a bit of good nourishment, that's perfect.]

It appears from this testimony that considerations of fairness and diplomacy are uppermost in the composer's mind at every stage of the process, to the extent that one verse is weighed against another in the effort to achieve a balanced result. And note the intent to throw in "a bit of good nourishment," to provide details whenever possible that will please the constituencies implicated in the violence, details invoking the heroic world and connecting the corrido protagonists to it.

In bringing his comments to a close, Contreras anticipates the corrido's impact on the community and he acknowledges that in some circumstances it is better not to compose and circulate a corrido:

Muchas ocasiones es conveniente y muchas ocasiones, no. Entonces, bueno, cuando esto va a tomar auge, cuando esto se va a hacer más grande, y que vaya a perjudicar a la ciudadanía misma, ¿sabe qué? Mejor, no. Se va levantando.

Inclusive, si usted, o alguien, alguien es mi amigo y le tocó la suerte de que ganó en un enfrentamiento, quién sabe con cuántos, con cuántas personas, de ley, que sean de la ley o que no sean de la ley. Pero es mi amigo, y este, digo no, ¿sabes qué? Debería de hacerle el corrido pero si lo hago lo voy a perjudicar. Porque en lugar de que vaya pasando un poquito al olvido esto, cada vez que escuchan este corrido, va a revivir esto.

¿Y qué es lo que va a pasar? Muchos jovencitos van creciendo y si están dolidos porque fueron de los perdedores, se va a incrementar el duelo. Y al rato van a andar buscando a mi amigo para desaparecerlo o ¿quién sabe que le vayan a hacer? Mejor no hago nada.

[Many times it's convenient and many times it isn't. So, well, when this is going to really catch on, when this is going to be a big deal, and it might endanger the general public, you know what? It's better not to. Things get out of hand.

Moreover, if you, or someone, someone is my friend and he was lucky enough
to win in an encounter, who knows with how many, with how many people, the
law, they could be the law or not the law. But he is my friend, and well, I say no,
you know what? I should write him a corrido but if I do it I am going to place
him in danger. Because instead of letting things fade a little into oblivion, every
time they hear this corrido, they are going to relive this.

And you know what will happen? Many young guys are growing up and if they
are hurt because they were on the losing side, their pain is going to increase. And
after a while they will be looking for my friend to get rid of him, or who knows
what they will do to him? It's better if I don't do anything.]

In these remarks, Contreras makes it clear that as a composer of corridos
he is sensitive to the impact of his productions not only on himself and on
those directly involved in the events to be narrated but also on the general
public. He asserts that composers must avoid placing the general public in a
state of risk. If the likely result of a particular corrido is deleterious to the public
interest, the composer is best advised to forego inventing and circulating that
corrido. In short, some episodes are so volatile that insulating devices are in-
sufficient to contain the escalating violence.

Onofre Contreras (*left*) with the author, Acapulco, 1996

Contreras gives a concrete example. A friend of the composer has triumphed in a violent encounter, with agents of the government or with personal rivals, and it is natural to write this friend a corrido celebrating his heroism and his good fortune. But is this a wise course of action? If one effect of the corrido would be to inflame the situation and place his friend in greater danger, then the composer should not write and publicize a corrido on this topic. Contreras's remarks make it abundantly clear that as a composer he looks beyond his own immediate well-being to assess the well-being of other individuals and indeed of *la ciudadanía* (the community) in deciding which events to write about and in devising the narrative text for a selected corrido topic. His goal is to write a timely corrido that will be received as an appropriate memorial to the events it narrates and that will meet at least a grudging acceptance on the part of all constituencies involved. Not a simple task, by any means, but as Contreras mentions, the composer has at hand a range of helpful techniques.

Hedging the Truth

One of the Costa Chica composers who gave generously of his time to help me understand these matters was Alvaro Guillén Bracamontes, widely known in Ometepec and Cuajinicuilapa as El Cobarde. El Cobarde, like Onofre Contreras, spoke about the perils of writing corridos in the aftermath of violent episodes. Both men had clearly pondered this topic many times. El Cobarde admitted that it can be dangerous to tell the truth and suggested that the composer operates in an environment in which it is not necessary to bluntly state the whole truth: "La gente sabe la verdad, la verdad. El compositor lo cambia un poquito para no meterse en dificultades" (People know the truth, the truth. The composer changes it a little so as to avoid difficulties).

El Cobarde described the procedures he used recently in working out a new corrido:

> Pues, nada más, conociendo los principios y fines del caso, que cómo empezaron, cómo fue, y todo eso. Para esto, un cliente mismo que estaba yo peluqueando me contó. Ya de allí se quedó en la mente, y ya después yo lo compuse.
>
> Y ya después, este, investigué con otros, de allí mismo porque yo tengo varios clientes de ese pueblo, son puros principales también como aquí, de allá. Y bajito la mano les fui sacando, y llegaron a la misma conclusión, lo mismo, todos dijeron lo mismo.
>
> Bueno, yo de allí, como ya me contaron todo, yo ya hice una recopilación, de allí voy sacando lo esencial, lo que yo creo conveniente para no meterme en problemas.

El Cobarde (*left*) instructs the author, Ometepec, 1989

[Well, just this, knowing the beginning and the end of the case, how things got started, how it went, and all that. For this, one of my clients whose hair I was cutting told me. From there it stayed in my mind, and later I wrote it.

And then later, I investigated with others, from the same place because I have various clients from that town, they are well-known people just like here, but from there. And without letting on, I was getting information from them, and they came to the same conclusion, the same, they all said the same thing.

Well, from there, as they told me the whole thing, I then put it all together, and from there I start bringing out the essential story, the part I think it is convenient to tell so that I don't get myself in trouble.]

El Cobarde is referring to a corrido he composed about a violent exchange in the nearby town of Azoyú. He calls it "El Corrido de la Quinceañera y los Tres Muertos" (The Corrido of the Quinceañera and the Three Deaths) or for short "El Oaxaqueño" (The Man from Oaxaca) after one of the protagonists in the song. Let us inspect the text of this corrido and some of El Cobarde's comments on it:

1. Voy a cantar una historia
   que sucedió allá en Guerrero,
   mataron a un oaxaqueño
   por la muerte de un becerro.

[I will sing the story
of what happened there in Guerrero;
they killed a man from Oaxaca
on account of the death of a calf.

2. La historia tuvo principio
   por causa de una chamaca,
   Rafael se la sacó
   a la fuerza de su casa.

The story had its beginning
because of a young girl—
Rafael stole her away
by force from her family.

3. El oaxaqueño se enojó
   y tenía mucha razón,
   al sacarla de su casa
   fue una gran humiliación.

The man from Oaxaca was angry
and he had ample reason,
for taking her from her house
was a serious humiliation.

4. Rafael justo se casó
   para borrar todo mal,
   el oaxaqueño enojado
   quiso menear el panal,
   le mató varios becerros
   los fue a matar al corral.

Rafael rightly got married
to remove any sense of wrong,
but the angry man from Oaxaca
wanted to shake the hive;
he killed him several calves;
he killed them in the corral.

5. Desde entonces se buscaban
   para poderse matar,
   el oaxaqueño decía:
   "No me les voy a rajar,
   dondequiera que lo encuentre
   yo sí lo voy a matar."

From then on they sought each other
in order to kill one another;
the man from Oaxaca said:
"I'm not going to back down—
wherever I might meet him
I will surely do him in."

6. Ese día la quinceañera
   regresaba de la misa,
   iba con toda la gente
   y don Fernando Bautista.

That day the girl of the party
was coming back from mass,
she went with all the people
and Don Fernando Bautista.

7. La misa se celebró
   ya estaba escrito ese día,
   y a los primeros balazos
   toda la gente corría.

The mass was celebrated;
that day was already marked,
and with the first shots fired,
all the people ran for cover.

8. Rafael se desvió
   y ya los traía en su lista,
   y el primero que mató
   fue don Fernando Bautista.

Rafael moved off to the side—
now he had them on his list;
the first one that he killed
was Don Fernando Bautista.

9. Esa fiesta iba a estar buena
   porque iba a tocar una orquesta,
   pero a Rafael no se espiaba
   detrás en una camioneta.

The party was to be a good one,
as a band was going to play,
but you couldn't see Rafael
out back in a pick-up truck.

10. La quinceañera lloraba
    al ver lo que sucedía,
    y lloraba por su fiesta
    que no iba a ser ese día.

The girl of the party cried
to see what was going on,
and she cried for her party
which couldn't be that day.

11. Rafael se defendía
    detrás de la camioneta,
    ya había matado al padrino
    faltaba el de Pinotepa.

Rafael defended himself
from behind the pickup truck;
he had already killed the godfather;
missing was the one from Pinotepa.

12. El oaxaqueño sin miedo
    su tres ochenta sacó,
    dando muerte a Rafael
    que en un tiempo lo ofendió.

The man from Oaxaca without fear
took out his three-eighty,
bringing death to Rafael,
who had once offended him.

13. Este caso sucedió
    y no crean que es el primero,
    esos hombres se mataron
    mero en Azoyú, Guerrero.

This case came to pass
and don't think it's the first time;
those men killed one another
right in Azoyú, Guerrero.]

The corrido tells of a bitter enmity triggered by a marriage-by-capture episode. We noted in an earlier chapter the argument that bride capture is a marker of afromestizo community, as reported by Gonzalo Aguirre Beltrán (1958). Here the Oaxaqueño has lost his daughter to a young man named Rafael, who took her "by force" from her home. Even though Rafael showed his honorable intentions by later marrying the young woman, the Oaxaqueño could not set aside his anger. Instead, he comes to Rafael's house to make trouble, "to shake the hive," and there kills some calves belonging to Rafael's family. One means of signaling hostile intentions in the vendettas of the Costa Chica is to kill livestock of an opponent, and many corridos describe such episodes. Rafael does not mistake the meaning of this gesture, and from that day on the two men, and by implication their families, exist in a state of open hostility.

The *fiesta quinceañera* is a lavish party thrown in honor of a girl who has just turned fifteen, and this one in Azoyú, inland from Guerrero's coast, serves as the occasion for this deadly drama. Rafael lies in wait behind in a pickup truck as the group winds its way from church to the party site. We know it was to be a fine party, with a live orchestra providing the music, and we momentarily experience the disappointment with this cruel turn of events from the perspective of the young woman. Her plans and hopes for the day are ruined as Rafael's bullets take down one member of the party but miss his main object, the Oaxaqueño. The corrido informs us that the man from Oaxaca is at last able to vent his anger against Rafael, who had previously offended him by stealing away his daughter. El Cobarde's corrido ends somewhat inconclusively, a sign that perhaps he was under some constraints in his composition.

As it happens, El Cobarde spoke to me at length about the process of composing this corrido. He recaptures the moment in the form of a recollected dialogue between himself and a group of his clients:

> Yo, como soy peluquero ¿verdad?, entonces, este, vinieron personas que son mero de allí del lugar donde sucedió el caso, tendría como quince días de que había sucedido el asunto.
>
> Entonces, este, me empezaron a contar y como buen compositor que soy pues en delante de ellos lo empecé a componer. Cuando ellos se fueron para su tierra allá en Azoyú yo ya llevaba como tres versos o cuatro en la mente.
>
> Estaba otro cliente aquí que estaba peluqueando que es de aquí, aquí mismo de Ometepec. Y me dijo, dice: "Tú eres bueno para fijar atención en la mente. . . ." Le digo: "Yo le aseguro que si pasado mañana pasa usted por la peluquería ya voy a tener el corrido con todo y música."
>
> Y sí, como a los tres o cuatro días pasó el señor y le digo: "Ven," que le pongo la grabadora y ya lo tenía el corrido con todo y música.

> [As I am a barber, right, so, well, people came who are exactly from the place there where the case happened, it was maybe two weeks after the thing happened.
>
> So, well, they started to tell me about it and like the good composer that I am, well, in front of them I started to compose. When they left for their home there in Azoyú I already had some three or four verses in my mind.
>
> There was another client here who was getting his hair cut who is from here, right here in Ometepec. And he told me, he says: "You are good at keeping things straight in your mind. . . ." I tell him: "I assure you that if you stop by the barber shop the day after tomorrow I will already have the whole corrido, complete with music."
>
> And sure enough some three or four days later the man passed by and I tell him: "Come over here." So I turn on the tape recorder and I already had the whole corrido, complete with music.]

I discussed with El Cobarde sensitive details in the corrido about the man from Oaxaca. As I had suspected, some considerations brought his corrido to an abrupt conclusion. I learned that El Cobarde was in possession of information vital to the story that he simply could not include in his narrative. The specific detail is the final outcome of the story, centering on the fate of Rafael. El Cobarde explained to me this detail as follows: "Por ejemplo, allí dice, a mí me dijeron que el que mató a uno de los principales de allí, viene la motorizada, lo detiene, y se lo entrega a sus familiares, y sus familiares lo mataron, los familiares del muerto, del otro que ya estaba caído. Como ellos son los principales de ahí. Entonces eso yo no lo puse allí" (For example, there they say, they told me that the one who killed a member of a leading family from there, the motorized police come, they detain him, and they deliver him to his relatives, and his relatives killed him, the relatives of the dead man, of the man who had already fallen. Since they are influential families there. So that I didn't put there).

When I asked my friend why he did not include that detail, his response was rapid and emphatic: "Ah, porque me mandan a quebrar a mí" (Ah, because they would send to have me broken). As El Cobarde let out a big laugh, I asked him if the authorities would send to have him killed, and he replied: "No, los de allá, como tienen mucho dinero, fácil" (No, the people from there, since they have lots of money, easy). I then asked El Cobarde if it was provident at times to avoid the truth, and he responded in these terms:

> Bueno, yo la dije pero de otra forma. No dije que lo agarraron y lo trajeron a su familia, no, porque allí ya era problema. Entonces yo lo dije en otra forma, dice el corrido. Ahí dice, dice, dice, "el oaxaqueño sin miedo," dice, "su tres ochenta sacó, dando muerto a un fulano que en un tiempo lo ofendió."
>
> Hasta allí no más. Pero no dije yo que lo agarraron la policía y le entregó a sus familiares. [Laughs.] Porque allí era ya meterse en líos.
>
> [Well, I told it (the truth) in another way. I didn't say that they grabbed him and brought him to the family, no, because that would be a problem. So I said it in another way, it says in the corrido. There it says, it says, "the Oaxaqueño without fear," it says, "took out his three-eighty, killing such and such a man who at one time had offended him."
>
> Just that much. But I didn't say that the police grabbed him and delivered him to the relatives. (Laughs.) Because that would have gotten me into arguments.]

El Cobarde acknowledges that the truth can be a source of difficulty in a case of this nature:

Porque decir la verdad muchas veces es peligroso. Porque como la policía estaba de acuerdo con los principales de allá, por eso agarraron al amigo ese y lo entregó a su familia, y ellos lo mataron, ya lo entregaron a la comisaría, ya muerto.

Así me dijeron de allá. Lo entregaron a la comisaría pero ya muerto. Y no más dijeron en el papel, dijeron que se había enfrentado con la policía, pero todo el mundo sabe que no es cierto. Porque eso fue en la calle, cuando se enfrentaron fue en la calle, todo el mundo vió.

[Because to tell the truth can often be dangerous. Because the police were in agreement with the influential families there, that's why they grabbed that friend and they delivered him to the family, and they killed him, they brought him to the police station, already dead.

That's what they told me from there. They brought him to the police station but already dead. And they just said on the paper, they said that he had shot it out with the police, but everybody knows that's not true. Because that was in the street, when they fought it out it was in the street, everybody saw it.]

El Cobarde, in defending his loyalty to the truth, makes reference to a lesser degree of truth-telling, the official account claiming that Rafael died in a shoot-out with the police. But he stresses that it is common knowledge how the man really died, since these events took place in a public arena. In bringing his commentary to a close, El Cobarde insists on a general understanding of the actual situation as a backdrop against which his selective and at moments covert handling of the story will not create any confusion.

The Teacher's Death

Another of El Cobarde's corridos entails a wider scope of controversy, and in this instance too I have the composer's explanation of strategies he used to avoid unwanted repercussions. The story behind El Cobarde's "La Muerte del Profesor" (The Death of the Teacher) involves elements in the state and federal government; it is a story that, with careless handling, could have added trouble to an extremely complicated situation. El Cobarde introduced the ballad to me with this prologue:

Ahora pues si quiere le canto el corrido de un individuo que, ése no fue matón. Pero que hizo historia aquí en Guerrero y parte de México. Fue profesor, ése, era profesor, y fue mi compañero de escuela. Ese lo mataron aquí, aquí, donde andan anunciando el circo ese.

En el campo, ahí le hicieron una carpa, un palenque, jugada de gallo; pero dicen que hicieron eso para poderlo agarrar, y de allí lo . . . [makes a gesture of shooting someone in the head] . . .

Según dice fue el mismo gobierno pues; sí, porque ya después se estaba descomponiendo mucho, porque era presidente del PRI aquí en Guerrero, era presidente del PRI aquí en Guerrero. Y era profesor. Y entonces pues por algo que ya no les convenía, pues lo mandaron a matar.

[Now if you like I will sing a corrido about a guy who, that guy was not a killer. But he made history here in Guerrero, and in part of Mexico. He was a teacher, that guy, he was a teacher, and he was my companion in school. They killed him here, here, where they are announcing the circus.

In the brush, there they put up a tent, a shelter, for a cockfight; but they say that they did this so they could grab him, and from there they . . . (makes a gesture of shooting someone in the head) . . .

They say it was the government, yes, because things were really falling apart afterward, because he was the president of PRI here in Guerrero, he was the president of PRI here in Guerrero. And he was a teacher. And so for some reason they didn't want him around anymore, so they sent to have him killed.]

In this prologue to his corrido, El Cobarde gives the main detail of the plot, a trap set in the form of a *palenque* (open-air shelter for cock-fighting). We learn too that the intended victim was a prominent member of the ruling party and that elements in the government are thought to have played a role in his murder. Here is the text of "La Muerte del Profesor" as El Cobarde sang it for me one January afternoon in 1989, in his barbershop with friends and clients on hand:

1. Voy a cantar un corrido
   permiso pido señores,
   en ese día viernes santo
   asesinaron a Abel Torres.

   [I will sing a corrido—
   I ask your leave, gentlemen;
   on that day of Good Friday
   they murdered Abel Torres.]

2. Se encontraba en el palenque
   apostando a los gallos,
   daba conchado a cualquiera
   pues conocía todo del gallo.

   He was inside the shelter
   betting on fighting cocks;
   he would match bets with anyone
   since he knew all about the cocks.

3. Por una apuesta traidora
   empezó la discusión,
   les gritaba: "Yo soy Torres
   de todita esta región."

   On account of a false bet
   the controversy began;
   he shouted: "I am Torres,
   known throughout the region."

4. Cuando salió del palenque
   ya lo tenían la emboscada,
   cuando le dieron de tiros
   se acercaba a la morada.

   When he came out of the shelter
   they already had the ambush;
   when they shot him down
   he was standing by the wall.

5. El traidor que lo mató
   poco debe hacer alarde
   nunca debe ufanarse,
   lo mató como un cobarde.

The traitor who did him in
should never boast of it,
nor should he take delight—
he killed him like a coward.

6. La muerte del profesor
   levantó una polvadera,
   nunca se sabrá el origen
   tenía enemigos dondequiera.

The death of the teacher
raised quite a cloud of dust;
we will never know the reason,
as he had enemies all around.

7. En su tierra tuvo pleitos
   con personas destacadas,
   fue para dar hasta la cárcel
   por una mala jugada.

In his hometown he had problems
with distinguished persons;
he even landed in jail
on account of a shady deal.

8. En el Tamal le odiaban
   porque fue muy violador,
   la chamaca que el quería
   le enseñaba luego el amor.

In Tamal they hated him
because he bothered the women;
the girl that he desired,
right there he made love to her.

9. Al entierro del profesor
   fue mucha gente de honor,
   también fueron los Aguirre
   que lo querían de corazón.

To the burial of the teacher
came many people of note;
the Aguirre family came too
because they really loved him.

10. Ya con ésta me despido
    mi canto se los irá,
    la muerte del profesor
    con el tiempo se sabrá.

Now with this I bid you farewell—
my song will come your way;
the death of the schoolteacher
in time will come to light.]

When I asked El Cobarde about the assassins of the schoolteacher, his response was quite interesting:

Como fue políticamente, no se sabe quien lo mató; como fue el mero gobierno. Por eso, nadie dice nada. Vieron, vieron cuando lo . . . [makes a gesture of shooting a pistol] . . .
Vieron mucha gente. Pero como se trata del gobierno: "No, yo no vi." Una persona, le cayó así a los pies, a unas personas, le cayó a sus pies. Y vieron, pero es el propio gobierno, no quieren decir nada porque mandan otro pistolero: "Ahora le toca para que no andes diciendo." [Laughs.]

[Since it was political, we don't know who killed him; it seems like it was the government itself. Because of that, nobody says anything. They saw it, they saw it when . . . (makes a gesture of shooting a person) . . .

Many people saw it. But because we are dealing with the government: "No, I didn't see it." One person, he fell like that at his feet, he fell right in front of several people. And they saw it, but it's the government itself, they don't want to say anything because they will send another gunman: "Now it's your turn so you won't go around talking." (Laughs.)]

There is a story untold in this ballad, as I discovered in conversation with a close relative of Abel Torres, the slain teacher. This gentle and intelligent young man, whom I will refer to as Ricardo,[1] also provided me with a great deal of insight into the code of blood revenge. He began his comments with the observation I occasionally got from members of losing factions in corrido tales, that he did not like the corrido. When I asked why, he explained: "Porque no dice la verdad" (Because it doesn't tell the truth). The particular detail that rankled with Ricardo was the way the corrido suggests that Abel Torres might have brought death upon himself due to prior indiscretions. Ricardo, like El Cobarde, claims that it is common knowledge who killed Abel Torres and why they killed him.

The hidden story that emerged in my conversation with Ricardo is a bitter rivalry between two powerful factions in Ometepec, the Aguirre and Torres families. Though Abel Torres had recently been elected leader of the PRI in Guerrero, the Aguirres had an even stronger grasp on the resources of the government, for one of their number was a close associate of the state governor. According to Ricardo, the Aguirres arranged for the death of Abel, in an effort to solidify their control over the politics of patronage in the state.

Ricardo described to me a series of events taking place in the wake of the killing. The group of brothers, uncles, and male cousins in the Torres clan held a kind of war council at a relative's place in Acapulco. They discussed plans of action to avenge the killing. In the midst of these discussions, an Aguirre family member who was linked in gossip to the killing presented himself to the Torres group and proclaimed his innocence. He managed to convince them that he had been falsely accused, and they let him go in peace. Ricardo told me that there was a strong desire to avenge Abel's death but at the same time an awareness that the Aguirres, with their direct access to the governor, would very likely call out the army in retaliation. As he put it, there was a fear that many Torres family members would die and not a single house would remain standing in Ometepec. A similar worry is present in El Cobarde's statement that "things were really falling apart" and these lines in his corrido: "La muerte del profesor / levantó una polvadera" (The death of the teacher / raised quite a cloud of dust).

At last, the Torres group decided against taking action against the Aguirres. As Ricardo described it, Abel's brothers started to demure on the grounds of concern for their immediate families. As one of them reportedly stated: "I would do it but I have two small children and I worry about their future." When these positions were staked out, it became easier for those less closely related to Abel to abstain from action. In the end, they decided to let the matter slip by, but that does not mean the Torres clan was pleased with the situation. El Cobarde's corrido, which came to be fairly well known on the Costa Chica, remains a source of uneasiness for Ricardo and for others in the Torres family.

When I spoke with El Cobarde about why his corrido does not identify Abel Torres's killers, he was quite clear on the matter:

No ve que allí dice, dice: "la muerte del profesor / con el tiempo se sabrá." No dice allá, "fue fulano y vengano." ¿Verdad? [Laughs.] La gente dijo, dijo que los principales de aquí lo mandaron a matar porque él iba a ser presidente, porque él era el presidente del PRI aquí en la Costa Chica, y los de aquí, no les convenían de que él fuera el presidente. Entonces solo así le quitaban, mandando a matar.

[Don't you see that it says there, it says: "the death of the teacher / will someday come to light." It doesn't say there, "it was so and so," right? (Laughs.) People said, they said that it was the main families from here who arranged to kill him because he was going to be president, because he was president of the PRI here on the Costa Chica, and some people here didn't want to see that happen. So only like this could they get rid of him, by having him killed.]

El Cobarde was frank about his likely fate had he inserted more information in the corrido: "Fácil, a mí, fácil me mandan a matar, facilito. Si aquél hasta fiesta le hicieron, al profesor le hicieron fiesta, pa' matarlo [laughs]" (Easily, easily they could have me killed, very easily. If they threw a party for him, for the teacher they threw a party, so they could kill him [laughs]).

But evident if not stated is the same concern that restrained the Torres family, the awareness that missteps in this volatile setting could trigger a general calamity. Against this backdrop, one can perceive calculated moves on El Cobarde's part. The Aguirres are named, but as loyal friends of the dead leader. There is not a whisper of their involvement in the plot, though one might read between the lines and wonder why their fondness for Abel Torres would need to be stated explicitly. The situation was so tense that El Cobarde felt compelled to deflect attention from the local rivalry by mentioning a series of problems Abel had accumulated in the region. The corrido hedges the issue of Abel's assassins by stating first that we will never know who did it and later that some day it will all come to light. In a gesture to the losing faction, El Cobarde stresses the heroic dimensions of Abel Torres, his love of fighting cocks and women, and his fierce rebuke to those who challenge him, and, what is more, El Cobarde dismisses as cowards those who shot him.

Healing through Song

We have seen that composing and publishing a corrido is fraught with difficulty. Although the genre comes equipped with verbal mitigators, such as the plea for artistic immunity and an editorial stance that most often evokes the common wisdom rather than a partisan agenda, composers also must make use of additional strategies to defuse potentially offensive situations. As Onofre Contreras explains, the composer can placate the losing party in the story by assimilating its representatives to the canon of heroic behavior. Both Contreras and El Cobarde point out the relative nature of truth and portray the composer as one who seeks the truth within this realm devoid of absolutes. Moreover, by selecting which events to treat and when to release newly composed corridos, composers avoid themes and moments that are simply too volatile to be contained.

It may be that considerations of self-preservation lie at the root of these measures, but I would argue that the issue goes beyond immediate self-interest. As Contreras noted, the composer must take into account the likely impact of a ballad on the well-being of his friends and at last on *la ciudadanía* (the general public). Concern for the general welfare may drive a composer to write and publicize a corrido on a particular theme or event, to refrain from doing so, or to frame an event in a specific manner. The key issue here is to recognize the healing mission of corridos in these situations of public trauma. Healing is accomplished on several levels, but the healing that most interests me is the reintegration of the body politic in the wake of disruptive violence. The corrido poet fashions a verbal monument that will enlist the support of most or even all the factions of the community. This monument proposes implicitly the continuity of community despite the wrenching impact of the violence that has shattered the collective tranquility.

In this light, writing and performing a corrido can be viewed as a rite of renewal. Véronique Flanet (1977) argues that the death of the *valiente* is akin to ritual sacrifice, bringing about a therapeutic release of social tension, and she views the performance of corridos as an integral phase in this process. But it makes more sense to construe episodes of personalized violence on the Costa Chica as social dramas, enacted and reenacted in the crux of regional conflicts as people live out the "scripts" their culture provides them. The corridos of the coast articulate the "stories" underlying these disruptive events as a prelude to constructing a consensual interpretation of their meaning. Along with celebratory and regulatory motifs, Costa Chica corridos contain therapeutic elements seeking revalidation of the social bond.

All sectors in the ballad process contribute to this effect. Composers avoid the radically divisive pieces of a story and highlight details that are likely to provide solace to the aggrieved parties. Performers bring forward only those corridos they estimate to be acceptable to a particular audience. Audience members make allowances for the performance of commemorative song and seek out nuances in song texts that include them in the embrace of community esteem. Such is the therapy embedded in the corrido that close relatives of a fallen hero may find comfort in it, and even, El Cobarde tells me, dance to corridos narrating the death of beloved friends and relatives. In the sweet strains of poetry set to music, in the companionship of people gathered in song, in the glow of an inclusive heroic vision, the Costa Chica corrido asserts the triumph of community over the partisan disputes that challenge it at every turn.

Note

1. I have elected not to reveal the actual name of my consultant in order to avoid any unwanted consequences.

8 Violence as Social Drama

> The phase structure of social drama is not the product of in-
> stinct but of models and metaphors carried in the actors' heads.
> It is not here a case of "fire finding its own form," but of form
> providing a hearth, a flue, and a damper for fire.
> —Victor Turner, *Dramas, Fields, and Metaphors*

Our inspection of ballad process on Guerrero's Costa Chica has brought to light a set of intertwined theses asserting a relationship between poetry and violence. These two realms of activity, seemingly drawn from opposite spheres of the human personality, now appear to be locked in an intimate embrace. The poetry of heroic action, in its celebratory mood, thrives upon the climate of violence in Costa Chica settlements. This violence is in turn fanned by the presence and stature of corrido poetry in these communities. The celebratory thesis, so prominent in the minds of those who produce and consume these ballads, suggests that the living ballad is nothing more than a reflection of the violent conditions in which it exists. But our inquiries into ballad process on the Costa Chica indicate that other themes are at play.

When leading corrido scholars like Vicente T. Mendoza (1954) and Améri-co Paredes (1993) spoke of the decline of the corrido tradition, they pointed to the shift in popular appetite away from homegrown, traditional entertainments. The arrival of mass communication and the disintegration of the village would remove the corrido from the lives of ordinary Mexicans. But the prediction of the corrido's decline entailed another important argument, the loss of ideological legitimacy. As the grass-roots chronicle of the great struggles shaping the nation, the corrido gives voice to the common man and woman swept away on the tides of Mexican history. Stories commemorating those who could not abide the *porfiriato*, of proud Mexicans who stood fast against the Texas Rangers, of the foot soldiers and popular leaders who "invented the revolution," these are stories worthy of veneration. But what do we make of corrido heroes after the revolution, who are most likely thought to be mere ruffians and rogues?

It would seem that the thesis of the corrido's demise results in part from a romancing of the past. Are fewer corridos being composed and sung today in greater Mexico? I doubt it, though a case could be made that the corrido as a living balladry is more restricted now than it was two or three generations ago. More basic to the perception of the corrido's decline may well be the end of revolutionary convulsion. The earlier stock of corridos dealt with men and women who were elevated as heroes in the national pantheon. The current stock of corrido heroes are more likely to be characterized as local toughs, criminals, *puros matones* (nothing but killers). There is value in distinguishing these historical periods, yet the distinction smacks of a double standard. After all, not every hero of the revolution was motivated by the ideals of social justice, nor is every hero of the modern corrido a rogue or a villain. Indeed, it was not until the "institutionalization" of the revolution well after the fighting had stopped that a purposeful ideology about it emerged.

Corridos of the Drug World

These issues are brought into clear focus in the controversy swirling around the narcocorrido of the borderlands linking the United States and Mexico. Sam Quinones, writing in the *Washington Post* on March 1, 1998, traces these ballads about the drug trade to the influence of Rosalino Sánchez. Chalino Sánchez, as he was called, came to the United States from Sinaloa and began recording corridos in Los Angeles in the 1980s about revenge killings associated with the underworld of his native state. He would compose ballads on commission, drawing on the Sinaloa tradition, and his clients came to include known figures in the drug business. After he was killed in 1992, apparently by Mexican police in Sinaloa, he became a cult figure in Los Angeles and an inspiration to musicians on both sides of the border.

As the example of Chalino Sánchez indicates, the current crop of corridos depicting intrigues of the drug mafia is an authentic reflex of a persisting ballad tradition in these regions. Precursors can be identified in the many corridos of contraband across the porous international boundary dating back as far as the beginning of the twentieth century (Paredes 1976) and produced continuously from that period (Herrera-Sobek 1979) to the present. The narcocorrido is a more polished sound, and it sometimes dispenses with traditional formulas, but its membership in the corrido family is hardly in doubt. The influence of mass communication, so feared by earlier commentators, is manifest in the narcocorrido, which has become something of a marketing phenomenon among young people in the borderlands. Bands like Los Tigres del Norte, Los Tucanes de Tijuana, Los Huracanes del Norte, and Los Rebeldes de Tijuana, to name only a few of the dominant ensembles of the 1990s, perform in large arenas to mass audiences and enjoy impressive record, cassette, and CD sales.

If the authenticity of the narcocorrido as a thriving offshoot of the corrido tradition is not in doubt, this contemporary musical explosion does encounter challenges to its legitimacy from another direction. A host of community leaders, most notably politicians, preachers, and teachers, have argued for the suppression of the narcocorrido on grounds that it adversely influences the thinking and behavior of its youthful followers. In cities and towns across northern Mexico and the southwestern United States, radio stations are banning the narcocorrido from the airwaves and civil authorities are denying the bands that perform it access to their arenas. But as of this writing, these efforts appear to be adding momentum to the narcocorrido craze. Much like attempts to suppress gangsta rap in the United States, a somewhat parallel cultural and commercial phenomenon, official disdain seems to accentuate the excitement and interest of fans.

The reaction against the narcocorrido is rooted in the celebratory thesis, the notion that these corridos are celebrating the deeds of the *traficantes* (drug traffickers) and thereby contributing to their prominence. As Sam Quinones wrote in the *Washington Post* on March 1, 1998: "Narcocorridos celebrate shootouts with *federales,* betrayals and executions and stories of how legendary traffickers fell and how cargoes of contraband got through." But drug dealers and their associates, like armed killers on the Costa Chica, are viewed by mainstream society as unworthy of admiration. They do not possess the stamp of legitimacy conferred by historical caveat on the heroes of the Mexican Revolution. Instead, they are seen as inappropriate models for young people, always within the celebratory premise that the corrido inspires emulation of the examples set by its protagonists.

This thesis is articulated clearly by those who are concerned with the impact of the narcocorrido, claiming that singers make "converts to the cause" who come to view the drug trade as "something not to fear or to shun, but to celebrate on the dance floor" (Kun 1997). Marta Rocha de Díaz, a Tijuana housewife who lives in a barrio hard-hit by drug-world rivalries, has organized opposition to the narcocorrido in her area. She compares the work of these songs to propaganda: "Young people are receiving constant subliminal messages glorifying the narcos, their cars, their girlfriends. These songs are very destructive. They are egging these kids on. Why don't authorities stop this propaganda?" (O'Connor 1997). Cited in the same newspaper article, Dr. Manuel Molina Bellina, director of a drug rehabilitation center in Tijuana, espouses a similar viewpoint: "The original corridos of the revolution ended with the tragic death of the hero. In narcocorridos, the trafficker prevails, and crime pays. The narco manages to stay alive, elude capture, get his drugs across the border, and vanquish authorities. The moral is that being a narco gives you immunity." One of Chicago's premier Latino/Latina radio stations, WTAQ, "La Mexicana," refuses to broadcast narcocorridos. Jose Alaniz, program director, disputes the argument that the songs do not influence their listeners. Using language similar to that employed by some observers of the corrido in Guerrero, he contends that "After one or two beers . . . they want to imitate these guys" (Moore 1997). Critics of the narcocorrido argue that it promotes a "culture of death."

Additional evidence of the celebratory thesis is found in the role apparently played by some drug dealers as sponsors of bands that compose and perform narcocorridos. Jesús García, an aspiring conjunto musician in Sinaloa, stress-

Los Dinámicos, Acapulco, 1996

es the importance of this sponsorship: "Any group that's going to make it big has to be sponsored by a narco. The band that doesn't have a sponsor behind them ends up playing in cantinas. We don't want to be playing in cantinas" (Quinones 1997). But is it true that the narcocorrido serves the purposes of the drug mafias? Does the celebratory mood prevail in this setting to the exclusion of other themes linking poetry to violence?

Certain immensely popular corridos lend some some credence to this theory. One of the hits of Los Tigres del Norte, a band composed mostly of brothers originally from Sinaloa, presents the narcotics trafficker in a positive light. In their "Pacas de a Kilo," a title that could translate as "One Kilo Packets," they portray an enterprising trafficker glorying in his success. This corrido is known to *conjuntos* throughout Mexico; I recorded it in February 1996 in Acapulco as it was sung by three talented young men, Los Dinámicos, the brothers Andrés and Rolando Cruz and their cousin Oscar Villasana, who entitled it "Vacas de a Kilo" (Cows by the Kilo). Here is the text that I recorded that evening:

1. Me gusta andar por la sierra	[I like to wander the high country;
me crié entre los matorrales,	I was raised in the thickets—
allá aprendí a hacer las cuentas	there I learned to do my sums
nomás contando costales,	just by counting burlap sacks;
me gusta burlar las redes	I like to make fun of the nets
que tienden los federales.	that are spread by federal forces.
2. Pegadito a la sierra	Right against the mountain
tengo un rancho ganadero,	I have a cattle ranch—
ganado sin garrapatas	cattle without any ticks—
que llevo pa' el extranjero.	that I bring across the border;
¡Qué chulas se ven mis vacas	how pretty are my cows
con colitas de borrego!	with their little lamb's tails!
3. Los amigos de mi padre	The friends of my father
me admiran y me respetan,	admire and respect me,
y en ciento cincuenta metros	and in 150 meters
levanto las avionetas,	I can lift off the little planes;
de diferentes calibres	of different calibers
manejo las metralletas.	I handle automatic guns.
4. El Tigre a mí me acompaña	El Tigre keeps me company,
porque ha sido un gran amigo,	as he has been a great friend,
maestro en la pista chicha	a master of the short runway

además muy precavido,	and a very clever man;
él sabe que en esta chamba	he knows that in this business
no es bueno volar dormido.	it's no good to sleep while flying.

5. Los pinos me dan la sombra	The pines give me shade,
mi rancho vacas de a kilo,	my ranch, cows by the kilo;
soy mediano de estatura	I am of average height—
amigo de los amigos,	a friend to all true friends;
perdonen que no acostumbro	forgive me, it's not my habit
decirles mis apellidos.	to tell people my last name.

6. Adiós sierras de Coahuila	Farewell, mountains of Coahuila
de Sinaloa y de Durango,	of Sinaloa and Durango,
de Sonora y Tamaulipas	of Sonora and Tamaulipas;
Chihuahua, te estás quedando,	Chihuahua, I leave you behind;
si me quieren conocer	if you want to get to know me
en Juárez me ando paseando.	I'm hanging out in Juárez.]

James Nicolopulos (1997:131) correctly remarks the distinctive character of this particular narrative, denoting it "a movie corrido" rather than a genuine "epic" text with direct links "to specific persons and events." Further, this song, couched in first-person narrative, deviates from the normal third-person corrido discourse. Nonetheless, it does correspond formally to the conventions of a corrido subcategory in which the singer tells his story, usually of vice and ruin, in first-person narrative. Here the protagonist speaks in a triumphant voice, confident in his career, polite and socially adept, admired by his father's friends, "a friend to all true friends." But he maintains a certain social distance, preferring not to use his full name and couching references to his trade in metaphors. His ranch is clearly unusual in some respects, producing "vacas de a kilo" and cows with lamb's tails. Those in the know can tell you that "lamb's tail" is slang for batches of high-grade marijuana. In this regard this song follows a trend in narcocorridos, and typical of corridos in general, of using esoteric terms to refer to the heroic worldview of the ballad community. In a recent hit by Los Tucanes, the singer mentions three animals that earn him his living, "mi perico, mi gallo, y mi chivo" (my parrot, my rooster, and my goat), with the subtext that these animals stand for marijuana, cocaine, and heroin. Still, the narrator in "Vacas de a Kilo" is forthright about his skill with automatic weaponry and his partner's ability to maneuver small aircraft, attributes that connect directly to the world of the drug trade.

"Pacas (or Vacas) de a Kilo" is a romance of the pastoral life with a modern twist. The great majority of narcocorridos are less idyllic. "El Avión de la

Muerte" (The Airplane of Death), also performed originally by Los Tigres del Norte, is far more typical of the narcocorrido. Here are the words as I have transcribed them from their 1989 commercial tape entitled *Triunfo Sólido* (Solid Triumph):

1. En Chihuahua lo agarraron
   sin tener una razón,
   y despúes lo torturaron
   sin tenerle compasión,
   a su amigo lo encerraron
   ya bordaron el avión.

   [In Chihuahua they detained him
   without having any cause;
   and after that they tortured him
   without showing any compassion;
   they locked up his good friend,
   then they boarded the airplane.

2. Ya con rumbo a Sinaloa
   Atilano les gritaba:
   "Ahora yo soy el que manda
   si quieren usen sus armas,
   quiero ver ese valor
   que en el suelo demostraban."

   Now on their way to Sinaloa
   Atilano shouted to them:
   "Now I'm the one in charge;
   if you like, use your weapons;
   I want to see that courage
   that you showed on the ground."

3. De la nave reportó
   todo lo que le habían hecho,
   que con pinzas machacaron
   partes nobles de su cuerpo,
   y que estrellaría el avión
   aunque muriera por eso.

   From the plane he gave account
   of all they had done to him—
   with pincers they had crushed
   the private parts of his body;
   and he would crash the plane,
   though he would die for that.

4. En la torre de control
   todo aquello se grababa,
   se oyen gritos de terror
   y tres hombres que lloraban,
   Atilano se reía
   y más los amenazaba.

   Inside the control tower
   all that was recorded;
   you could hear the shouts of terror
   and three men who were crying;
   Atilano was just laughing
   and more he threatened them.

5. El teniente y los soldados
   de su acción se arrepentían,
   torturaron a un gran gallo
   pensando que no lo sabían,
   en el avión de la muerte
   se estuvieron aquel día.

   The lieutenant and the soldiers
   repented of their deeds;
   they tortured a fine fighting cock
   thinking that nobody knew;
   on the airplane of death
   they found themselves that day.

6. El teniente le decía:
   "Mi mujer me está esperando."

   The lieutenant said to him:
   "My woman is waiting for me."

Atilano contestó:	Atilano gave an answer:
"Ahora vamos a estrellarnos,	"Now we are going to crash;
yo tambien tengo mujer	I also have a woman
y se quedará llorando."	and she will have to cry."

7. Llegando a Badiraguato	Arriving at Badiraguato
helicópteros se alzaban,	the helicopters lifted off;
iba a estrellarse al cuartel	he was going to crash at the base,
por la escuela no hizo nada,	for the school he didn't do it;
los boludos se bajaron	the soldiers went back down—
sienten que se los llevaba.	they see he had them beaten.

8. Dijo adiós a sus amigos	He said farewell to his friends,
camaradas de aviación,	his comrades in aviation;
y después allá en el cerro	and later there in the mountains
se estrelló con el avión,	he crashed into the other plane;
en Chihuahua y Sinaloa	in Chihuahua and Sinaloa,
gran recuerdos les dejó.	great memories he left them.]

This corrido tells a tale of intrigue in which a man victimized by the authorities extracts revenge, though he too must perish in the event. Atilano is unfairly arrested and brutally mistreated by the soldiers. The tables are turned when he gains the upper hand as pilot of a small plane with the very same soldiers on board. Now in control of the situation, he denounces his torturers over the aircraft's radio and informs them that they will soon perish. The corrido poet features the stunned reaction of the soldiers when they realize they are going to die and the determination of the hero, who is described as "un gran gallo." This corrido dispenses with the opening and closing formulas, though the hint of a *despedida* is present in the closing reference to the great memories the hero has left behind. But the main body of the narrative is classic corrido discourse, with its mix of clauses forwarding the story and poignant episodes of reported speech.

"El Avión de la Muerte" is rooted in historical events. Starting in the late 1970s and continuing into the next decade, a region in the Sierra Madre where the states of Sinaloa, Durango, and Chihuahua meet became a center for the production and dissemination of illicit substances, particularly marijuana and opium. According to news accounts, Operation Condor was started to combat the growing drug trade in the region. With assistance from the CIA and the Chilean secret police, the Mexican military mounted an offensive that disregarded basic human rights. Eventually many of the major drug players were forced to relocate to Guadalajara, though the hidden ravines and canyons of the region remained a prime zone for the cultivation of marijuana and poppies.

In the midst of these operations, according to the testimony of Samuel M. Hitt (1994), a prominent drug trafficker named Atilano was captured, tortured, and then "forced to fly his private plane under heavy guard to Sinaloa for further questioning. During the flight, he crashed his plane into a military escort plane, killing everyone aboard both planes. This incident and human rights protests ended Operation Condor." A news dispatch from Reuters captures the futility of the scene: "On the edge of Badiraguato, a sleepy town in the foothills of the Sierra Madre, stands a fortress-like military barracks which could serve as a monument to victories in drug battles that failed to change the course of the war" (Debusmann 1988).

In light of such conflicting evidence, what can we determine regarding the stance of the narcocorrido toward the drug world it describes? Guillermo Hernández (1992:229) strikes a note of caution on this theme, warning that narcocorridos avoid taking any overt stance. But intentions of corrido poets can be interpolated from their selection and handling of plots. As in "El Avión de la Muerte," most narcocorridos deal with desperate situations leading to violent death. It is worth noting that Los Tigres del Norte produced a video for their twenty-ninth album, *Jefe de Jefes* (The Boss of Bosses; 1997), on the grounds and in the cells of Alcatraz, the former maximum-security prison in San Francisco Bay, seeking to convey visually a message printed on the CD liner notes: "Life has many roads but he who is bad has only one destiny . . . the hospital, the prison, or the cemetery." This moral position is advanced in their corridos through strategies associated with the regulatory function. It may be that, as on the Costa Chica, people respond most readily to a celebratory message and discover only upon reflection the deeper undercurrent of social commentary embedded in these ballads.

The link between corridos and *mafiosos* is by no means restricted to the north; as Onofre Contreras told me, "eso ya está metido en todas partes" (that is now entrenched everywhere). He spoke of occasions in Acapulco when he has performed corridos for people involved in the drug trade. One of his corridos, "Los Tres del Oscuro" (The Three in the Gray Car), relates the story of three fellows who attempt to avoid a police check on the coastal highway near Zihuatanejo by placing their gray car inside a trailer truck loaded with coconut husks. When the officers ask them if they have seen a gray car, they reply, truthfully, "Yes, it's behind us," and are allowed to pass. Eventually the officers realize their mistake and come to apprehend them. Contreras told me he had been playing corridos for those men not long before their fateful run up the coast. He asserted with confidence: "A la mafia les gustan mucho los corridos" (The drug mafia really likes corridos). We have seen that songs from the northern repertoire are known to corrido singers in Guerrero, some of whom (like Contreras) have adopted the *charro* look associated with the *norteño* lifestyle and worked the accordion, typical of the northern sound, into their musical ensembles.

This is neither the time nor the place to undertake a thorough investigation of the narcocorrido. It would prove interesting to track in this balladry the interplay of celebratory, regulatory, and therapeutic elements. Here I introduce the controversy generated by the narcocorrido in an effort to refine arguments we have been developing with regard to poetry and violence on Mexico's Costa Chica. Collating the two cases deepens the discussion of the purported "decline" and "decadence" of the corrido. The genre's perceived falling from grace emerges in this light as a complex matter, imbued with assumptions and ambivalences about the trajectory of Mexican history. It appears that the discourse and mission of the corrido remains largely unchanged; what has changed are the historical circumstances. Birthed in a lapsarian world after the revolution, the contemporary corrido is forced to recount tales of tainted heroes of regional conflicts in the south and drug trafficking in the north. Yet there is always the chance that the narcocorrido and the living ballad of the Costa Chica will acquire a new legitimacy, as the romancing of the past encompasses their historical periods.

Social Drama and the Corrido

If community resides in a heroic vision that outlasts the individuals who died in partisan strife, does this imply the triumph of the celebratory thesis? The ballad community, however, perseveres through a collective embracing of the heroic ethos, which is refined in the regulatory function of heroic poetry. Poetry about violence heals by invoking the wellsprings of the ballad community, its heroic ethos, celebrated in the corpus of regional corridos. Yet this ethos is tempered and refined in the ballads. These poets, as the conscience of their communities, tap into the common wisdom to admonish and constrain, praise and condemn. Their songs are created, in many instances, to preserve calm, defuse tension, and promote social harmony. In bringing this inquiry to a close, I employ the fruitful construct of *social dramas* in assessing the interplay of our three theses, diverging in their take on poetry about violence yet converging in the ballad process.

The singing of corridos in the Costa Chica ballad community marks a critical phase in constantly unfolding social dramas. Victor Turner (1967) initially developed his concept of the social drama in addressing conflicts arising among Ndembu villagers in Africa. He noted that conflicts could be isolated as units of social process with a recurrent temporal structure. These episodes tended to be dramatic in their organization of time and space; like violent events commemorated in Costa Chica corridos, Ndembu quarrels exhibited chronological structures divisible into acts and scenes. It was only later that Turner recognized the presence of social dramas in other settings, eventually coming to think of the social drama as a unit that "can be isolated for study in societies at all levels of scale and complexity" (1974:33). For Turner (1986:33), the social drama is "an objectively isolable sequence of social interactions of a conflictive, competitive, or agonistic type."

In his writings, Turner repeatedly highlights the interplay of narrative and social drama. One of the puzzles he poses is "how to account for the fact that the social drama is processually 'structured' before any story about it has been told" (1986:33). Our examination of corridos on Mexico's Costa Chica offers some insight here. These ballads play a double role in the social dramas of the region, as narrative projections of key event sequences and as instruments in the enactment of their phase structures. Turner's phases of breach, crisis, redressive action, and reintegration encompass a cycle of rupture and repair that is portrayed in corrido poetry and completed through the performance of corridos. In pursuing this analysis, it will be necessary to take note of the corrido as a *reflection* of social process and as a *form* of social process. In Turner's formulation, social dramas begin with a "*breach* of regular, norm-governed social relations" (1974:38). The typical pattern on the Costa Chica involves a killing or an attempted killing. Turner (1974:38) notes that "there is always something altruistic about such a symbolic breach," and this observation tallies with the perpetrator's frequent sense that justice is on his side. As in Turner's analysis, what might appear an act of wanton violence or rank criminality can attain, in the heroic worldview, the status of legitimate self-realization. As we have seen, the celebratory thesis finds merit in even those actions that stem from the deadly combination of drink, *machismo,* and weaponry.

The next phase in social dramas is the *crisis,* a dangerous moment in which "there is a tendency for the breach to widen and extend until it becomes coextensive with some dominant cleavage in the widest set of relevant social relations to which the conflicting or antagonistic parties belong" (Turner 1974:38). In settlements along the Costa Chica this process of alignment and realignment in the wake of a violent action is all too familiar. We have seen that in extreme cases, the crisis phase threatens to overwhelm entire towns and villages. As the perception of crisis gathers force, people are forced to choose between competing loyalties, to signal emphatically their abandonment of the cause, or to flee to safer territory. Like the dark clouds of an approaching storm, the mounting aura of crisis acquires a malevolent presence of its own, obliging all the affected parties to adjust to its imperatives. Costa Chica corridos offer many vistas on this phase of the drama, portraying consultations, vows of mutual allegiance or defiance, and similar machinations as the impact of an initial act of violence spreads. As Turner (1974:39) notes and the corridos confirm, the crisis "cannot be ignored or wished away."

Next comes the phase of *redressive action,* which in Turner's scheme involves steps taken "to limit the spread of crisis" through such devices as informal mediation, legal proceedings, and "the performance of public ritual" (1974:39). Turner recognizes the possibility that these efforts may fail, leading to a "regression to crisis" (1974:41). It is significant that the Costa Chica corridos, as reflections of social process, give rather scant attention to these ameliorative remedies, which play a crucial role in limiting the fallout from violent episodes. The heroic vision of the corrido directs our attention to the legitimate quest for vengeance, working to prolong the crisis phase as one retributive deed follows another. Turner (1974:41) mentions that regression to crisis can trigger "endemic, pervasive, smouldering factionalism," a common result on the Costa Chica that is prominently displayed in regional corridos.

Finally, social dramas come to rest in either "the *reintegration* of the disturbed social group" or "the social recognition and legitimization of irreparable schism between the contesting parties" (1974:41). Corrido narratives devote considerable attention to arrangements intended to legitimate a new status quo after an outbreak of violence. There is little scope for reconciliation in these narratives, which feature instead the drawing of lines for further rounds of combat or efforts to limit the options available to hostile parties. One dying hero after another warns of a successor who will reap vengeance, of a *brosa* or gang that will avenge his death. A number of corridos spell out in detail the efforts made to contain further rounds of violence, efforts that sometimes extend to securing the compliance of the nation's president. The phase of reintegration, as portrayed in corrido narratives, has the look of arranging a temporary truce as competing parties explore their options for successive engagements.

Costa Chica corridos are expressive and artistic renderings of social dramas. Their narratives highlight public and stylized conflicts, selecting elements that sustain and confirm a heroic perspective. In this role they conserve in narrative a specific slant on social dramas and provide a blueprint for appropriate behavior in future confrontations. As mirrors of culture these ballads encapsulate core attitudes, values, and expectations of the ballad community. But corridos are not merely artistic reflections of social process; they are instruments or *forms* of social process as well. Composing and performing corridos is a means of reintegrating the disturbed social group, a social ritual effecting a revalidation of community in the aftermath of disruptive events. By defining appropriate uses of violence, lauding them, and criticizing inappropriate uses, the corrido poet articulates or indexes a moral code that is shared by members of the ballad community. This invocation of common ground enables corrido performances, as forms of social process, to promote both the redressive and the reintegrative phases of social dramas, in line with what Turner labels the "performance of public ritual."

Naturally, the celebratory theme in corrido narratives is ever-present, always threatening to perpetuate a state of crisis. Commentators in the ballad community are well aware of the inflammatory potential of the material. In illustrating this point, they frame extreme scenarios like this one: a teenager hears a corrido telling of a slight suffered by his family a generation previous and resolves to avenge the wrong. But I have developed in these chapters another line of thinking, one that emphasizes the role of the critical faculty and the healing potential in corrido narratives. As social events that bring people together in the exploration and articulation of social solidarity, corrido performances renew and strengthen the bonds of community. Corrido poets see themselves as guardians of the collective well-being, as authors who consciously craft their narratives to appease the wounded feelings of those who have suffered reverses in the social dramas of the day.

The corrido is a multifaceted artistic object that eludes simplistic categorization. The crafting and singing of corridos unleashes celebratory, regulatory, and therapeutic elements that radiate throughout the ballad community and achieve their conflicting and complementary potential in varying degrees. The people of Mexico, inheritors of heroic poetry from their diverse ancestry, have elaborated a ballad practice commemorating the turmoil and struggle involved in forging and refining a modern nation. On the northern frontier, as on the southern coast, this ballad tradition persists uninterrupted. Examination of the Costa Chica ballad community reveals complex patterns of interaction between life and song, between violence and poetry. The theses developed in this study propose three distinct responses to the initial query, Why do we find poetry and violence, seemingly so different in kind, bound together in such intimacy in the world's societies?

The Costa Chica case suggests that important social factors account for this conjunction of opposites. Inspection of the corridos composed and performed on Mexico's southern coast reveals that this narrative poetry simultaneously celebrates, regulates, and heals the violence afflicting these communities. As selective renderings of these social dramas, and as instruments in their denouement, Costa Chica corridos provide invaluable access to the web of attitude and sentiment implicated in the violent episodes affecting this region of Mexico.

Thinking about Violence

Although violence has always been with us, we live in a moment when inquiry into the causes and conditions of social violence has acquired a special urgency. In addition to the routine litany of violent behavior, we have been confronted more recently with episodes that challenge a previous conceptual framework attributing violence to mentally ill people within our society and to remorseless enemies on the outside. The bombing of the federal building in Oklahoma City highlighted the existence of domestic terrorists who were willing to take the lives of men, women, and children in pursuit of their political objectives. And the outbreak of mortal violence in our public schools awakened us to darkness in the very heart of the American dream.

Can the ballads on Mexico's Costa Chica tell us anything about violence affecting young people in the cities, suburbs, and towns of the United States today? Can the approach to poetry and violence, as articulated in the foregoing chapters, provide a useful orientation to the disturbing incidents so much in the news? My object here is not to provide tidy solutions, for these are not yet within our reach, but rather to suggest areas of concern.

I have already stated my belief that the controversy swirling around rap music, especially gangsta rap, resembles the ongoing debate about narcocorridos. Stylistically these two narrative traditions are worlds apart. Gangsta is deliberately abrasive, in-your-face, laced with profanity, and couched in aggressive first-person narrative. The narcocorrido, in contrast, preserves the melodic flair of Mexican balladry and presents more low-key narratives in third-person tellings. But when we evaluate the functions served by these traditions, the parallels are striking: in both cases, we have a culture of violence that is apparently celebrated in a companion tradition of verbal narrative. In gangsta rap, as in narcocorridos, we have poets and performers implicated to a significant degree in the lifestyle they portray in their artistic creations. Major rap artists have died for their commitment to this lifestyle, as did the young man who invented the narcocorrido, Chalino Sánchez. Moreover, both gangsta rap and the narcocorrido are fueled by commercial interests. And finally, both of these popular expressive forms have generated a furious debate about their contribution to further violence, a debate that has tended to emphasize the celebratory thesis to the exclusion of the other two functional paradigms proposed here. Do these highly commercialized expressive forms accentuate the celebration of violence? Are there regulatory and therapeutic dimensions to the narcocorrido and gangsta rap, and if so, how prominent are they?

What about the cycles of youth violence affecting our schools over the last few years? Can our model linking poetry to violence be of any service here? Missing in this instance is an enveloping artistic narrative like corrido or rap. The anguished search for explanations of school violence has centered on issues such as the availability of guns, the impersonality of large public institutions, the weakening of parental involvement, and the impact of mass media products featuring predatory scenarios. In the absence of a poetic narrative tradition, we will have to expand the analysis in search of relevant phenomena in other cultural arenas. Perhaps through close inspection of the communities these young men belong to and the expressive forms that shape them, we can best approach these issues. On this score, we note a significant point of contrast with the Costa Chica setting, where immediate and extended families are the social locus of violence and responses to violence. In suburban America the indicated community is not the family but rather the peer group that forms as a refuge from the family and other institutions.

The social world of the two young men who took lives at Columbine High School was composed of a select group of like-minded peers (the so-called trench coat mafia) and an amorphous collection of virtual peers connected through Internet chat rooms and bulletin boards. These adolescent communities are deeply engaged in a popular culture absorbed with violence, destruction, and murder, and it is this involvement that most closely approximates, at least from a functional perspective, the role of poetry and music in the narcocorrido and gangsta rap traditions. I note in passing that these young men who kill are often consumers of gangsta rap.

What elements of the analysis presented in these pages transfers to tragic events like those in Pearl, Mississippi; West Paducah, Kentucky; Jonesboro, Arkansas; Springfield, Oregon; and Littleton, Colorado? We can view these episodes as social dramas with the familiar cycle of breach, crisis, redress, and reintegration. There is thus little difficulty in transferring our discussion of the phenomenology of violence to these events, featuring as they do perpetrators, victims, and witnesses. Many details of individual and social psychology, as treated in our discussion of the corrido, apply without much difficulty to these shootings. It will take more ingenuity to account for celebratory, regulatory, and therapeutic functions, but I believe these too are present in the deadly scenes being played out in public schools. In short, I contend that our model offers a useful framework for assessing violence in the schools. I cannot fully explore this claim here, but let me touch on a few intriguing points.

It is worth noting that most of these episodes involve one or a few adolescent males taking revenge for perceived wrongs. In this regard, our discussion of the psychology of the perpetrator fits very well. Just as the corrido hero sets out in search of revenge—a quest that leads to antisocial acts—these young men seek revenge on the institutions and individuals they perceive as having wronged them. It seems that these young men also experience an untenable situation that they believe can be corrected only through the application of violent means. They contrive plans to obtain vengeance, which for them (as for corrido heroes) may well coincide with the notion of justice. These plans lead to tightly organized, inherently dramatic shootings. As in any violent scene, the victims are shaken loose from their normal routine and are forced to contend with a desperate situation imposed on them by the flow of events. And as in other violent settings, a sense of loss and disruption spreads from the epicenter of violence to affect the many layers of witnesses, both immediate and remote. Also, as in all instances of violence, the urge to verbalize about the event is irrepressible, leading to immediate narrative that is later replaced with seasoned tellings.

Accepting that much of this apparatus transfers with ease, let us turn to the more problematic issue of celebratory, regulatory, and therapeutic elements discovered in the corridos of Mexico's Costa Chica. I suspect we should examine the array of expressive forms that count in the lives of these young men. Principal among them are the products made available to young people by the commercial entertainment industry. If we take up the celebratory thesis, it appears that perpetrators of school violence find inspiration in these commercial products, much as the corrido hero is inspired by lessons drawn from the corpus of traditional corridos. Newspaper accounts of school violence indicate a deep involvement of the perpetrators in video games, Internet links, and commercial music that foreground the thrill of violent action. In fact, some of these games allow the consumer to experience the unleashing of violence, as the player walks through a virtual scene and uses the controls to destroy enemies as they appear on the screen. It seems that perpetrators of school violence, much like those who aspire to fame on the Costa Chica, imbibe inspiration and even practical formulas from their exposure to these imaginative resources. There is speculation that the young killers at Columbine High mastered the notion of "one-shot kills" partly through their exposure to mass entertainment products.

Video games such as Doom, Quake, and Blood, favored by several of the young men implicated in school shootings, concentrate on the visual depiction of violence, something that is of course impossible in corrido or rap. These games accentuate what are called "gibs" (short for "giblets"), signifying the chunks of flesh sent flying through the impact of bullets, grenades, and bombs, and those who program the games have made use of increasingly powerful computers to create increasingly more realistic effects (Keegan 1999:36). In this regard, these extreme video games part company with the corrido, which, as we have seen, takes note of violent action but does not dwell on it.

It would seem that the corrido and the violent video game hold in common a heroic vision of the world, and this is true to a degree, but here too one can note a significant point of contrast. The corrido world is populated by flawed human beings drawn into conflict with one another, a world where the concepts of "good" and "evil" have little application. The world of Doom, on the other hand, features a marine stationed on the moon laying waste to evil adversaries. The corrido presents a world of relativity, and corrido poets strive for objectivity in their authorial stance. The world of the video game is one of absolutes, where the crusading hero may represent humanity's last chance for salvation. These points of divergence indicate the possibility of a heightened celebratory impact in these video games, an almost intoxicating absorption in the role of "first-person shooter" as evil rivals and monsters are graphically dismembered. Some components of contemporary popular culture seemingly move beyond celebration to achieve glorification or even glamorization of violence, unfettered by any plausible moral constraints. Judging by recent trends in American cinema and television, the graphic portrayal of violence is nearly as addictive as nicotine.

But what of the celebratory effect of being commemorated in a ballad, of having one's name spoken all across the country? I have seen no evidence to date that any of these young men were involved in anything comparable to a ballad tradition that could be expected to celebrate their deeds. It stands to reason that they might gain some notoriety among their peers, and this factor could be a partial incentive to them. But I would argue that the medium for the spread of their fame is not an artistic form of expression, but rather a journalistic one. Young men who take guns and bombs to their schools are no doubt aware that if they succeed in carrying out their plans, their drastic actions will be headline news throughout the world. Journalistic coverage admittedly lacks the gravitas of commemorative verse, but it has proven to be very effective in spreading the news—more effective than the ballad process could ever be. And the splashy formats of CNN and the network news, with their striking icons and dramatic replays, have appropriated something of the affective power of traditional expressive genres.

In an eerie twist on the Columbine episode, we have testimony from the lips of the young killers indicating they were highly conscious of the prospect of achieving fame through media coverage. On video segments the boys made shortly before their murderous campaign, one of them is heard to say that "directors will be fighting over this story." The other then speculates: "Steven Spielberg . . . Quentin Tarantino" (Gibbs and Roche 1999:42). Steeped in the violent side of American popular entertainment, these young men apparently had little difficulty imagining themselves as heroes in a brutal and bloody plot like those of their favorite movies.

There are good reasons to explore the implications of the model developed in these pages in relation to school violence. We have seen that the celebratory thesis comes into play and helps identify some aspects of the motivation underlying these apparently irrational modes of behavior. But what about the regulatory thesis and the thesis that expressive forms might contribute to healing? As we think through the regulatory thesis, we can inquire to what extent video games, music, television shows, and movies sketch out a moral universe within which to evaluate the effects of violence? If they do so, how believable is it? It may be that these media products, driven primarily by the profit motive, lack the regulatory thrust underlying celebration of heroic deeds in Costa Chica corridos. It is disturbing to note, in this light, that one of these games, Blood II, actually rewards the player for killing civilians (Keegan 1999:40).

Turning now to the healing function, we can note the reluctance of our individualistic, iconoclastic society to indulge in communal rituals. Naturally, religious and civic institutions are in place to ease the suffering and cope with the dislocation occasioned by violent actions. We can also observe in the aftermath of these terrible events a number of seemingly spontaneous actions, such as writing and reciting verse and depositing flowers and memorabilia near the scenes of violent deaths. This reaching toward poetry for making verbal memorials affirms that verbal commemoration is a natural and powerful response to the experience of violence. But here in the United States we lack a direct equivalent of the corrido poet, who is called on to craft verbal narratives that will soothe and restore community.

I pursue this discussion not to prefer one social practice to another, but rather to seek enlightenment in a very difficult setting. After all, for all the healing work of the corrido, for all its regulatory pieces, young men on the Costa Chica, and on Mexico's northern frontier, continue to engage in violence. As of the moment, we have no antidote for the propensity toward violence that runs so deep in the human psyche. But it is wise to muster all available resources, in the spirit of carrying out that least violent of gestures, which is to try to understand the causes of violence. It is plausible to think of violence on the Costa Chica, like violence on the grounds of public schools in the United States, as a social drama partially amenable to analysis and interpretation. Perhaps the main contribution of this line of thinking is to direct our attention to celebratory, regulatory, and therapeutic possibilities in the expressive culture surrounding this matrix of violence.

To be clear, we cannot claim that involvement in these expressive forms automatically leads to immersion in violent action. Obviously, most of the young people who listen to corridos, to narcocorridos, or to gangsta rap never act out the violence they depict. By the same token, most of the young men and women engaged in the popular culture of our times will never be inspired to carry bombs or guns to their schools. But we must acknowledge a significant association between youth violence and a cultivation of expressive forms whose focus is on violence. In the company of other factors, artistic renderings of violence can influence young people to turn upon their peers, teachers, and families. And it seems just as likely that the promise of notoriety through graphic and extensive press coverage—or perhaps a movie with a famous director—might act as a stimulant to violence in these settings. It does not strain the imagination to suggest that youthful killers view themselves as actors in social dramas, much like the corrido hero determined to avenge a wrong while claiming a name for himself. It is in this convoluted domain of human motivation that our discussion of poetry and violence on Mexico's Costa Chica is likely to offer the most useful insights into the universal problem of human violence.

Note on the Recording

The CD holds eleven corridos culled from the hundreds of performances I have recorded in the towns and villages of the Costa Chica and in Acapulco. In making the selections, I tried to balance a set of criteria: the corrido's merit as a sample of the tradition; the musical virtues of the performance; and the condition of the audio document. I also favored corridos that are presented and discussed in this book. I have arranged the selections in chronological groups, moving from 1972 to 1989 to 1996.

The CD was digitally remastered from my field recordings by Guy Hardy at the American Indian Studies Research Institute at Indiana University. It benefited from technical assistance provided by Alan Burdette, Patrick Feaster, and John Fenn. I appreciate as well access granted to the facilities of SAVAIL, the sound and video lab at Indiana University's Department of Folklore and Ethnomusicology.

1. "Antonio Veles"

Performed by Audón Ramón Juárez (lead voice), Celedonio Mejía (second voice), Alfredo Salado (violin), and Sabino Serrano (guitar) at the Gallardo home in Cruz Grande, Guerrero, on August 11, 1972.

Voy a cantar un corrido	[I will sing a corrido—
no se vayan a enojar,	please do not be angry;
la gente de Antonio Veles	the people of Antonio Veles
no se ha podido arreglar,	have not been able to settle,
la gente de Antonio Veles	the people of Antonio Veles
no se ha podido arreglar.	have not been able to settle.

Antonio estaba en Cuilutla
y tenía gente a su lado,
lo mismo los cuilutecos
que tenían gallo jugado,
por no saberse tantear
la existencia le han quitado.

Antonio vive en Cuilutla
que tenía gente a su lado,
por no saberse tantear
la existencia le han quitado,
por no saberse tantear
la existencia le han quitado.

Un día martes de por cierto
cuando Emilio muy confiado,
iba a mudar su caballo
donde estaba Perso Gago,
pero no se daba cuenta
que lo espiaban sus contrarios.

Cándido lo vió venir
y se tiró una risada:
"Emilio, ya vienes muerto
aquí está quien te deseaba,
Emilio, ya vienes muerto
aquí está quien te deseaba."

Cándido tiró un balazo
pero muy bien apuntado,
cuando Emilio se dió cuenta
porque ya estaba tirado,
de plano no tuvo tiempo
que hubiera contestado.

Antonio escuchó el balazo
y se quedó pensativo,
le dijo a sus compañeros:
"Se me hace que ha muerto Emilio."
Allí le dijo a Virginio Nava:
"Quiero que me des auxilio."

Antonio pegó el arranque
perdió el amor a su vida:

Antonio was in Cuilutla
and he had people at his side;
the same thing, the Cuilutecos—
they had a real tough fighter;
for not knowing how to figure,
they have put an end to him.

Antonio lives in Cuilutla
and he had people at his side;
for not knowing how to figure
they have put an end to him,
for not knowing how to figure
they have put an end to him.

It was on a Tuesday for certain
when Emilio, so sure of himself,
went out to move his horse
to where Perso Gago was,
but he never was aware
that his rivals were watching him.

Cándido saw him arrive
and he tossed off a loud laugh:
"Emilio, you're already dead;
here's the one who wanted you,
Emilio, you're already dead;
here's the one who wanted you."

Cándido fired a shot,
and very well aimed it was;
Emilio figured it out
when he was already down;
he just didn't have any time
or else he would have answered.

Antonio heard the gunfire
and he fell into deep thought;
he said to his companions:
"It seems that Emilio is dead."
There he said to Virginio Nava:
"I want you to lend me a hand."

Antonio hit the throttle;
he lost his love for life:

"Si vino mi tío Eliodoro
de una vez que se decida."
Con su escopeta en las manos
perdió el amor a su vida.

En el topón que se dieron
Antonio salió corriendo,
con su escopeta en las manos
todavía se iba sonriendo:
"Ya no cuenten con mi vida
porque ya me voy muriendo."

Manuelo Peláez gritaba
al público y todo al grito:
"Tú me tenías que pagar
la muerte de mi hermanito."
Y metió otros dos balazos
con una cuarenta y cinco.

Amigo Rosa Garzón
ya la llevaba ganada,
pero no se daba cuenta
que allá andaba Virginio Nava,
las nueve postas le entraron
las nueve de retrocarga.

Ya me voy a despedir
perdonen lo mal trovado,
ya se murió Antonio Veles
siendo gallo resacado,
en la puerta del campo santo
allí lo dejaron tirado.

Ya me voy a despedir
perdonen lo mal trovado,
ya se murió Antonio Veles
siendo gallo resacado,
las muchachas de Cuilutla
huerfanitas se han quedado.

"If my Uncle Eliodoro came,
he should join in right away."
With his shotgun in his hands
he lost his love for life.

In the clash that followed,
Antonio came out running
with his rifle in his hands;
he even came along smiling:
"No longer count on my life
because I am already dying."

Manuelo Peláez shouted
to all present and fully shouted:
"You were going to pay me
for the death of my little brother."
And he sunk in two more bullets
with a forty-five pistol.

Friend Rosa Garzón
already had it won,
but he didn't realize
Virginio Nava was there;
nine bullets entered him,
nine from a breech-loading rifle.

Now I will say farewell—
please forgive any poor verse;
Antonio Veles has died
being a tough fighting cock;
at the cemetery gate
there they left him lying.

Now I will say farewell—
please forgive any poor verse;
Antonio Veles has died
being a tough fighting cock;
the young ladies of Cuilutla
have now become little orphans.]

2. "Tomás Marín"

Performed by José Figueroa in Ometepec on August 5, 1972.

Les voy a cantar un corrido señores, perdonarán, este corrido es compuesto del pueblo de San Nicolás.	[I will sing you a corrido— gentlemen, forgive me; this corrido is composed from the town of San Nicolás.
El pueblo de San Nicolás ya se está poniendo el plan, allí pagaban dos mil pesos que agarraran a Tomás.	The town of San Nicolás is already making a plan; there they paid two thousand pesos so they would capture Tomás.
Ese caso estuvo serio por la fiesta de un rosario, él andaba muy confiado pòrque andaba en los rezados.	That case was a serious one: at a rosary celebration, he went around without worry, as he was among those praying.
Así es que ya estaba preso luego mandaron a ver, que ya Tomás estaba preso que lo fueran a traer.	And so he was already captured; they told them to come and see that Tomás was already captured; they should come and take him away.
Allí los ricos de Tapextla ya les prestaban dinero, que lo lleven a Tomás para el estado de Guerrero.	There the rich people of Tapextla, now they were lending them money, so they would bring Tomás into the state of Guerrero.
De Tapextla lo sacaron pa'l pueblo de San Nicolás, porque llegando a la raya allí lo iban a matar.	They took him from Tapextla to the town of San Nicolás because, arriving at the border, there they were going to kill him.
Cuando le estaban tirando el sargento se sonrió, ya todos ya le tiraron cuantas penas se recibió.	When they were firing at him the sergeant was all smiles; then they all shot at him; so many wounds he received.
El se sacó la pistola y un tiro le disparó, le tiró a la mera frente comoquiera no le dió.	He took out his pistol and fired one shot at him— he fired right at his forehead; even so, he didn't get him.
Allí dieron la media vuelta todititos la risada: "Ahora sí, Tomás Marín ya te cargó la fregada."	There they spun around, all of them laughing loudly: "Now for sure, Tomás Marin, now your goose is cooked."

Así que ya se habían ido Tomasito hasta se rió: "Mamá, no se ha de espantar todavía estoy vivo yo."	Then when they had all left Tomás even let out a laugh: "Mother, you need not worry for I am still alive."
Ese Pipino Noyola llegó hasta San Nicolás: "Ahora que Tomás murió ¿qué si hacemos un fandango?"	That Pipino Noyola arrived at San Nicolás: "Now that Tomás is dead let's have ourselves a party."
Dijo Alfredo Fuentes pero con una apureza: "Si Tomás ya se murió dispararemos cerveza."	Alfredo Fuentes said, but in a tremendous hurry: "If Tomás is dead let's go toss down some beers."
Cuando le llega una carta que Tomás no estaba muerto, que Tomás no estaba muerto lo que estaba solo herido.	When he receives a letter it seems Tomás was not dead, it seems Tomás was not dead, that he was only wounded.
Allí dijo Alfredo Fuentes: "Que se termine este baile, si Tomás no se murió que si lo barre con él."	There Alfredo Fuentes said: "Let this dance be done; if Tomás did not die maybe we should finish him off."
Allí dice Tomás Marín: "Traigo la sangre caliente, la muerte de mi papá me la paga Alfredo Fuentes."	There says Tomás Marin: "My blood is boiling over; the death of my father will be paid by Alfredo Fuentes."
Ya me voy a despedir señores, perdonarán, aquí termina el corrido de Alfredo Fuentes y Tomás.	Now I will take my leave— gentlemen, forgive me; here ends the corrido of Alfredo Fuentes and Tomás.]

3. "Chicharrón"

Sung by Pablo and Laurencio Gallardo at the home of the Gallardo family in Cruz Grande, Guerrero, on August 5, 1972.

Voy a cantar un corrido lo molesta al corazón, les voy a dar a saber la muerte de Chicharrón, les voy a dar a saber la muerte de Chicharrón.	[I will sing a corrido— it troubles the heart; I will let you know about the death of Chicharrón, I will let you know about the death of Chicharrón.

Un día domingo por cierto
le estaban formando el plan,
Licho con Pedro Berdeja
Balta con Matía Guzmán,
Licho con Pedro Berdeja
Balta con Matía Guzmán.

La mujer que lo entregó
fue de su misma pandilla,
buen dinero se ganó
Victoria la Tarequía,
buen dinero se ganó
Victoria la Tarequía.

Iban cargando un difunto
que lo iban a sepultar,
luego eligieron el punto
donde lo habían de matar,
luego eligieron el punto
donde lo habían de matar.

Adentro de una cantina
lo tiró Matía Guzmán,
han parado a una esquina
allí estaba su hermano Juan,
han parado a una esquina
allí estaba su hermano Juan.

Pedro Palacio cayó
con su cerrojo en las manos,
quebrado de la cintura:
"No le tiren a mi hermano."
Quebrado de la cintura:
"No le tiren a mi hermano."

Uno de sus compañeros
se llamaba Zalapa,
y ese era Rufino Diego
en su caballo alazán,
y ese era Rufino Diego
en su caballo alazán.

Gritaba Rufino Diego
y en el grito les decía:
"'Ora sí, Matía Guzmán

It was a Sunday for certain
they were making the plan—
Licho with Pedro Berdeja
Balta with Matía Guzmán,
Licho with Pedro Berdeja
Balta with Matía Guzmán.

The woman who delivered him
was from his own band;
good money she made,
Victoria la Tarequía,
good money she made,
Victoria la Tarequía.

They were carrying a corpse
that they were going to bury,
then they chose the spot
where they would murder him,
then they chose the spot
where they would murder him.

Inside of a cantina
Matía Guzmán shot him;
they have stopped at a corner,
there was his brother Juan,
they have stopped at a corner,
there was his brother Juan.

Pedro Palacio fell
with his shotgun in his hands,
broken at the waist:
"Don't shoot at my brother,"
broken at the waist:
"don't shoot at my brother."

One of his companions
was named Zalapa,
and that one was Rufino Diego
on his chestnut mare,
and that one was Rufino Diego
on his chestnut mare.

Rufino Diego shouted
and in the shout he told them:
"Now for sure, Matía Guzmán,

se juntó la misma cría,	the same breed has come together,
'ora sí, Matía Guzmán	now for sure, Matía Guzmán,
se juntó la misma cría."	the same breed has come together."
Barrio de Cahuatitán	The barrio of Cahuatitán
ahora es pura sonrisa,	now is nothing but smiles;
si Pedro estuviera vivo	if Pedro were alive
hubiera muerto Ceniza,	Ceniza would have died,
si Pedro estuviera vivo	if Pedro were alive
hubiera muerto Ceniza.	Ceniza would have died.
Dijo Candelario Río:	Candelario Río said:
"La culpa la tengo yo,	"I am the one to blame;
en este velorio mío	in this wake of mine,
el diablo aquí se esmeró,	the devil cleaned up here,
en este velorio mío	in this wake of mine,
el diablo aquí se esmeró."	the devil cleaned up here."
Cuando lo iban a enterrar	When they went to bury him
su caballo iba de luto,	his horse was dressed in mourning;
a las arenas del mar	to the sands of the sea
fueron a hacer el sepulto,	they went to make the grave,
a las arenas del mar	to the sands of the sea
fueron a hacer el sepulto.	they went to make the grave.
Ya me voy a despedir	Now I will take my leave—
me palpita el corazón,	my heart is beating fast;
se murió Pedro Palacio	Pedro Palacio is dead
sobrenombre el Chicharrón,	of the last name Chicharrón,
se murió Pedro Palacio	Pedro Palacio is dead
sobrenombre el Chicharrón.	of the last name Chicharrón.]

4. "Tiene Lumbre el Comal" (The Hearth Has Live Embers)

Composed by Lucio Arizmendi and performed by Los Hermanos Arizmendi (Benito, Isidro, and Raul) at Miguel Arizmendi's home in Acapulco on June 27, 1972.

¡Cuidado la judicial de Acapulco!	[*A warning to the judicial police of Acapulco!*
Escuchen este corrido	Listen to this corrido—
el hecho fue verdadero,	this thing really happened;
la judicial de Acapulco	the judicial police of Acapulco
fue presa en Ejido Nuevo.	were imprisoned in Ejido Nuevo.
Año del sesenta y seis	In the year of '66,
grabado en mármol y cuarzo,	engraved in marble and quartz,

fue a las tres de la mañana
del día veintiuno de marzo.

Cuando entró la judicial
el pueblo estaba dormido,
sonando los M-1
por las orillas de Ejido.

Con tan raro despertar
los habitantes de Ejido,
preguntaban con pesar:
"Señores, ¿qué ha sucedido?"

Y luego de investigar
todo quedaba aclarado,
la honorable judicial
a un hombre había asesinado.

Y por encima del pueblo
pisando su dignidad,
gritaban: "Ríndanse todos,
somos de la autoridad."

Creyendo que con injurias
los dejarían asustados,
y en menos que canta un gallo
ya estaban acorralados.

Demostrando con agallas
que nada les asustaba,
se fajaron, Valentín
el Zarco y Sabino Nava.

¡Vámonos, Lucio!

La policía sub-urbana
y la defensa rural,
con el respaldo del pueblo
desarmó a la judicial.

Depositaron las armas
que eran de la autoridad,
en casa 'e Máximo López
pa' mayor seguridad.

Dieron aviso a Acapulco
de lo que había acontecido,

it was at three in the morning
on the twenty-first of March.

When the judicial police entered
the town was sound asleep;
sounding the M-1 rifles
around the edges of Ejido.

With such a strange awakening
the inhabitants of Ejido,
they were asking with concern:
"Gentlemen, what has happened?"

And after looking into it
everything became clear;
the honorable judicial police
had assassinated a man.

And on top of the people,
trampling their dignity,
they shouted: "Surrender, everyone,
we are the authorities."

Believing that with insults
they would have them frightened,
and in less than a cock's crow
they were already surrounded.

Showing they had guts,
that nothing frightened them,
they were fighting—Valentín,
El Zarco, and Sabino Nava.

Let's go, Lucio!

The suburban police force
and the rural defense,
with the support of the town,
disarmed the judicial police.

They deposited the weapons
which belonged to the authorities
in the house of Máximo López,
for better security.

They sent word to Acapulco
about what had occurred;

y en el camino del Treinta
el parte fue detenido.

and along the road to El Treinta
the delegation was detained.

Llegaron los federales
dizque para apaciguar,
y en vez de ayudar al pueblo
lo comenzó a desarmar.

The federal army arrived
supposedly to keep the peace,
and instead of helping the people
they began to disarm them.

La judicial protegida
por la fuerza federal,
en represalia detuvo
a los guardias del lugar.

The police under protection
of the federal forces,
in reprisal they detained
the militia of the place.

Y lo que hicieron con ellos
en el puerto de Acapulco,
si tiene nombre me callo
pa' no gritar un insulto.

And what they did with them
in the port city of Acapulco—
if it has a name I am silent
in order not to shout an insult.

Al señor Máximo López
sin tener culpa en verdad,
por sostener su inocencia
lo golpearon sin piedad.

As for Mr. Máximo López,
without really being to blame,
for maintaining his innocence
they beat him without mercy.

Así quedó demostrado
que la justicia en Guerrero,
es pa'l que está en el poder
o de'l que tiene dinero.

So it was revealed
that justice in Guerrero
is for those who are in power
or for those who have the money.

Hoy el pueblo se pregunta
¿en quién debemos confiar
si nuestras autoridades
nos vienen a asesinar?

Today the people are asking,
In whom can we trust
if our authorities
come to assassinate us?

Y que no se les ocurra
a los de la judicial,
pasar por Ejido Nuevo
pues tiene lumbre el comal.

And let it not occur
to those of the judicial police
to stop by Ejido Nuevo,
as the hearth still has live embers.]

5. "Sidonio"

Performed by Ernesto Gallardo and Alejandro Mejía in Cruz Grande on January 28, 1989.

Voy a cantar un corrido
escúchenlo con esmero,
le cayeron a Sidonio

[I will sing a corrido—
listen to this with care;
they fell upon Sidonio

al punto de la costadero,
lo sacaron a balazos
con mucha gente del cerro.

Sidonio no quería creer
que Santa Rosa pesaba,
pidiéndoles de favor
la pasara de la barra,
porque esa gente de Lorenzo
la verdad estaba muy brava.

Teófilo la Chichacola
era un hombre y no se rajaba,
en la barra de Chautengo
tenía la sombra pesada,
la escopetita del doce
seguido se las tronaba.

Ese Pipino Lorenzo
se cubrió por los retoños,
porque le escuchaba el habla
a su compadre Sidonio,
quería que saliera afuera
para meterle unos plomos.

¡Lo quería mucho!

Pedro García les gritaba:
"Todavía esto no es de creer,
éntrenle aquí está su padre
aquí traigo el cero-seis,
no lo compré pa' mi padre
voy a vengar a José."

Estaba sencillo.

Ese Filimón Lorenzo
le gritaba de valor,
con una pistola super
le gritaba, Filimón:
"Yo soy de tus enemigos
no tomes otra cuestión."

Prisco Soto se murió
según ya eso era su siño,
(esa era su mujer de ellos)

by the edge of the coastal highway;
they drew him out with bullets
with several men from the highlands.

Sidonio didn't want to believe
that Santa Rosa was for real,
asking them as a favor
they should hand her over,
because those people of Lorenzo's,
in truth, they were very angry.

Teófilo la Chichacola
was a man who didn't back down;
among the gang of Chautengo
he cast a heavy shadow;
that twelve-gauge shotgun,
he fired it off right away.

That Pipino Lorenzo,
he took cover in the brush
because he could hear the voice
of his *compadre* Sidonio;
he wanted him to come outside
so he could fill him with lead.

He was really fond of him!

Pedro García shouted:
"This still can't be for real;
come on in, here is your father,
here I've got the aught-six—
I didn't buy it for my father,
I will avenge José."

It was easy.

That Filimón Lorenzo,
he shouted with valor,
with his super pistol
he shouted, Filimón:
"I am one of your enemies,
don't take it any other way."

Prisco Soto died—
it seems his time was at hand;
(she was the woman of those people)

no le tiraron a ella	they didn't shoot at her,
le tiraron al marido,	they shot at her husband instead;
según no quería morir	it seems he didn't want to die,
pero ya eso era su siño.	but his time was already at hand.

| *Su siño como dice, "Ahí te va."* | *It's like, "There you go."* |

Ya me voy a despedir	Now I will take my leave—
escúchenlo con esmero,	listen to this with care;
le cayeron a Sidonio	they fell upon Sidonio
al punto de la costadero,	by the edge of the coastal highway;
lo sacaron de balazos	they drew him out with bullets
con mucha gente del cerro.	with several men from the highlands.]

6. "Pedro el Chicharrón"

Performed by Juvencio Vargas with his daughter, Meche, at their home in Acapulco on February 4, 1989.

Voy a cantar un corrido	[I will sing a corrido—
me permitan su atención,	allow me your attention;
de esos hombres pocos nacen,	few men like these are born—
hombres de mucho valor,	men of great resolve;
el que nace no se logra	those who are born don't last,
como Pedro el Chicharrón,	like Pedro el Chicharrón,
el que nace no se logra	those who are born don't last,
como Pedro el Chicharrón.	like Pedro el Chicharrón.

Ese Pedro el Chicharrón	That Pedro el Chicharrón—
era hombre y no se rajaba,	he was tough and wouldn't back down;
que si el gobierno le caiba	if the government fell upon him
con el gobierno peleaba,	with the government he would fight;
le decía a sus compañeros	he was saying to his companions
que hasta risa le causaba,	that it just made him laugh,
le decía a sus compañeros	he was saying to his companions
que hasta risa le causaba.	that it just made him laugh.

Bajaba Zeta Martínez	Zeta Martínez came down
a rumbo de Espinalillo:	on his way to Espinalillo:
"Voy a ver al Chicharrón	"I am going to see Chicharrón;
que lo quiero para amigo,	I want him to be my friend;
me lo encargó el comandante	the commander gave me the job—
que lo quiere muerto o vivo,	he wants him dead or alive,
me lo encargó el comandante	the commander gave me the job—
que lo quiere muerto o vivo."	he wants him dead or alive."

Cuando el general llegó
Pedrito estaba sentado,
estaba cuidando las armas
un ladito de la puerta,
y de toditito el parque
que lo estaba asoleando,
y de toditito el parque
que lo estaba asoleando.

Le contesta el Chicharrón:
"Dejes de estar molestando,
lárguese con esas armas
ya no me esté usted enfadando,
no vaya a venir el diablo
y me vaya a estar achuchando,
no vaya a venir el diablo
y me vaya a estar achuchando."

Otro día por la mañana
su compadre lo invitó:
"Vamos a echarnos un trago
pero con ordenamiento,
ahora que estás desarmado
te ayudo en tu sentimiento,
ahora que estás desarmado
te ayudo en tu sentimiento."

Luego sacó su cerrojo
también su reglamentaria,
y le decía a su compadre:
"De eso ya ni diga nada,
voy a tirar de balazos
por si acaso hay emboscada,
voy a tirar de balazos
por si acaso hay emboscada."

Allí le dijo su compadre
al llegar a la cantina:
"Que nos sirvan una copa
de mescal o de tequila."
El Chicharrón pensativo
porque ya lo presentía,
El Chicharrón pensativo
porque ya lo presentía.

When the general arrived
Pedrito was sitting down,
he was taking care of his weapons,
just beside the door,
and of all his ammunition—
it was drying in the sun,
and of all his ammunition—
it was drying in the sun.

Chicharrón answers him:
"Stop making trouble here;
get out of here with those weapons
and quit making me angry;
I hope the devil doesn't come
and make me lose my patience,
I hope the devil doesn't come
and make me lose my patience."

The next day in the morning
his *compadre* invited him out:
"Let's go have a drink
but in an orderly way;
now that you are disarmed
I'll help you through your trouble,
now that you are disarmed
I'll help you through your trouble."

Then he took out his mauser,
also his forty-five luger,
and he was telling his *compadre:*
"Don't even speak about that;
I am going to fire some shots
just in case there is an ambush,
I am going to fire some shots
just in case there is an ambush."

There his *compadre* told him
on arriving at the cantina:
"Serve us each a drink
of mescal or of tequila."
Chicharrón was full of thought
because he knew what was coming,
Chicharrón was full of thought
because he knew what was coming.

Pedro al sentir el balazo	When Pedro felt the bullet
dió la vuelta y luego dijo:	he turned around and then spoke:
"Ya me chingastes, compadre	"Now you have screwed me, *compadre;*
salte a matarte conmigo,	come over and let's have it out,
con esta reglamentaria	with this forty-five luger
van a ser ocho contigo,	it'll be eight bullets for you,
con esta reglamentaria	with this forty-five luger
van a ser ocho contigo."	it'll be eight bullets for you."
Su compadre cayó adentro	His *compadre* fell inside
y Pedro al pie de una palma,	and Pedro at the foot of a palm;
le gritaba a su querida:	he shouted to his girlfriend:
"Te quedas, negra del alma,	"You'll stay behind, darling girl,
vas a abrazar a otros hombres	you will embrace other men
que no sabes ni como hablan,	and you don't even know how they speak,
vas a abrazar a otros hombres	you will embrace other men
que no sabes ni como hablan."	and you don't even know how they speak."
Decía Pedro el Chicharrón	Pedro el Chicharrón spoke
cuando estaba agonizando:	when in the throes of death:
"Arrímate, Crescenciana	"Come close, Crescenciana,
que ya me estoy acabando,	as I will soon meet my end;
te quiero morder el brazo	I want to bite your arm
pa' que te andes acordando,	so you will always remember,
te quiero morder el brazo	I want to bite your arm
pa' que te andes acordando."	so you will always remember."
Decía Pedro el Chicharrón:	Pedro el Chicharrón said:
"De este mundo me despido,	"I take my leave of this world;
lo que les encargo muchachos	what I ask of you boys
que me troven un corrido,	is that you write me a corrido,
pa' que quede de recuerdo	so it can be a reminder
a toditos mis amigos,	for every one of my friends,
pa' que quede de recuerdo	so it can be a reminder
a toditos mis amigos."	for every one of my friends."]

7. "Ernesto Quiñones"

Performed by Artemio Aguirre and friends during a bohemio *at his house in Aca-pulco on January 16, 1989.*

Voy a cantar un corrido	[I will sing a corrido
de la palomilla brava,	about a very fierce gang;
quisieron matar a Ernesto	they wanted to kill Ernesto
pero no le hicieron nada,	but they couldn't touch him,

quisieron matar a Ernesto
pero no le hicieron nada.

they wanted to kill Ernesto
but they couldn't touch him.

Su mujer le preguntó:
"Ernesto, ¿pa' dónde vas?"
"Voy en busca de estos cabrones
que me vinieron a matar,
voy en busca de estos cabrones
que me vinieron a matar."

His woman asked of him:
"Ernesto, where are you going?"
"I'm going to find those bastards
who came here wanting to kill me,
I'm going to find those bastards
who came here wanting to kill me."

Empezó la tirotea
como a las doce del día,
una sola polvadera
y hasta las vacas corrían,
una sola polvadera
y hasta las vacas corrían.

The battle of guns began
around twelve noon in the day—
just one big cloud of dust
and even the cows took off running,
just one big cloud of dust
and even the cows took off running.

A los primeros balazos
todos creían que era fuete,
Juvencio y sus dos hermanos
peleaban contra de siete,
Juvencio y sus dos hermanos
peleaban contra de siete.

With the first shots fired
they thought it was firecrackers;
Juvencio and his two brothers
were fighting it out with seven,
Juvencio and his two brothers
were fighting it out with seven.

El amiguito Pachuca
no sirve pa' compañía,
con un rozón en la nalga
decía que ya se moría,
con un rozón en la nalga
decía que ya se moría.

Dear little friend Pachuca,
he is not a good companion,
with just a scratch on his buttocks
he was saying that he was dying,
with just a scratch on his buttocks
he was saying that he was dying.

El amiguito Pachucas
corría como chachalaca,
en la estampida que dió
allí se montó en una vaca,
en la estampida que dió
allí se montó en una vaca.

Dear little friend Pachuca,
he ran about like a pheasant,
in the stampede that took place
there he was riding a cow,
in the stampede that took place
there he was riding a cow.

Ernesto les ensuplicó
tirado en la pura playa:
"Tiren con valor muchachos
Juvencio que no se vaya,
tiren con valor muchachos
Juvencio que no se vaya."

Ernesto asked of them
stretched out on the sandy beach:
"Shoot bravely, boys—
Juvencio must not get away,
shoot bravely, boys—
Juvencio must not get away."

Ese Juvencio Moreno	That Juvencio Moreno,
ese sí le viene guango,	he sure has the balls,
porque defendió su vida	because he defended his life
debajo de un palo de mango,	beneath a mango tree,
porque defendió su vida	because he defended his life
debajo de un palo de mango.	beneath a mango tree.
Ya me voy a despedir	Now I will say farewell
de la palomilla brava,	to the gang that was so fierce;
quisieron matar a Ernesto	they wanted to kill Ernesto
pero no le hicieron nada,	but they couldn't touch him,
quisieron matar a Ernesto	they wanted to kill Ernesto
le hicieron pura chingada.	but they couldn't do shit to him.]

8. "Apolonio"

Performed by Juvencio Vargas (lead vocal) and Rogelio Calvo (violin) in a cantina in Pinotepa Nacional on February 12, 1989.

Voy a cantar un corrido	[I will sing a corrido,
señores, perdonarán,	gentlemen, by your leave,
señores, perdonarán,	gentlemen, by your leave;
se comprometió Apolonio	Apolonio got into trouble
por defender a Fabián,	for defending Fabián,
por defender a Fabián.	for defending Fabián.
Desde el puerto de Acapulco	From the port of Acapulco
Fabián le mandó a decir,	Fabián sent word to him,
Fabián le mandó a decir,	Fabián sent word to him,
que si no lo acompañaba	saying wouldn't he come along
a perseguir al Barril,	to chase after El Barril,
a perseguir al Barril.	to chase after El Barril.
Y entonces dice Apolonio:	And then Apolonio says:
"'Ora sí, me voy a rajar,	"This time I'll have to back down,
'ora sí, me voy a rajar,	this time I'll have to back down;
porque estoy escaso de parque	because I am low on ammo,
no te puedo acompañar,	I cannot come along with you,
no te puedo acompañar."	I cannot come along with you."
Entonces dice Fabián:	Then Fabián tells him:
"Me engañas con la verdad,	"You're playing tricks with me,
me engañas con la verdad,	you're playing tricks with me;
si le escribo a mi patrón	if I write off to my boss
dos cajas me va a mandar,	he will send to me two cartons,
dos cajas me va a mandar."	he will send to me two cartons."

Entonces dice Apolonio:
"'Ora sí, no veo la hora,
'ora sí, no veo la hora,
con mi escopeta del doce
la que le nombro La Tora,
la que le nombro La Tora."

Ahí la brosa de Fabián
parecía unas buenas siervas,
parecía unas buenas siervas:
"Pa' ese lugar no vamos
porque existe una reserva,
porque existe una reserva."

Entonces dice Fabián:
"Te mando un maldonareño,
te mando un maldonareño,
que les vaya a amanecer
al estado oaxaqueño,
al estado oaxaqueño."

Ya me voy a despedir
señores, perdonarán,
señores, perdonarán,
se comprometió Apolonio
por defender a Fabián,
por defender a Fabián.

Then Apolonio says:
"Now I can hardly wait,
now I can hardly wait—
with my twelve-gauge shotgun,
the one I call La Tora,
the one I call La Tora."

There the gang of Fabián
looked just like a herd of deer,
looked just like a herd of deer;
"Let's not go to that place—
they have reinforcements there,
they have reinforcements there."

Then Fabián says:
"I'll send a man from Maldonado,
I'll send a man from Maldonado,
he should come to you at dawn
to the state of Oaxaca,
to the state of Oaxaca."

Now I will say farewell,
gentlemen, by your leave,
gentlemen, by your leave;
Apolonio got into trouble
for defending Fabián,
for defending Fabián.]

9. "Moisés Colón"

Performed by Tomás Navarrete (lead voice and accordion), Tomás Mayo (backup vocals and guitar), and Jesús Navarrete (backup vocals and guitar) at the edge of the bay in front of Silvia's Restaurant in Acapulco on February 12, 1996. See the transcription on pp. 131–33.

10. "Palemón Mariano"

Performed by Taurino Colón (lead voice) and Agustín Mayo (lead guitar) in Cuaji on April 11, 1996.

Voy a cantar un corrido
me duele mi corazón,
les voy a contar la historia
de Luciano y Palemón,
les voy a contar la historia
de Luciano y Palemón.

[I will sing a corrido—
my heart it is aching;
I will tell you the story
of Luciano with Palemón,
I will tell you the story
of Luciano with Palemón.

Palemón toda esa noche
se hallaba desconsolado,
porque ya la ingrata muerte
se le acercaba a su lado,
porque ya la ingrata muerte
se le acercaba a su lado.

Cutberto cuando lo amarró
también el amigo Puleyo,
cuando Palemón murió
esos corrieron de miedo,
cuando Palemón murió
esos corrieron de miedo.

Ese Cutberto Salinas
es el que insiste a Luciano:
"Me matas a Palemón
porque lo traigo de encargo,
me matas a Palemón
porque lo traigo de encargo."

Ahí Palemón ya se iba
bien montado en su caballo:
"Le dirán que ya me fuí
cuando recuerde Librado,
le dirán que ya me fuí
cuando recuerde Librado."

Toda la gente decía
allí Jesús Vargas nos dió,
mataron a Palemón
porque Salinas mandó,
por causa de dos caballos
hasta su vida perdió,
por causa de dos caballos
hasta su vida perdió.

Pobre de la venterita
del miedo hasta se orinaba,
arrancó pa'onde Fidencio
se metió abajo la cama,
arrancó pa'onde Fidencio
se metió abajo la cama.

Palemón all that night
was in a restless mood,
for now ungrateful death
was coming to his side,
for now ungrateful death
was coming to his side.

Cutberto, when he got him,
also friend Puleyo—
when Palemón did die
those guys ran off in fear,
when Palemón did die,
those guys ran off in fear.

That Cutberto Salinas,
he's the one insisting to Luciano:
"Kill Palemón for me
because I have him on order,
kill Palemón for me
because I have him on order."

Palemón was already going
well mounted on his horse:
"Tell him I already left
when Librado remembers,
tell him I already left
when Librado remembers."

All the people were saying,
there Jesús Vargas got us;
they killed Palemón
just as Salinas ordered;
on account of two horses
he lost even his life,
on account of two horses
he lost even his life.

The poor little barmaid,
out of fear she wet her pants;
she took off to Fidencio's place;
she crawled in under the bed,
she took off to Fidencio's place;
she crawled in under the bed.

Ya me voy a retirar	Now I will withdraw;
amigos, yo me despido,	friends, I say farewell;
murió Palemón Mariano	Palemón Mariano has died
en el pueblo de Cortijo,	in the village of Cortijo,
murió Palemón Mariano	Palemón Mariano has died;
lo mató su fiel amigo.	his own good friend did him in.]

11. "Matías Rojas"

*Composed by Juan Saguilán and performed by Juan Saguilán (voice and guitar)
and Teódulo García (accordion) in Cuajinicuilapa on May 5, 1996.*

Voy a cantar un corrido	[I will sing a corrido—
muchachos no se hagan bola,	boys, don't crowd so close;
en el barrio de Las Crucitas	in the barrio of Las Crucitas
murió Genaro Noyola,	Genaro Noyola died,
también sus dos compañeros	also his two companions,
y se murió Matías Rojas.	and Matías Rojas died.
Genaro se fue de Maguey	Genaro took leave of Maguey
pero no se fue de en balde,	but he didn't go in vain;
se llevó el ajonjolí,	he took the sesame seeds
del maestro Adelaido,	of the teacher Adelaido,
se llevó el ajonjolí	he took the sesame seeds
del maestro Adelaido.	of the teacher Adelaido.
Cuando venían pa' Maguey	As they came from Maguey
pasaron por Copalilla,	they passed by Copalilla;
ahí quitaron dos armas	there they took two weapons
y asaltaron a Eloila,	and they assaulted Eloila,
ahí quitaron dos armas	there they took two weapons
y asaltaron a Eloila.	and they assaulted Eloila.
Luego que llegó a Las Cruces	When they came to Las Cruces
Genarito los reinaba,	Genarito was calling the shots;
pensaba matar a Vilo	he was planning to kill Vilo
y llevarse su entenada,	and steal his daughter-in-law,
pensaba matar a Vilo	he was planning to kill Vilo
y llevarse su entenada.	and steal his daughter-in-law.
Luego que rondeó Las Cruces	As he went around Las Cruces
Genaro estaba en su ley,	Genaro was having his way;
pero no se daba cuenta	but he was not aware
que habían dado parte a Maguey,	they had sent word to Maguey,
pero no se daba cuenta	but he was not aware
que habían dado parte a Maguey.	they had sent word to Maguey.

Genaro se acobardó
cuando vió a sus enemigos,
ahí dice el maestro Chencho:
"Todavía lo tienen vivo."
Ahí dice el maestro Chencho:
"Todavía lo tienen vivo."

El Grande ha señalado a Herlindo
y Herlindo se reculó,
Matías como traiba bueno
luego se le encaminó:
"Y al cabo que sí me matas
nos vamos juntos los dos."

A los primeros balazos
luego formaron su fila,
Sotero, Erasmo y Leobardo
arrancaron pa' las pilas,
Sotero, Erasmo y Leobardo
arrancaron pa' las pilas.

Dice Manuel Saguilán:
"Oye, ¿cómo está esa cosa?
Me dicen que está baleado
Ismael López Mendoza,
también salió Mario Melo
y Bustamante Zorrosa."

Mandaron a traer al Chego
por orden del presidente,
y le daban la pistola
mejor se llevó un machete,
y le daban la pistola
mejor se llevó un machete.

Ya me voy a despedir
porque todo está en la ley,
ese caso sucedió
en el pueblo del Maguey,
ese caso sucedió
en el pueblo del Maguey.

Genaro lost his nerve
when he saw his enemies;
there the teacher Chencho says:
"They still have him alive,"
there the teacher Chencho says:
"They still have him alive."

El Grande has pointed to Herlindo
and Herlindo turned it down;
as Matías came well armed
right there he took it on:
"And if in the end you kill me
the two of us will leave together."

With the first shots fired
then they formed their line;
Sotero, Erasmo, and Leobardo,
they took off for the troughs,
Sotero, Erasmo, and Leobardo,
they took off for the troughs.

Manuel Saguilán says:
"Listen, what's going on here;
they tell me they are wounded—
Ismael López Mendoza,
the same for Mario Melo
and Bustamante Zorrosa."

They sent for Chego to come
on orders from the mayor
and they handed him a pistol
but he opted for a machete,
and they handed him a pistol
but he opted for a machete.

Now I will say farewell,
as all is by the law;
this case came to pass
in the town of Maguey,
this case came to pass
in the town of Maguey.]

Works Cited

Aguirre Beltrán, Gonzalo. 1958. *Cuijla: Esbozo etnográfico de un pueblo negro*. Mexico City: Fonda de Cultura Económica.

————. 1972. *La población negra de México*. Mexico City: Fonda de Cultura Económica.

Arendt, Hannah. 1970. *On Violence*. New York: Harcourt, Brace.

"Los asesinos de Dr. Barajas preparaban una matanza de policías." *El Excelsior*. 1952. Aug. 25.

Avitia Hernández, Antonio. 1989. *Corridos de Durango*. Mexico City: Instituto Nacional de Antropología e Historia.

Barry, Phillips. 1933. "Communal Re-creation." *Bulletin of the Folk-Song Society of the Northeast* 5:4–6.

Barthes, Roland. 1977. *Roland Barthes*. Trans. Richard Howard. London: Hill and Wang.

Basauri, Carlos. 1943. *Breves notas etnográficas sobre la población negra del distrito de Jamiltepec, Oaxaca*. Mexico City: Primer Congreso Demográfico Interamericano.

Boehm, Christopher. 1984. *Blood Revenge: The Enactment and Management of Conflict in Montenegro and Other Tribal Societies*. Philadelphia: University of Pennsylvania Press.

Bowra, C. M. 1952. *Heroic Poetry*. London: MacMillan.

Buchan, David. 1970. *The Ballad and the Folk*. London: Routledge and Kegan Paul.

Bustamante Alvarez, Tomás. 1987. "Periodo 1934–1940." In *Historia de la Cuestión Agraria Mexicana: Estado de Guerrero 1867–1940*. Universidad Autónoma de Guerrero. Mexico City: Imprenta de Juan Pablos. 335–436.

Chadwick, H. M. 1912. *The Heroic Age*. Cambridge: Cambridge University Press.

Chadwick, H. M., and Nora Chadwick. 1932. *The Ancient Literature of Europe.* Vol. 1 of *The Growth of Literature.* Cambridge: Cambridge University Press.

Child, Francis James. 1994. "1874 Essay from Johnson's Universal Cyclopaedic and Atlas." *Journal of Folklore Research* 31:214–24.

Coffin, Tristram. 1957. "Mary Hamilton and the Anglo-American Ballad as an Art Form." *Journal of American Folklore* 70:208–14.

Colín, Mario. 1972. *El corrido popular en el estado de México.* Mexico: Editorial Imprenta Casas.

Debusmann, Bernd. 1988. "In Fight against Drugs, Authorities Win Battles but Lose War." Reuters. July 8.

De los Angeles Manzano, María. 1991. *Cuajinicuilapa, Guerrero: Historia Oral (1900–1940).* Mexico City: Ediciones Artesa.

Derrida, Jacques. 1988. *Limited Inc.* Evanston, Ill.: Northwestern University Press.

De Vries, Jan. 1963. *Heroic Song and Heroic Legend.* London: Oxford University Press.

Douglas, Mary. 1968. "The Social Control of Cognition: Some Factors in Joke Perception." *Man,* n.s. 3:361–76.

Eliot, T. S. 1934. *Selected Essays.* London: Faber and Faber.

Entwistle, William. 1939. *European Balladry.* Oxford: Clarendon Press.

Finnegan, Ruth. 1977. *Oral Poetry.* Cambridge: Cambridge University Press.

Flanet, Véronique. 1977. *Viviré, si Dios Quiere: Un estudio de la violencia en la mixteca de la costa.* Mexico City: Instituto Nacional Indigenista.

Fletcher, Richard. 1989. *The Quest for El Cid.* Oxford: Oxford University Press.

Friedrich, Paul. 1981. *Agrarian Leadership and Violence in Mexico.* Chicago: University of Chicago Center for Latin American Studies.

Garibay, Ricardo. 1978. *Acapulco.* Mexico City: Grijalbo.

Gerhard, Peter. 1993. *A Guide to the Historical Geography of New Spain.* Norman: University of Oklahoma Press.

Gibbs, Nancy, and Timothy Roche. 1999. "The Columbine Tapes." *Time.* December 20. 40–51.

Gilligan, James. 1996. *Violence: Reflections on a National Epidemic.* New York: Vintage Books.

Githiora, Chege. 1994. "Afromexican Names: A Trail of History and Kinship." *Conexões* 6:1, 4–5.

Gómez Maganda, Alejandro. 1960. *Acapulco en mi vida y el tiempo.* Mexico City: Libro Mex.

González Obregón, Luis. 1945. *México viejo y anecdótico.* Mexico City: Colección Austral.

Greenberg, James. 1989. *Blood Ties: Life and Violence in Rural Mexico.* Tucson: University of Arizona Press.

Guardino, Peter. 1996. *Peasants, Politics, and the Formation of Mexico's National State.* Stanford: Stanford University Press.

Gummere, Francis Barton. 1959. *The Popular Ballad.* New York: Dover.

Gutiérrez Avila, Miguel Angel. 1988. *Corrido y violencia entre los Afromestizos de la Costa Chica de Guerrero y Oaxaca.* Chilpancingo, Mexico: Universidad Autónoma de Guerrero.

Hall, Raymond. 1999. "The Afromestizo on Mexico's Atlantic Coast: Ethnicity through Festival, Food, and Dance." Ph.D. diss., Indiana University.

Héau de Giménez, Catalina. 1990. *Así cantaban la revolución.* Mexico City: Grijalbo.

———. 1998. "Ballads of the Mexican Revolution." Lecture delivered at Indiana University. Apr. 22.

Hernández, Guillermo. 1992. "El corrido ayer y hoy: Nuevas notas para su estudio." In *Entre la Magia y la Historia: Tradiciones, mitos y leyendas de la frontera,* comp. José Manuel Valenzuela Arce. Mexico City: Gráfica, Creatividad y Diseño.

Hernández Moreno, Taurino. 1996. "Los 'armeros' de la Costa Chica: Una historia de poder regional." *Amate: Arte, Cultura y Sociedad de Guerrero* 5:20–24.

Herrera-Sobek, María. 1979. "The Theme of Drug Smuggling in the Mexican Corrido." *Revista Chicana-Riqueña* 7:49–61.

———. 1990. *The Mexican Corrido: A Feminist Analysis.* Bloomington: Indiana University Press.

Herzfeld, Michael. 1985. *The Poetics of Manhood: Contest and Identity in a Cretan Mountain Village.* Princeton: Princeton University Press.

Hitt, Samuel M. 1994. "Testimony April 25, 1994 Samuel M. Hitt." Federal Document Clearing House.

Hobsbawm, Eric. 1969. *Social Bandits.* New York: Dell.

Hodges, Donald. 1995. *Mexican Anarchism after the Revolution.* Austin: University of Texas Press.

Illades, Carlos, with Marta Ortega. 1989. *Guerrero: Textos de su Historia.* Mexico City: Instituto de Investigaciones Dr. José María Luis Mora. Gobierno Estado Guerrero.

Jacobs, Ian. 1982. *Ranchero Revolt: The Mexican Revolution in Guerrero.* Austin: University of Texas Press.

Johns, Christina. 1995. *The Origins of Violence in Mexican Society.* Westport, Conn.: Praeger.

Keegan, Paul. 1999. "A Game Boy in the Cross Hairs." *New York Times Magazine.* May 23. 36–41.

Kerrigan, John. 1996. *Revenge Tragedy: Aeschylus to Armageddon.* Oxford: Clarendon Press.

Kun, Josh. 1997. "Narcocorridistas." *Village Voice.* Dec. 2.

Kuri-Aldano, Mario, and Vicente Mendoza Martínez. 1987. *Cancionero popular mexicano.* Mexico City: SEP.

Ladd, D. Robert, Jr. 1980. *The Structure of Intonational Meaning.* Bloomington: Indiana University Press.

Lewis, Laura. 2000. "Blacks, Black Indians, Afromestizos: The Dynamics of Race, Nation, and Identity in a Moreno Mexican Village (Guerrero)." *American Ethnologist* 24. In press.

———. n.d. "Of Ships and Saints: History, Memory, and Place in the Making of Black Mexican Identity." Ms.

López Barroso, Epigmenio. 1967. *Diccionario geográfico, histórico y estadístico del distrito de Abasolo, del estado de Guerrero.* Mexico City: Impresos Anáhuac.

Lord, Albert. 1960. *The Singer of Tales.* Cambridge, Mass.: Harvard University Press.

McCarthy, William. 1990. *The Ballad Matrix: Personality, Milieu, and the Oral Tradition.* Bloomington: Indiana University Press.

McDowell, John. 1972. "The Mexican Corrido: Formula and Theme in a Ballad Tradition." *Journal of American Folklore* 85:205–20.

———. 1975. "La rebelión cristera de México: Enfoque sociológico." *Comunidad* 52:232–45.

———. 1981. "The Corrido of Greater Mexico as Discourse, Music, and Event." In *"And Other Neighborly Names": Social Process and Cultural Image in Texas Folklore,* ed. Roger Abrahams and Richard Bauman. Austin: University of Texas Press. 44–75.

———. 1992. "Folklore as Commemorative Discourse." *Journal of American Folklore* 105:403–23.

Meeker, Michael. 1979. *Literature and Violence in North Arabia.* Cambridge: Cambridge University Press.

Memije Alarcón, Salvador. 1995. Epicoplas: Controversias, Bombas y Décimas. Chilpancingo, Mexico: Promociones y Publicidad "CANDY."

———. 1992. *El folklore literario en Guerrero.* Chilpancingo: Todos Empresos de Guerrero.

Mendoza, Vicente T. 1939. *El romance español y el corrido mexicano: Estudio comparativo.* Mexico City: Ediciones de la Universidad Nacional Autónoma.

———. 1954. *El corrido mexicano: Antología, introducción y notas.* Mexico City: Fondo de Cultura Económico.

Menéndez Pidal, Ramón. 1939. *Los Romances de América y Otros Estudios.* Madrid: Espasa-Calpe.

Meyer, Jean. 1976. *The Cristero Rebellion: The Mexican People between Church and State.* Cambridge: Cambridge University Press.

Moedano, Gabriel. 1988. "El corrido entre la población afromestiza de la Costa Chica de Guerrero y Oaxaca." In *Jornadas de Homenaje a Gonzalo Aguirre Beltrán.* Instituto Veracruzano de Cultura. 119–28.

Molina Alvarez, Daniel. 1987. "Periodo 1920–1934." In *Historia de la Cuestión Agraria Mexicana: Estado de Guerrero 1867–1940.* Universidad Autónoma de Guerrero. Mexico City: Imprenta de Juan Pablos. 221–333.

Moore, Gary. 1997. "Popular Ballads Called Narco-corridos Are Taking the Image of Drug Smuggling to a New High." *Chicago Tribune.* Nov. 18.

Nicolopulos, James. 1997. "The Heroic Corrido: A Premature Obituary?" *Aztlán* 22:115–38.

O'Connor, Anne-Marie. 1997. "Ballads about Drug Cowboys Proving Popular in Mexico; Some Criticize Trend, but Others Defend Storytelling Tradition." *Dallas Morning News.* Jan. 12.

Olivera de Bonfil, Alicia. 1994. *La literatura cristera*. Mexico City: Coleción Divulgación.

Paredes, Américo. 1958. *"With His Pistol in His Hand": A Border Ballad and Its Hero*. Austin: University of Texas Press.

———. 1963. "The Ancestry of Mexico's Corridos: A Matter of Definitions." *Journal of American Folklore* 76:231–35.

———. 1971. "The United States, Mexico, and Machismo." *Journal of the Folklore Institute* 8:17–37.

———. 1973. "José Mosqueda and the Folklorization of Actual Events." *Aztlán* 4:1–30.

———. 1976. *A Texas-Mexican Cancionero: Folksongs of the Lower Border*. Urbana: University of Illinois Press.

———. 1993. "The Mexican Corrido: Its Rise and Fall." *Folklore and Culture on the Texas-Mexican Border*. Ed. Richard Bauman. Austin: University of Texas Press. 129–42.

Paz, Octavio. 1959. *El laberinto de la soledad*. Mexico City: Fondo de Cultura Económica.

Quinones, Sam. 1997. "Narcocorridos." Pacific News Service. Dec. 1.

———. 1998. "Narco Pop's Bloody Polkas." *Washington Post*. Mar. 1.

Ramos, Samuel. 1962. *Profile of Man and Culture in Mexico*. Trans. Peter Earle. New York: McGraw-Hill.

Ravelo Lecuona, Renato. 1987. "Periodo 1910–1920." In *Historia de la Cuestión Agraria Mexicana: Estado de Guerrero 1867–1940*. Universidad Autónoma de Guerrero. Mexico City: Imprenta de Juan Pablos. 81–219.

Reed, John. 1914. *Insurgent Mexico*. New York: D. Appleton.

Renwick, Roger. 1980. *English Folk Poetry: Structure and Meaning*. Philadelphia: University of Pennsylvania Press.

Reynolds, Dwight. 1995. *Heroic Poets, Poetic Heroes: The Ethnography of Performance in an Oral Arabic Tradition*. Ithaca: Cornell University Press.

Richmond, Edson. 1989. *Ballad Scholarship: An Annotated Bibliography*. New York: Garland.

Salazar Adame, Jaime. 1987. "Periodo 1867–1910." In *Historia de la Cuestión Agraria Mexicana: Estado de Guerrero 1867–1940*. Universidad Autónoma de Guerrero. Mexico City: Imprenta de Juan Pablos. 9–79.

Santamaría, Francisco. 1992. *Diccionario de Mejicanismos*. 5th ed. Mexico City: Editorial Porrúa.

Sargent, Helen Child, and George Lyman Kittredge. 1904. *English and Scottish Popular Ballads*. Boston: Houghton-Mifflin.

Serrano Martínez, Celedonio. 1989. *La bola suriana: Un espécimen del corrido mexicano*. Chilpancingo: Gobierno del Estado de Guerrero.

Simmons, Merle. 1957. *The Mexican Corrido as a Source for Interpretive Study of Modern Mexico*. Bloomington: Indiana University Press.

———. 1963. "The Ancestry of Mexico's Corridos." *Journal of American Folklore* 76:1–15.

Smith, C. Colin. 1964. *Spanish Ballads*. Oxford: Pergamon Press.

Stanford, Thomas. 1968. *Catálogo de Grabaciones del Laboratorio del Sonido del Museo Nacional de Antropología*. Instituto Nacional de Antropología e Historia. Mexico City: Imprenta Madero.

Tibón, Gutierre. 1961. *Pinotepa Nacional: Mixtecos, negros y triques*. Mexico City: UNAM.

Los Tigres del Norte. 1989. *Triunfo Sólido*. FonoVisa FPC-8831.

———. 1997. *Jefe de Jefes*. FonoVisa FD 80714 CS.

Turner, Victor W. 1967. *The Forest of Symbols: Aspects of Ndembu Ritual*. Ithaca: Cornell University Press.

———. 1974. *Dramas, Fields, and Metaphors: Symbolic Action in Human Society*. Ithaca: Cornell University Press.

———. 1986. *The Anthropology of Performance*. New York: PAJ Publications.

Vasconcelos, José. 1958. "La Raza Cósmica." In *Obras Completas*. Mexico City: Libreros Mexicanos Unidos.

Vásquez Añorve, Francisco. 1974. *El Ayer de mi Costa*. Puebla, Mexico: Editorial Periodística e Impresora de Puebla.

Vizcaino, Rogelio, and Paco Ignacio Taibo II. 1983. *El socialismo en un solo puerto*. Coedición Extemporáneos/Información Obrera. Mexico City: Coleción el Overal Azul.

Whetten, Nathan. 1948. *Rural Mexico*. Chicago: University of Chicago Press.

Whitmer, Barbara. 1997. *The Violence Mythos*. Albany: State University of New York Press.

Index

Chilena (musical form), 6, 42, 49, 55, 66, 111–12, 121n3
Chilpancingo, Guerrero, 70, 77, 90, 140, 167
Chocotí (regional clan), 44–45
Cimarron (escaped slave), 100, 115–16
"El Ciruelo," 70, 92
"Claudio Bahena," 64, 69n1
El Cobarde (Alvaro Guillén Bracamontes): biographical sketch of, 54–56; on *brosas*, 135–37; on celebratory thesis of violence, 146; composition method of, 55–56; compositions and performances of, 172n9; on ethnicity in Costa Chica, 105–7; on factual truth in corridos, 185–97; mentioned, 73; on regulatory thesis of violence, 159
Cockfighting, 7, 48–49, 109, 156, 181–82, 192
Colombiana (musical form), 42, 66
Colón, Juan, 64. *See also* "Juan Colón"
Colón, Moisés, 73, 95, 105, 128–35, 146, 172n10
Colón, Taurino, 73, 128–29
Comadres (women in ritual kinship relation), 172n9. *See also Compadres*
Commemorative discourse, 16, 24–25, 60, 67, 122
Compadres (men in ritual kinship relation): *comadres* and, 172n9; gang loyalty and, 127–28; obligation to God and, 157; violence between, 5, 21, 154–55
Composition and composers: accountability to public and, 64, 175–85; aesthetic concerns and, 24, 28–29, 31; composition on request, 63; composition process, 27–28, 44, 46, 50, 185–86, 189–90; cooperative process, 57; *corridistas* in revolutionary armies, 124; *cuadrado* (squared, well-formed) quality, 62; *dueños* (owners) of corridos, 176–77, 180; emotional detachment from violence and, 56; ethnic influences on, 105–6; experimentation with form and, 59; historical obligation and, 62, 177–80; kinship obligation and, 60; management of social equilibrium and, 180–91; melodic distinctiveness, 63; "mirroring" of heroic lifestyle and, 65; musical form of corrido, 28–29; sources of ideas, 55, 62; talent divinely inspired, 50, 64; treatment of volatile subjects and, 83, 93, 174–77, 180–85, 191–96; *trovadores* (composers), 27–28, 50, 54–64; vulnerability of composers, 175–78, 194–96. *See also* Poetics; Textuality
Contreras, Onofre: biographical sketch of, 54; on celebratory thesis of violence, 138–39;

composition method of, 62–63; compositions of, 37n6; on idealism of heroes, 127; on *machismo*, 164; on narcocorridos, 206–7; on sensitivity to corrido subjects, 178, 180–84, 196
Copala, Guerrero, 37n9
Corrido: artifactual treatment of, 50–51, 96; cockfighting compared to, 7, 48–49, 109; as collective representation, 24, 49–50, 55, 70; compared to newspaper, 144–46, 177, 214–15; compared to personal recollection, 145–46; consensual politics and, 102, 198–99; decline of, 70, 198, 207; as factual account, 36–37, 57, 60, 144–45, 177–80, 185–91; as feminine genre, 7–8; insider vs. outsider understanding of, 44–45; interpretive and moral dimensions of, 149–50; musical form of, 29; national character and, 26, 74, 198–99; origin of, 25–27, 43; recordings of, 180, 200, 204; social equilibrium in, 16, 18, 180–85, 196; as symbol of local identity, 47–48, 69, 76; volatile themes in, 83, 93, 174–77, 180–85, 191–96. *See also* Ballad; Celebratory thesis; Composition and composers; Narrative; Performance; Poetics; Regulatory thesis; Speech; Textuality; Therapeutic thesis
—related forms: general description of, 55; *bambuco*, 55; *bola suriana* (Costa Chica variant), 28–29; *bolero*, 42, 66; *chilena*, 6, 42, 49, 55, 66, 111–12, 121n3; *colombiana*, 42, 66; *corrido de bravíos*, 6; *corrido de valentías*, 6; *corrido trágico*, 6, 55, 98; epic poetry, 7, 65, 122–23, 126; gangsta rap, 200, 211–12; *huapango*, 55; *mañanita* (corrido subgenre), 124; "movie corrido," 203; narcocorrido, 70, 98, 199–207; *ranchera* corrido, 26; *son*, 26–27; Spanish broadside ballad, 26; Spanish *romancero*, 25–26, 47, 72, 74, 76; *vals peruano*, 55; video games, 213–14
"El Corrido de la Quinceañera y los Tres Muertos" ("El Oaxaqueño"), 186–91
Cortez, Hernán, 78
Costa Chica: African influences in, 8–9, 82, 97, 103–4; *amigos* (tough corrido characters) in, 55, 67; "¡Así es la costa!" 40, 48, 174; *bajos* (peripheral settlements) in, 55, 104–5; as ballad community, 47, 73–76, 95–96; *blanquito* settlements in, 14; class structure in, 84–85, 93–95, 102, 104; colonial period in, 77–79; compared to Costa Grande, 84–85, 95–96; corridos heard on radio in, 47; *costeños* (cos-

JOHN H. MCDOWELL is a professor of folklore, director of the Folklore Institute, and chair of the Department of Folklore and Ethnomusicology at Indiana University. He is the author of *"So Wise Were Our Elders": Mythic Narrative of the Kamsa, Sayings of the Ancestors: The Spiritual Life of the Sibundoy Indians,* and *Children's Riddling.*

Music in American Life

Race, Rock, and Elvis   *Michael T. Bertrand*
Theremin: Ether Music and Espionage   *Albert Glinsky*
Poetry and Violence: The Ballad Tradition of Mexico's Costa Chica   *John H. McDowell*

Folklore and Society

George Magoon and the Down East Game War: History, Folklore, and the Law
   Edward D. Ives
Diversities of Gifts: Field Studies in Southern Religion   *Edited by Ruel W. Tyson, Jr.,*
   James L. Peacock, and Daniel W. Patterson
Days from a Dream Almanac   *Dennis Tedlock*
Nowhere in America: The Big Rock Candy Mountain and Other Comic Utopias
   Hal Rammel
The Lost World of the Craft Printer   *Maggie Holtzberg-Call*
Listening to Old Voices: Folklore in the Lives of Nine Elderly People   *Patrick B. Mullen*
Wobblies, Pile Butts, and Other Heroes: Laborlore Explorations   *Archie Green*
Transforming Tradition: Folk Music Revivals Examined   *Edited by Neil V. Rosenberg*
Morning Dew and Roses: Nuance, Metaphor, and Meaning in Folksongs   *Barre Toelken*
The World Observed: Reflections on the Fieldwork Process   *Edited by Bruce Jackson and*
   Edward D. Ives
Last Cavalier: The Life and Times of John A. Lomax, 1867–1948   *Nolan Porterfield*
Steppin' on the Blues: The Visible Rhythms of African American Dance   *Jacqui Malone*
The Bonny Earl of Murray: The Man, the Murder, the Ballad   *Edward D. Ives*
Polish-American Folklore   *Deborah Anders Silverman*
Poetry and Violence: The Ballad Tradition of Mexico's Costa Chica   *John H. McDowell*

Typeset in 10.5/13 Minion
with Gill Sans Ultra and Dizzy display
Designed by Dennis Roberts
Composed by Jim Proefrock
at the University of Illinois Press
Manufactured by Thomson-Shore, Inc.

University of Illinois Press
1325 South Oak Street
Champaign, IL 61820-6903
www.press.uillinois.edu